JESUS: A PORTRAIT

Also by Gerald O'Collins:

Easter Faith
The Lord's Prayer

JESUS: A PORTRAIT

♦

GERALD O'COLLINS SJ

ORBIS BOOKS

Maryknoll, New York 10545

Founded in 1970, Orbis Books endeavors to publish works that enlighten the mind, nourish the spirit, and challenge the conscience. The publishing arm of the Maryknoll Fathers and Brothers, Orbis seeks to explore the global dimensions of the Christian faith and mission, to invite dialogue with diverse cultures and religious traditions, and to serve the cause of reconciliation and peace. The books published reflect the views of their authors and do not represent the official position of the Maryknoll Society. To learn more about Maryknoll and Orbis Books, please visit our website at www.maryknoll.org.

First published in Great Britain in 2008 by
Darton, Longman and Todd Ltd
1 Spencer Court
140-142 Wandsworth High Street
London SW18 4JJ

First published in the USA in 2008 by
Orbis Books
P.O. Box 308
Maryknoll, New York 10545-0308

Printed and bound in Great Britain.

Library of Congress Cataloging-in-Publication Data

O'Collins, Gerald.
Jesus : a portrait / Gerald O'Collins.
p. cm.
Includes bibliographical references.
ISBN 978-1-57075-783-9
1. Jesus Christ--Biography. I. Title.
BT301.3.O36 2008
232.9'01--dc22
2007044172

♦

CONTENTS

◆

PREFACE

It is Jesus Christ alone we must present to the world.
Outside of this, we have no reason to exist.

Pope John Paul I,
speaking on the last day of his life
to Cardinal Bernardin Gantin

S OME OF WHAT ONE sees on television about Jesus or reads in
articles and books about him seems quietly evasive. At times
producers and writers raise issues of merely historical interest, or
allege that official 'cover-ups' have hidden the 'real truth' for
many centuries. Or else they get caught up in secondary and
even merely trivial matters. They will do anything but face the
challenge in the ultimate religious drama created by the life,
death, and resurrection of Jesus. Last Christmas, for instance, I
sat through two hours of a programme that was all too ready to
indulge eccentric theories about such things as the location of
Bethlehem. Shifting the birthplace of Jesus from Bethlehem in
Judea to an alternative 'Bethlehem' in Galilee on frivolous 'evidence' seemed to do nothing more than parallel the nineteenth-
century attempt by General Charles George Gordon (1833–85)
and others to relocate the site for the death and burial of Jesus (to
'Gordon's Calvary' and the 'Garden Tomb') away from the well-
authenticated 'Holy Sepulchre'.

In the past, but seemingly much less today, some literary
critics would spend their time on such secondary questions as
the geography of Scotland or the latest visitors to the court of
Elizabeth I, rather than face what Shakespeare presented in the
tragic destiny of *Macbeth* and in the deliciously beautiful language of *Twelfth Night*. This kind of evasion lives on in the work

of those who present Jesus or write about him but avoid at all costs a face-to-face encounter with the Jesus witnessed to and disclosed by Matthew, Mark, Luke, and John.

FOUR PORTRAITS

The Gospels pack a lot into their portraits of Jesus, and do so in their own characteristic ways. Given the extraordinary nature of their experience of Jesus, it was almost inevitable that the first Christians would more than once tell that story in the form of Gospels which were to be recognised as the heart of the new Christian Scriptures. Add too the fact that the Gospels came from one eyewitness (John) and from three other evangelists who took much of their material from different eyewitnesses. Mark drew especially on Simon Peter; Luke (as well as using Mark's Gospel and Q, a collection of the sayings of Jesus) relied on a number of eyewitnesses (Luke 1:2), who included women (Luke 8:1–3); Matthew drew on eyewitnesses, as well as on Mark and Q. The eyewitness testimony of the Twelve played a major role in the formation of all three of the Synoptic Gospels (Matthew, Mark, and Luke).[1]

The four portraits may be classified into more representational and historical (Matthew, Mark, and Luke) or more impressionistic and concerned to develop characteristic effects produced by Jesus (John). The first three evangelists at points modify the traditions derived from eyewitness testimony to Jesus (e.g. the longer form of the Lord's Prayer found in Matthew 6:9–13), occasionally retroject into the lifetime of Jesus traditions which come from the post-Easter period (e.g. Matthew 18:20), and are largely (but by no means entirely) responsible for the contexts in which they place the sayings and doings of Jesus. Yet their testimony provides reliable access to the history of what Jesus said, did, and suffered. At the same time, these evangelists have their spiritual and theological messages to announce; they are not to be reduced to mere compilers of traditions that they have drawn from eyewitnesses or otherwise inherited.

One of them, Luke, presses on to write a second volume, the Acts of the Apostles, in which he presents the continuing impact that the risen Christ and the Holy Spirit exercised in the mission and life of early Christianity. Yet the Christians' ongoing experience of the exalted Christ and his Spirit continued to result from the past history of Jesus and did not dissolve it. From the opening chapters of his Gospel to the end of Acts, Luke makes it clear that the history of Jesus was decisively important for the Church's life and preaching. In his life, death, and resurrection, Jesus proved the source of *salvation* for the world and the basis of Christian identity (Acts 4:10–12; 28:31).[2]

John's Gospel emerged from decades of prayerful, theological contemplation, which took Luke's work a stage further by merging two horizons: the *memory* of Jesus which the author recalled from a past that ended with Good Friday, Easter Sunday, and the appearances of the Risen One, and his continuing *experience* of the exalted Lord through to the end of the first century. In a lifelong process of understanding and interpretation, the author of the Fourth Gospel gained deeper insights into the meaning of the events in which he had participated, which had deeply formed him, and which he reflectively remembered. Like some wonderful modern paintings, his portrait of Jesus plays down some features in Jesus' activity (e.g. the preaching of the kingdom, his parables, and the exorcisms) and develops other features (e.g. Jesus' encounters with individuals, his questions, and his self-presentation). The masterpiece, which is the Fourth Gospel, brings out what was to some extent implicit in the life of Jesus and displays for the readers the deep truth about him.

To portray Jesus adequately is an impossible dream (John 20:30; 21:25). Unlike his near contemporary Marcus Tullius Cicero (106–43 BC), he left no letters or other personal documents. The only time he was remembered as writing anything came when he 'wrote with his finger on the ground' (John 8:6–8). This was in response to some scribes and Pharisees who had caught a woman in adultery and wanted Jesus to agree to her being stoned. According to several later manuscripts, Jesus wrote on the ground nothing about himself but 'the sins of each of them'. Jesus did not bequeath to his followers any written instructions, and he lived in almost total obscurity, except for the brief period of his public ministry. According to the testimony provided by the Synoptic Gospels, that ministry could have lasted as little as a year or eighteen months. John implies a period of two or three years. Even for the brief span of that ministry, much of the chronological sequence of events (except for the baptism of Jesus at the start and his passion at the end) is, by and large, irretrievably lost. The fact that, explicitly and for the most part, Jesus did not proclaim himself but the kingdom of God, as well as the fact that he left behind no personal papers, makes access to his interior life difficult. In any case the Gospels rarely mention his motives or deal with his states of mind. These sources make it hard (but not impossible) to penetrate his inner life. But they do allow us to reconstruct much of the message, activity, claims, and impact of Jesus in the final years of his life, as well as glimpsing every now and then his feelings and intentions. Jesus himself never wrote, but he continues to speak through the writings of the evangelists.[3]

THREE STAGES

In drawing on the Gospels, I use the obvious and widely accepted scheme of *three stages* in the transmission of testimony to Jesus' deeds and words: (1) the initial stage in his earthly life when his disciples and others spoke about him, repeated to others his teaching, and began interpreting his identity and mission; (2) the handing on by word of mouth or in writing (including the use of notebooks) of testimony about him after his death and resurrection; and (3) the authorial work of the four evangelists later in the first century. I agree that one can use such criteria as multiple (independent) witness in arguing that testimony to particular deeds and words derives substantially from the first stage: i.e. from the history of Jesus himself. When I draw on the Gospels, I will indicate whether I understand some passage to testify to what Jesus said or did at stage one, or whether the passage seems to illustrate rather what a particular evangelist at stage three (and/or the tradition behind him at stage two) understood about Jesus' work and identity. I cannot stop to justify why I hold some deed or saying to have its historical origin in what Jesus said or did. But I will cite only examples for which such justification is available.

EYEWITNESS TESTIMONY

In a remarkable recent contribution to New Testament studies, Richard Bauckham (see note 1) has argued persuasively that the four Gospels provide an appropriate and credible means of access to the historical Jesus (stage one), since they derive from the testimony of eyewitnesses (both major ones like Peter, the Twelve, Martha and Mary, and minor ones like Bartimaeus in Mark 10). For decades many scholars have imagined stage two to be a long process of anonymous, collective, and mainly oral transmission that separated the original eyewitnesses from those who wrote the Gospels. Bauckham recognises how the period between Jesus and the final composition of the Gospels (stage three) was spanned by the continuing presence and testimony of those who had participated in the story of Jesus: namely, the original eyewitnesses. Until the final years of the first century, these authoritative living sources continued to provide first-hand witness to Jesus.

In demonstrating that the traditions (both oral and written) about the words and deeds of Jesus were attached to known and named eyewitnesses and those who enjoyed direct personal links with such eyewitnesses, Bauckham probes both the internal evidence from the New Testament and the external evidence from Papias of Hierapolis, Justin Martyr, and other early Christian sources. He sets his argument within a careful study of the ancient standards for writing history and 'lives' (such as the Gospels) that can be gleaned from Josephus, Lucian, Polybius, and others. He proposes that many of the named characters in the Gospels were eyewitnesses and were known in the circles in which the traditions about Jesus were originally transmitted. They included Mary Magdalene, Joanna (one of the sources for Luke), and Cleopas (of the Emmaus story in Luke 24). Some, like Jairus (Mark 5:21–43) and Simon of Cyrene (Mark 15:21) could well have remained eyewitness sources for particular stories. The Twelve were especially qualified to testify to the public history of Jesus, since they had participated in it from its early stages to its end and beyond (in the Easter appearances). The Synoptic evangelists drew on the first-hand experience of this group, who were pre-eminently 'eyewitnesses and ministers of the word' (Luke 1:2).

Bauckham produces plausible (internal and external) evidence to rehabilitate the case for Simon Peter being the major eyewitness source behind the Gospel of Mark. The naming of Peter creates an 'inclusion' that holds together the Gospel from 1:16–18 right through to 16:7. Readers can share the eyewitness perspective which the testimony of Peter embodied. Bauckham identifies the anonymous disciple of John 1:35–40 with the beloved disciple of John 21:24, the ideal witness to Jesus who was with him 'from the beginning' (John 15:27) and who 'saw the glory' of the incarnate Word of God (John 1:14). This establishes the major 'inclusion' in the Fourth Gospel, even though an 'inclusion' involving the chief shepherd, Peter, is not abandoned. He is present from Chapter 1 to Chapter 21, yet within the even wider involvement of the beloved disciple. That disciple spent hours with Jesus before Peter even set eyes on Jesus (John 1:35–42). Bauckham puts a strong case for the author of the Fourth Gospel being the beloved disciple, who is not to be identified with John the son of Zebedee or any other member of the Twelve. He was an individual disciple, a close follower of Jesus and is not to be dissolved into a merely representative figure.

This learned and precisely argued book makes a strong case for all four Gospels being close to eyewitness reports of the words and deeds of Jesus. Between the earthly story of Jesus (stage one) and the writing of the Gospels (stage three), the original eyewitnesses played a central and authoritative role in guiding the transmission of the traditions about Jesus (stage two). Bauckham's book should help put an end to the unfounded impression that a long period of creative, collective development of the Jesus-traditions preceded the work of the evangelists.

This landmark volume illuminates helpfully the obvious difference between the Synoptic Gospels and John. Not having been eyewitnesses themselves, the first three evangelists remained close to the ways in which the original eyewitnesses told their stories of Jesus and handed on his sayings. They allowed themselves only a small degree of freshly created interpretation. The Fourth Gospel, however, offered a more extensively interpreted version of the story of Jesus. Through a more delineated plot, greater selectivity of the events recorded, and the fashioning of lengthy discourses and debates, this Gospel became a strongly reflective interpretation of Jesus' identity and mission. This was the way in which one central eyewitness understood what he and others had personally experienced. When testifying to the history of Jesus in which he had participated so closely, the beloved disciple allowed himself a higher degree of interpretative appropriation precisely because he had been an eyewitness.

EXPERIENCE AND INTERPRETATION

The pursuit of the earthly history of Jesus (stage one) should not lead us to foster the illusion that our research could yield some nuggets of original 'facts' about Jesus, historical data which somehow preceded all later doctrinal interpretations, beliefs, and affirmations about him. Human experience and, as we shall see, personal knowledge are never like that. No one (and no instrument, not even the most sophisticated camera) can ever record and communicate the non-interpreted, unmediated 'hard' reality of somebody (or, for that matter, of something). Historically there never was an uninterpreted, 'untheological' Jesus. Here, as elsewhere, there never was a kind of 'view from nowhere', a 'given' that was not yet interpreted. 'Fact' and interpretation are inseparable.

Right from their earliest encounters with him, the beloved disciple, Peter, Mary Magdalene, Joanna, and others among the first disciples, necessarily interpreted Jesus and their experience of him. When the evangelists came, decades later, to put the testimony and traditions into gospel shape, they were handling material in which, so to speak, the input from Jesus himself and various responses to him were inextricably intertwined. It cannot be otherwise with our human experience of an historical figure. Not even oral reports from the very first meetings with someone can ever give us the 'pure' story of that person, free from any significance that becomes attached to him or her. No one's reality can ever be captured and exhausted through such initial acquaintance, nor by subsequent research.

Mark, Matthew, and Luke manifested their personal attitude towards and relationship with Jesus, now risen and exalted in glory. There are no good grounds for holding that any of these three evangelists enjoyed personal contacts with Jesus during his earthly existence. They were and remain, however, central figures in the whole story of transmitting the response which Jesus evoked and of creating further response. That response includes Christian worship in all its diversity; creeds and other official doctrines; millions of lives which have taken their inspiration from Jesus (and, in particular, the lives of those who teach us by their shining, saintly example); preaching and theological reflection on Jesus; and all the art, literature, and films that have come into existence around him. As with other figures in human history, the response that Jesus has evoked and continues to evoke belongs essentially to his integral story. This book will attend, here and there, to some of this response: in particular, to the ways artists, writers, and saints have responded to Jesus.

THE MYSTERY OF JESUS' PERSON

Whenever we seek to know another person and, so to speak, paint his portrait, we are grappling with an elusive mystery. Even with those who constantly live with us, we would delude ourselves if we imagined that their total personal reality were available for our 'impartial' inspection. Perhaps we can 'know' one-dimensional characters in lesser films, dramas, and novels. Real persons, as well as characters in great dramas, novels, and epic poems, always remain, at least partly, elusive mysteries. If this holds good for any human beings, whether they live in the present or the past, Christian believers expect it to be very much more true in the case of Jesus. His question to Philip, 'Have I been with you so long, and yet you do not know me?' (John 14:9), goes beyond a mere reproach to touch a profound truth about the mystery of his person. Could anyone ever hope to know him adequately, either then or now?

Let us recall also the way in which knowing other persons (as much or more than knowing any reality) is always an exercise of personal knowledge. This means that we must reckon not only with the elusive mystery of the other person but also with the inevitably subjective nature of our own knowledge, above all when it is a question of our experiencing and knowing the reality of other persons. Admittedly we can read the Gospels now with all the resources of modern scholarship. These resources enrich and clarify what we know about the historical reality of Jesus' words and deeds as well as about the events directly connected with him. Yet knowledge of persons always means, at least minimally, our *knowing someone*, not simply our *knowing about* him or her. Our personal knowledge of 'the other' always goes beyond the merely empirical and publicly accessible data. Knowing other persons, whether they belong to the past like Confucius, Socrates, Martin Luther, and Teresa of Avila or share life with us today like our friends and relatives, is much more than simply knowing a certain number of 'facts' about them. Our own (subjective) relationship to and evaluation of those persons is always necessarily involved. There is simply no way of knowing any reality and, above all, other persons in a 'purely objective' fashion.

The subjective nature of our knowledge, in particular our historical knowledge and knowledge of other persons, should not be reduced to the mere fact that we are historically and culturally conditioned. Such conditioning expresses but also conceals the deepest desires (for life, meaning, and love) and primordial questions (about such matters as suffering and evil of all kinds) that shape our existence but here and now find only, respectively, fragmentary fulfilment and provisional answers. Inevitably these desires and questions come into play whenever we encounter other persons, all the more when the encounter assumes deep importance for us and the other person is richly significant to us. Such moments bring the meeting of two mysteries – mine and his or hers.

MYSTERY AND PROBLEM

The classic distinction drawn by Gabriel Marcel (1889–1973) between a problem and mystery bears on this point. Getting to know any person and, in particular, someone of world stature and significance is always much more than a mere problem to be solved; it is a mystery to be wondered at and grappled with. It is at our peril that we approach our knowledge of Jesus as a problem to be solved by honesty and scholarship rather than as a mystery (or rather *the* mystery) with which to engage ourselves for a lifetime.[4]

We are all part of the history of Jesus and his mystery – whether we realise this or not. This necessary involvement of ourselves in his full and unfolding story rules out attempts to tackle the history of Jesus as if it were no more than a mere problem 'out there' or 'back there', standing quite apart from our personal existence. Really knowing another person in depth – and, especially, Jesus – always demands that we relate to and participate in another personal mystery.

TESTIMONY AND ITS INTERPRETATION

The testimony embodied in the Gospels and coming from eyewitnesses provides the substance for this book. Like all testimony, the Gospels invite us to enter a situation of interpersonal communion and trust with the witnesses. Because we relate to these witnesses and trust them, we know Jesus. The testimony coming from eyewitness participants (e.g. Simon Peter, Mary Magdalene, and the beloved disciple) and from those in immediate contact with such eyewitnesses (e.g. Luke) is utterly indispensable if we wish to know and understand Jesus and his history.

The Gospels refer back to Jesus, his earthly reality, and his significance for salvation and divine self-revelation. Yet what they say about him also acts as a mirror for interpreting our own lives. The stories of his birth, life, death, and resurrection have constantly evoked in Christian believers and others the 'I was/

am there' feeling. When heard during community worship or meditated on during personal prayer, these stories invite their hearers and readers to interact imaginatively with them. Thus such texts function not only as windows on the history of Jesus but also as critical mirrors that reflect and challenge the ways we view ourselves, our community, and our world.

This preface has aimed at explaining and, if needs be, justifying what follows: a personal portrait of Jesus that is also a vital mirror of ourselves. I begin with his beauty, a theme which St Augustine of Hippo (354–430) used when drawing together the story of Christ. I dedicate this book to two dear friends: Brendan Walsh, who suggested my writing it, and Michael Jones, who gave me the laptop on which it was written.

Gerald O'Collins sj
St Mary's University College
Twickenham (London)
2 October 2007

Chapter 1

♦

THE BEAUTY OF JESUS

Without beauty, the good becomes a burden and truth
becomes a useless and empty labour. It is in beauty that
truth and the good find their supreme revelation.

Divo Barsotti, The Spirituality of Beauty

A T A SPECIAL CONSISTORY in Rome, held in 2001, Cardinal
Godfried Daneels, Archbishop of Malines-Brussels, told his
brother cardinals that the way into the culture of our times was
through an appeal to beauty. By that door we can bring contemporary people to a sense of the truth and goodness of God. If
we approach God and the divine attributes directly, our audience may remain sceptical. Like Pontius Pilate, they can say,
'What is truth?' While attracted by goodness and its ideals, they
can feel put off by their own sense of sinful inadequacy. The door
to God through beauty, the cardinal suggested, is the way to let
the Christian message enjoy a renewed impact.

How would the cardinal's advice look when applied to Jesus?
Approaching the story of Jesus through his human and divine
beauty will have its powerful impact. We gladly give our hearts
to what is beautiful. We fall in love with beautiful men and
women. Those people who are beautiful possess an instant
appeal. We hope that they are also good and truthful, but it is
their beauty that catches and holds our attention. Jesus is the
beauty of God in person. When we fall in love with his beauty,
we are well on the way to accepting his truth and imitating his
goodness.

St Augustine of Hippo (354–430) knew through his personal
experience the power that beauty exercises over our hearts and

1

feelings. In his *Confessions* he addresses God as the divine Beauty reaching him through his five senses – through the sense of hearing, sight, smell, taste, and touch: 'You *called* and *cried* to me and broke open my deafness. You *sent forth your beams* and *shone* upon me and chased away my blindness. You *breathed fragrance* upon me, and I drew in my breath and now pant for you. I *tasted* you, and now hunger and thirst for you. You *touched* me and I burned for your peace.'[1] The coming of Christ meant that human beings could now literally hear, see, smell, taste, and touch the very incarnation of the divine Beauty. The infinitely beautiful God had reached out to us and become in person available through our five senses.

It is not surprising then that Augustine spelt out in terms of beauty (and not of goodness and truth) the major stages of Christ's story. In a homily on a royal wedding song that we know as Psalm 45, St Augustine declared: 'he [Christ] is beautiful in heaven; beautiful on earth; beautiful in the womb; beautiful in his parents' arms; beautiful in his miracles; beautiful under the scourge; beautiful when inviting to life ... beautiful when laying down his life; beautiful in taking it up again; beautiful on the cross; beautiful in the sepulchre; beautiful in heaven.'[2] This eloquent passage from Augustine takes us 'from heaven to heaven' – that is to say, from Christ's pre-existent life 'in heaven' 'before' the incarnation to his 'post-existent' life when risen from the dead. At every stage in that story, beauty characterises Christ, even when he is laying down his life on the cross. Others might have said 'Christ is good/true in heaven, good/true on earth' and so forth, but not Augustine. The wonderful framework he provides for summarising Christ's entire story comes in terms of beauty, and Augustine does so out of the communicative wealth of the Scriptures.

Two things stand out in this list from Augustine: the echoes from St John's Gospel and the sense that it may be difficult to recognise beauty in the passion of Christ. First, 'laying down his life' and 'taking it up again' obviously echo the language of John (10:17–18), a Gospel on which Augustine commented in 124 'tractates'[3] and which he often quoted or echoed in other writings. Second, since he seems concerned about the difficulty (and the importance) of accepting that Christ was also beautiful in the passion, Augustine repeats this point four times: 'beautiful under the scourge', 'beautiful in laying down his life', 'beautiful on the cross', and 'beautiful in the sepulchre'. The beauty of Christ powerfully revealed in his suffering is integral to his total story. Those who curated the 'Seeing Salvation' exhibition, which drew so many visitors to London in 2000, obviously shared that conviction. From the 79 paintings and other objects displayed, 22 were placed in two sections dealing directly with Christ's passion. Further works of art concerned with the passion turned up in other sections, right from the first one, 'Sign and Symbol'. The *Agnus Dei* (Lamb of God), a painting by Francisco de Zurburán (1598–1664) lent by the Prado in Madrid, showed a lovely lamb with its feet tied, lying on a butcher's slab and standing out against a dark background. It conveyed a powerful sense of what human sin did to the Lamb of God in his work of redemption, and set the tone for many visitors to the exhibition.

Many have quoted from *The Idiot* by Fyodor Dostoyevsky (1821–81) the dictum 'beauty will save the world' and rightly see in Prince Myshkin, a saintly stranger who returns to Russia, an effective symbol of the innocent and beautiful Christ. But not all have noticed the novel's connection with the passion and with John's Gospel. On his way to Florence, where he wrote this work, Dostoyevsky stopped in Basel to see *The Dead Christ* by Hans Holbein the Younger (1497–1543). Deeply moved by this tragic painting, he introduced references to it at key points in the novel, which ends in deeper darkness than any of his other novels. A letter from 1867 shows how he held together this sense of tragedy with the beauty of Christ as portrayed by John: 'There is only one perfectly beautiful person, Christ, so that the appearance of this immeasurably, infinitely beautiful person … is an infinite miracle. That is the sense of the entire Gospel of John; it finds the whole miracle in the incarnation alone, in the manifestation of the beautiful alone.'[4]

Augustine would have applauded this view of John's Gospel. It underpins excellently the summary of Christ's story we quoted above from Augustine. To that summary we now turn.

'BEAUTIFUL IN HEAVEN, BEAUTIFUL ON EARTH'

The Old Testament frequently highlights something very similar to the divine beauty: namely, the 'glory of God' or the radiant, powerful presence of God. When Jerusalem is restored, the luminous presence of God will appear over the city, which is called to reflect 'the glory of the Lord' and welcome home her children (Isaiah 60:1–5). Talk of the shining glory of God goes together with the biblical scenarios of fire and light. It is in a flame of fire out of a bush that God speaks to Moses (Exodus 3:1–6). The New Testament goes beyond speaking of God as 'dwelling in unapproachable light' (1 Timothy 6:16) to declare simply: 'God is light' (1 John 1:5).

Drawing on St Thomas Aquinas (about 1225–74), Jacques Maritain (1882–1973) describes beauty as follows: 'For beauty three things are required: in the first place integrity or perfection (*integritas sive perfectio*) . . . in the second, proportion or harmony (*proportio sive consonantia*); in the third, clarity (*claritas*), for there is splendour in all objects that are called beautiful.'[5] This third element of beauty comes close to the scriptural language of God's shining radiance or 'glory'.

Even if no biblical author ever expressly says that 'God dwells in unapproachable beauty' or that 'God is beauty', some scriptural texts directly celebrate the peerless beauty of a divine personification, Lady Wisdom. Solomon is pictured as declaring this 'pure emanation of the glory of the Almighty' to be 'more beautiful than the sun'. He 'became enamoured of her beauty' and desired 'to take her' as his bride and teacher (Wisdom 7:25, 29; 8:2, 9). She is understood to be the agent of divine creation and all its beautiful works. From 'the greatness and beauty' of these created things comes 'a corresponding perception of their Creator', who is the very 'Author of beauty', and hence of Lady Wisdom, who is the radiantly beautiful 'reflection' or 'spotless mirror' image of God the Creator (Wisdom 7:26; 13:3–5). Here the Scriptures come close to joining Augustine in characterising God as 'the Beauty of all things beautiful' (*Confessions*, 3.6; see 9.4).

By opening his list with 'beautiful in heaven, beautiful on earth', Augustine pointed to the glory and beauty that Christ possessed in his pre-existence and then manifested in his incarnation. The prologue of John displays Christ as the very incarnation of the divine glory and beauty. It first calls him six times 'light' or 'the true light', and so encourages readers to think of Christ pre-existing in divine glory or beauty. It is in these terms, then, that John coherently portrays the incarnation: 'the Word became flesh and lived among us, and we have seen (contemplated) his glory (beauty)' (John 1:14). The Gospel of John proves to be nothing less than a drawn-out contemplation of the divine glory/beauty revealed in the person of Christ (e.g. John 2:11), which reaches its high point when Thomas gazes at the risen One and confesses: 'My Lord and my God' (John 20:28).

Along the way Jesus describes himself as 'the Light of the world' (John 9:5), equivalently as the radiant and beautiful presence of God in the world, and also as 'the good Shepherd' (John 10:11, 14). Although it is normally translated 'good', the Greek adjective used here, *kalos*, also means beautiful. It is applied in the Book of Wisdom to Lady Wisdom; she is both beautiful and good. Christ is likewise good and beautiful in his pre-existence, in his incarnation, and as the beautiful Shepherd in laying down his life and taking it up again.

This beauty is God's way of appealing to human beings and calling them back into union with the divine life. Dionysius the Pseudo-Areopagite, an anonymous Christian writer of the late fifth or early sixth century, supposed that the Greek word for 'call', *kalein*, had given rise to the noun for beauty, *kallos*, and its connected adjective *kalos*. He understood the call of divine beauty to occur above all through the incarnation of the Son of God. As divine beauty in person, Christ heals human brokenness, restores meaning, and recreates relationships with God and others.[6]

'BEAUTIFUL IN THE WOMB, BEAUTIFUL IN HIS PARENTS' ARMS'

While John accounts best for the starting point, when Augustine begins itemising the stages at which the beauty of Christ was manifested, we turn to Luke and Matthew for the next stage: the conception and birth of Jesus. When they open their Gospels with the 'infancy narratives', they do not directly describe the beauty of Christ either in his mother's womb or after his birth. In Luke's narrative, however, the beauty of the Holy Child in Mary's womb is implied by the joy that pervades the meeting between Mary and her pregnant relative Elizabeth. The presence of the beautiful Christ Child, still unborn, binds Mary and Elizabeth together in an ecstasy of joy that shines through what they say and is shared by the unborn child (John the Baptist) in the womb of Elizabeth (Luke 1:39–56). Elizabeth praises Mary, and Mary praises God. Each mother has learned from heaven about the child of the other: Mary from the angel Gabriel, and Elizabeth from the Holy Spirit when she is 'filled' with the Spirit and the child in her womb leaps prophetically. By mentioning twice that leaping (Luke 1:41, 44), the evangelist calls attention to the fact that, even in the womb, John joyfully goes before his glorious Lord.

After his birth the beauty of the Christ Child emerges indirectly and through various heavenly and earthly protagonists in the nativity story: for instance, through the angels, awesomely beautiful heavenly visitors. As 'the glory/beauty of the Lord' illuminates the fields at night with divine radiance, the otherworldly beauty of the angels mirrors that of the Holy Child whose birth they announce (Luke 2:8–14). His beauty is also suggested by the joy of the shepherds. They rush to Bethlehem, and find Mary, Joseph, and the Child lying in the manger. They leave 'glorifying and praising God for all that they had heard and seen' (Luke 2:15–20). Luke also introduces the impact on two old people who meet Jesus when he is brought to the Temple in Jerusalem. Simeon and Anna have waited so long for this moment. They delight in the beautiful Christ Child and can now die in peace (Luke 2:25–38). In Matthew's infancy narrative, the Magi 'rejoice with extremely great joy' when they finally arrive at the goal of their journey and can present the new-born Jesus with their gifts (Matthew 2:10–11). A sense of the divine beauty threads its way through many details in the nativity story that Luke and Matthew tell in their own ways and in dependence on different traditions.[7]

Composers, poets, and artists have taken a cue from this biblical language and introduced the theme of beauty into their versions of the nativity. In his *Christmas Oratorio* Johann Sebastian Bach (1685–1750) acclaimed the birth of 'the most beautiful of all human beings'. St Robert Southwell (about 1561–95) adapted the scriptural language of fire and love in his image of 'a pretty Babe all burning bright' who appears on Christmas Day ('The Burning Babe'). Christian artists have excelled themselves in depicting the loveliest Child, whose beauty is reflected in the beauty of his Mother as she holds him in her arms or gazes upon him with intense love. One thinks of the paintings of Bartolomé Esteban Murillo (1617–82), with his delicate colours and ethereal forms, Raphael Sanzio (1483–1520), and other classical Italian painters.

'BEAUTIFUL IN HIS MIRACLES, BEAUTIFUL WHEN INVITING TO LIFE'

Augustine sums up the story of Jesus in his ministry as being 'beautiful in his miracles' and 'beautiful when inviting to life'.

Once again the Gospel writers make no attempt to describe directly the exquisite appearance of Jesus. But even though they never tell us what he looked like, they certainly suggest his wonderful beauty through their accounts of his impact on others. People flocked to him. If ever there was a magnetic, attractive personality, he was it. Beauty shone through him. Mark has Peter and his companions say to Jesus, 'everyone is searching for you' (Mark 1:37). In Matthew's Gospel, Jesus says to his audience: 'Come to me all you who are weary and are carrying heavy burdens, and I will give you rest' (Matthew 11:28). If the poor and overburdened accept his light yoke, they will find enduring peace. As beautiful, divine Wisdom in person,[8] Jesus invites his poor and overburdened hearers to accept him and his message; thus they will find enduring peace. He hardly needs to invite his audience to come to him. They know from others, or have already themselves experienced, how tender, welcoming, and comforting he proves to be. They want to stay in his presence and share in the mysterious grace of his person. The sick and the sinful receive from him healing and a joyful wholeness.

The preaching of Jesus reported by Matthew and Luke provides grounds for concluding that Jesus thought of himself in terms of wisdom and made it possible for his followers to recognise him as divine Wisdom come in person. This was tantamount to acknowledging him as the divine Beauty.[9] Echoing the Book of Wisdom, the Letter to the Hebrews would call him 'the reflection of God's glory' (Hebrews 1:3).[10] As one should expect, the resurrection and the coming of the Holy Spirit transfigured what early Christians believed about Jesus. Nevertheless, their beliefs regularly reached back to the ministry of Jesus and to what they remembered him saying, or at least implying, about himself. These memories helped them to see in him the radiant splendour of the divine beauty.

During his lifetime one group in their special way sensed that beauty in him. Children were drawn to the joy of Jesus' lovely presence. In the rural society of ancient Galilee, children were sent off as soon as possible to take care of sheep and in other ways prove themselves to be producers and not merely consumers. Since they did not know the Torah, they were low on the religious and social scale. Yet Jesus showed himself their special friend; he delighted in their company; he worked miracles in favour of children (Mark 5:35–43; 7:24–30).[11] When his disciples tried to keep them away, Jesus took some children into his arms, blessed them, and declared that the kingdom of heaven belonged to them. Children heard him hold them up as models for adults: 'Whoever does not receive the kingdom of God as a little child will never enter it' (Mark 10:13–16). To illustrate the new attitude towards God that he required, Jesus singled out little children. He did not say, 'unless you become like priests and prophets, you will never enter the kingdom of God'. He expected all people to show a trusting, childlike attitude towards their heavenly Father. For Jesus, the seeming incapacity of children turned out to be their greatest asset. The fact that they had nothing to give or to show in order to enter the kingdom of heaven made them receptive to whatever God offered them. They could accept and appreciate the unique gift that they had not worked to deserve.

An American-Italian film that was first shown in December 1999, *Jesus*, ended with a striking tribute to Jesus (played by a very handsome actor Jeremy Sisko) as the beautiful friend of children.[12] The film took its viewers through Jesus' life, death, and resurrection, and then leapt forward nearly two thousand years to the waterfront of modern Valletta (Malta). His long, chestnut hair now cropped, Jesus stood there in jeans as a crowd of small children ran up to him. The film ended with him taking a tiny child in his arms and walking off with the others crowded around him. The beautiful Jesus exited with the beautiful children.

Before leaving the beauty of Jesus manifested in his ministry, we should recall three further items: (1) his baptism, (2) his transfiguration, and (3) his self-presentation as the bridegroom.

Jesus' baptism

Matthew, Mark, and Luke make much of the baptism of Jesus, an event rich in detail and not least in its manifestation of the Trinity. Many painters have caught something of the special grace and beauty of that moment – not least Piero della Francesca (c. 1416–92) in *The Baptism of Christ* on permanent exhibition in the National Gallery (London). John's Gospel, however, does not relate the episode of Jesus' baptism, but merely alludes to it (John 1:32–34). This may be why Augustine does not insert as a logical marker at the start of the ministry of Jesus 'beautiful in his baptism'. He is very oriented towards the Gospel of John and ready to follow its lead.

Jesus' transfiguration

According to the Synoptic Gospels, Peter, James, and John went up a high mountain with Jesus and saw him 'transfigured', as the divine glory gleamed through him. His face shone like the sun, and two heavenly figures (the prophet Elijah and the law-giver Moses) talked with him (Mark 9:2–8; Matthew 17:1–8; Luke 9:28–36). The disciples reacted not only with astonished awe but also with a desire to prolong the vision of the radiantly beautiful Lord that they were experiencing. As he was naming the moments when the divine beauty of Christ shone through, Augustine could well have added, 'beautiful in the transfiguration'. But the Gospel of John did not encourage him to do so. Rather than narrate a specific episode of transfiguration, John let the transfiguration pervade, so to speak, the whole story: from the incarnation through to the death and resurrection. The entire life of Christ disclosed his divine glory to people at large (above all through what John calls 'the signs'); the transfiguration was not limited to a specific event on a mountain that involved only three close disciples of Jesus.[13]

Jesus as the bridegroom

The Synoptic Gospels report words of Jesus which imply that, in the joyful time of salvation, he had come as 'the bridegroom' for his followers (Mark 2:19–20; Matthew 9:15; Luke 5:34–35). The Parable of the Wise and Foolish Bridesmaids, which presents the coming of the kingdom as the coming of the bridegroom and the need to be prepared for this awesome event (Matthew 25:1–13), left its audience with the question: Who was this mysterious bridegroom if not Christ himself? This language evoked many Old Testament passages, such as the psalm which prompted Augustine's reflections on the beauty of Christ. An ode for a royal wedding, Psalm 45 highlights the glory, majesty, and beauty of the king: 'You are the most handsome of men; grace is poured upon your lips ... Gird your sword on your thigh, O mighty one, in your glory and majesty' (Psalm 45:2–3).

Christians were to apply this spousal language to the union between Christ and the Church (e.g. Ephesians 5:25–33). The Bible ends with the Book of Revelation and its promise of marriage between the gloriously beautiful Christ and his Church (Revelation 21–22). The awesome splendour of the exalted Christ has already been evoked in the vision with which that book begins (Revelation 1:9–20). The theme of Christ as the supremely beautiful bridegroom, for whom we are all waiting, was to have a long future, not least in the way that mystics would draw on the Song of Songs to describe their ecstatic union with the divine Spouse.

'BEAUTIFUL UNDER THE SCOURGE'

Augustine can seem audaciously paradoxical when he writes of Christ being 'beautiful under the scourge' and 'beautiful on the cross'. Has Augustine forgotten Isaiah and those words about the servant of God being cruelly disfigured, devoid of attraction, and even repulsive – a passage in which Christian tradition from the start saw the suffering and death of Christ (Isaiah 52:13–53:12)? What Augustine appreciates, however, is how the crucified Jesus in a radically subversive way challenges all the normal indices of beauty. As Tom Casey remarks, 'the beauty of Christ is visible most of all at what is seemingly the ugliest moment of all: Jesus' tortured death on the cross. The beauty that shines in the form of Christ at that moment is the beauty of infinite love.' Casey moves on to articulate the 'call' of that crucified beauty: 'This beauty seeks to touch people and to transform them, to awaken and draw them. The response it elicits is not sensual and momentary but all-encompassing, one that embraces the individual's entire existence. This beauty is a light that pierces the heart.' Those who contemplate this crucified beauty are called 'to re-shape and mould anew an entire life so that it may conform to this new standard of beauty'.[14]

In their narrative fashion, the Gospels show Christ's crucified beauty at work. Women gather around the cross and attend the death of Jesus. The Roman centurion who has been in charge of the crucifixion blurts out his confession ('indeed this man was the Son of God') – a confession in which, according to Matthew, the other soldiers join (Matthew 27:54). An outsider, Joseph of Arimathea, boldly comes on the scene to give Jesus a reverent and honourable burial (Mark 15:42–47). Quite visibly the passion accounts in Matthew, Mark, and Luke show the prophecy in John's Gospel coming true: in his death Jesus would 'gather into one the children of God who had been scattered' (John 11:51–52). In his dying and death on the cross, the Beautiful Shepherd already touches, draws, and re-shapes human lives.

In a laconic, implicit way St Paul concurs with this. It is precisely in his most eloquent passage about the crucifixion (1 Corinthians 1:18–2:5) that he calls Christ 'the power of God and the wisdom of God' (1 Corinthians 1:24).[15] But Paul appreciates that we face here a mysterious, hidden wisdom. Otherwise, how could 'the rulers of this age' have 'crucified the glorious Lord' (1 Corinthians 2:8)? The divine wisdom, glory, and beauty revealed and at work in Christ's passion were in no way self-evident. Here Christians face perhaps the sharpest challenge to their faith. They are summoned to recognise beauty in the weak and suffering men and women with whom Christ identifies himself (Matthew 25:31–46). His passion continues in them until the end of history. In the words of Blaise Pascal (1623–62), 'Jesus will be in agony until the end of the world.'[16] One might adapt Paul's teaching about power being made perfect in weakness (2 Corinthians 13:4), and say that the power of Christ's beauty is manifested perfectly in the weakness and ugliness of the crucifixion.

Countless Christians and others have seen the *Pietà* by Michelangelo (1475–1564) in St Peter's Basilica (Rome), or at least a photograph or replica of it. Created when the sculptor was in his early twenties, this dramatically intense work represents the Virgin Mary holding the body of her Son across her lap and heartbroken at his death. Yet the physical beauty of the two bodies takes away something of the grief and suffering from an emotionally charged scene. Later in life Michelangelo carved other versions of the *Pietà*. One is kept in the museum of the cathedral in Florence. Michelangelo himself mutilated and abandoned it, only for the work to be restored and completed by a mediocre artist. Another is the Rondanini *Pietà* (in the Castello Sforzesco, Milan), on which he was still working a few days before his death when he was almost ninety.

The work in Florence places Nicodemus above and Mary Magdalene on the left, both helping the Virgin Mary to support the body which has been taken down from the cross. Her face is close to the face of her dead Son, and she is interlaced with him in a painful union that merges the two bodies physically and spiritually. This physical and spiritual union comes through even more powerfully from the unfinished splendour of the Rondanini *Pietà*, which folds the body of the Virgin into that of the dead Christ. The work expresses the spiritual, inner, even divine beauty of suffering, rather than the external beauty of a young athlete dying in the prime of his life.

11

Few, if any, among Western painters have equalled Rembrandt (1606–69) in his ability to portray the beauty of Christ in his passion and death. The Dutch artist's images of Christ standing before Pilate, moving towards Calvary, or nailed to the cross itself let a mysteriously haunting beauty gleam through the pain and weakness of the suffering Jesus. The power of Christ's beauty is manifested in the horror of his crucifixion, when he seems abandoned and powerless.

'BEAUTIFUL IN THE RESURRECTION'

Augustine calls Christ beautiful 'in laying down his life' and 'beautiful in taking it up again' – language that echoes what Jesus says about himself in John 10. Through his death and resurrection he is revealed as the beautiful/good Shepherd, who 'knows his own', calls them by name, and is known by them (John 10:3–4, 14). We find this mutual knowledge spectacularly exemplified a few chapters later in John's Gospel, when the risen Christ calls Mary Magdalene by name. She recognises his voice and clings with love to her beautiful Master, now gloriously risen from the dead (John 20:16–17).

Angels are present in the Easter stories of all four Gospels and provide an image of heavenly beauty that accompanies and mirrors the new risen life of Christ. The angelic beauty that reflects the beauty of the risen Christ reaches its high point in Matthew's 'angel of the Lord': 'His appearance was like lightning and his clothing white as snow' (Matthew 28:3). In his majestic beauty this angel functions as a kind of double for the risen Christ. But Jesus himself is not described in any of the Easter narratives of the Gospels. It is left to another book in the New Testament to evoke directly the awesome beauty of the resurrected and exalted Lord, whose 'face was like the sun shining with full force' (Revelation 1:16). No wonder then, that, when the Book of Revelation portrays the heavenly Jerusalem, it reports a vision of the future in terms of the glorious splendour of God and his Son: 'The city has no need of sun or moon to shine on it, for the glory of God is its light, and its lamp is the Lamb' (Revelation 21:23).

St Paul writes of the glory/beauty of God on the face of the risen Christ, connecting our chance of knowing this radiant glory with the primeval act by which God first created light: 'It is the God who said, "Let light shine out of darkness", who has shone in our hearts to give the light of the knowledge of the glory of God in the face of Jesus Christ' (2 Corinthians 4:6). What the crucifixion and resurrection bring to all believers – the knowledge of the divine glory – sets them apart from Moses. When Moses prayed to see the divine glory, God warned him: 'You cannot see my face; for no one shall see me and live.' The Lord went on to say: 'See, there is a place by me where you shall stand on the rock; and while my glory passes by, I will put you in a cleft of the rock, and I will cover you with my hand until I have passed by; then I will take away my hand, and you will see my back. But my face shall not be seen' (Exodus 33:20–23). The passage contains bold anthropomorphisms – the Lord's hand and back. The writer wants to stress that, even for the favoured Moses, God may be vividly present but remains hidden. Paul, however, appreciates how faith and baptism bring a unique illumination, knowledge of God's glory revealed in the face of his risen Son. As the Revealer *par excellence*, Christ communicates God's beauty and loving goodness. Since God is love and beauty, Jesus is that love and beauty in person.

'BEAUTIFUL IN HEAVEN'

Augustine closes his list with the risen and exalted Christ being 'beautiful in heaven', but this final marker differs from the opening 'beautiful in heaven'. The incarnation and what it involves sets the subsequent story off from the 'beautiful', eternal pre-existent life of the Son of God. Through his life, death, and resurrection he is now beautiful in a new way – for human beings and their world. 'He is beautiful for us', we could say. Augustine's whole commentary on Psalm 45 (that enfolds his list of moments displaying Christ's beauty) is deeply concerned with the impact of Christ's glorious beauty on those who require redemption. Augustine would agree with Dostoyevsky's dictum 'beauty will save the world', but might well have added: 'it is beauty that is already saving the world'. We are not what we are meant to be; through the beauty of the exalted Christ we are led to the truth and goodness we so desperately need.

Other early Christian writers agreed on the present impact of Christ now 'beautiful in heaven'. Clement of Alexandria (c. 150–c. 215) wrote: 'Our Saviour is beautiful, and is loved by those who desire true beauty' (*Stromata*, 2.5). Apropos of Colossians 1:15 ('the image of the unseen God'), St Basil the Great (c. 330–79) assured his readers: 'in the blessed sight of the image [the Son] you will see the inexpressible beauty of the archetype [the Father]' (*De Spiritu Sancto*, 9.23). Over the centuries several major anthologies entitled *Philocalia* ('love of what is beautiful') drew on Basil and other Greek Fathers of the Church to encourage the 'prayer of the heart' and other practices of the spiritual life centred on Christ who is now 'beautiful in heaven'. Let me cite one final voice.

In a famous sermon, Gerard Manley Hopkins (1844–89) said: 'There met in Jesus Christ all that can make man lovely and loveable.' No wonder then that he went on to admit: 'I look forward with eager desire to seeing the matchless beauty of Christ's body in the heavenly light.' Yet 'far higher than beauty of the body', Hopkins added, 'comes the beauty of his character'. He ended his sermon by urging the congregation to praise the beautiful Christ over and over again in their hearts.[17]

THE FACE OF CHRIST

This chapter has used as a launching pad a list from Augustine which summarises the entire story of Christ in terms of beauty. But, if this book purports to be 'a portrait' of Jesus, what about his face? What did he look like? In many cultures, judgements about beauty are strongly linked with facial symmetry, and the modern film industry has led many to equate beauty at least in part with facial beauty. Those who highlight the beauty of Jesus can be asked to swing around and address the question: What did his face look like? It could seem a strange state of affairs to have nothing to say in answer to this question.

Sadly for many people, however, the Gospels rarely mention the face of Jesus and even then do not tell us what it looked like. In his version of the transfiguration, Matthew writes that the face of Jesus 'shone like the sun' (Matthew 17:2); Luke simply says that 'the appearance of his face' changed (9:29); Mark says nothing specifically about the face of Jesus and merely states in general that Jesus was 'transfigured' (Mark 9:2). Luke twice (9:51, 53) writes of Jesus 'setting his face to go to Jerusalem'. Other references to the face of Jesus belong to the passion stories. In the garden 'he fell on his face' (Matthew 26:39). When he was being interrogated by Annas, one of the temple police struck Jesus on the face (John 18:22). According to Mark, at the end of the hearing before the chief priests, elders, and scribes, some of them 'covered the face' of Jesus and struck him (Mark 14:65). In Matthew's account, they 'spat in his face' (Matthew 26:67). The Gospels have little to say then about the face of Christ. What they do say emphasises, more than anything else, the tragic beauty of Christ's face that is spat upon, blindfolded, and struck. Occasionally the Gospels comment on some 'look' on the face of Jesus. Mark supplies a number of examples of this. Before curing a man with a withered hand, Jesus looks around 'with anger' at those who think it outrageous to heal someone on the Sabbath (3:5). A woman who has been suffering from haemorrhages touches the cloak of Jesus and is cured. He is aware that 'power has gone forth from him' and 'looks around' to see who has touched him (5:25–32). Before feeding the five thousand, Jesus 'looks up to heaven' and then blesses and breaks the loaves (6:41). He looks lovingly at a rich man and invites him, 'come, follow me' (10:21). These and other examples of the look on Jesus' face show us, we could say, his face in action but do not describe it.

Since the Middle Ages, however, Christian artists have turned Christ's face into 'the face of all faces'. For each of the stages listed by Augustine, except for the pre-existence, they have supplied innumerable examples: for the Christ Child, Jesus in his ministry, the suffering Christ, and the glorious Lord. Images of the face of Christ were everywhere in medieval Europe. It was his suffering face that predominated – through copies of the *Veronica* in the West and the *Mandylion of Edessa* in the East, until the face on the Shroud of Turin established itself in Christian imagination from the end of the fourteenth century.[18]

Everyone has their favourite example. Mine is *The Calling of Matthew,* a painting by Caravaggio (1571–1610) kept in the Church of St Louis in Rome. The look on the face of the beautiful Christ calls Matthew to a new life. In turn, the light on the face of Matthew shows that he has recognised the beautiful Light of God who has come into the world (John 1:9; 9:5). The divine face and the human face meet in a moment of creation and re-creation.

15

Chapter 2

♦

GOD'S KINGDOM IN PERSON

[The name of Jesus] is honey in our mouths; it is melody
in our ears; it is jubilation in our hearts.
    St Bernard of Clairvaux, Sermo XV In Canticum

He [Jesus] was conscious of a vocation from God to proclaim this kingdom, and the record shows him as single-
mindedly devoted to that vocation, even to the point at
which it brought him to death.
    John Macquarrie, Jesus in Modern Thought

THIS CHAPTER BEGINS TO explore the stage that Augustine
summarised as 'beautiful in his miracles' and 'beautiful
when inviting to life'. But we must first say something about the
years that preceded that public ministry.

PREPARATION FOR PREACHING

Along with other dates with which he tags his opening chapters,
Luke writes that 'Jesus was about thirty years of age when he
began his work' (3:23). What happened during those years before
Jesus was baptised by John, spent a stint in the desert, and began
his public ministry? We might reply in general that Jesus
embodied the message of the divine kingdom before preaching
it. His life at Nazareth expressed in advance the hidden, humble
quality of the kingdom. But can we say anything specific?

Luke twice speaks of the Christ Child growing up and
becoming older, bigger, wiser, and more blessed by God (Luke
2:40, 52). Jesus followed the normal laws of human growth by

16

advancing from childhood to manhood. This growth made Jesus the sublime Mediator of God's kingdom that we see him to be at his fully mature and adult stage. Through his hidden years, his life of faith developed strongly and clearly, so that the Letter to the Hebrews could sum up his human story as that of One who had begun and run perfectly the race of faith (Hebrews 12:1–2). In his public ministry he showed himself unconditionally committed to the reign of God which was breaking into the world. When he spoke about faith, his words reflected the kind of faith that lay behind his life of service: for instance, 'if you had faith as a grain of mustard seed, you could say to this mulberry tree, "Be rooted up and be planted in the sea", and it would obey you' (Luke 17:6).[1] Jesus had grown in an intense faith that put him uniquely at the disposition of God. When he assured the father of the epileptic boy, 'all things are possible to him who believes', that was an invitation to share his own faith. He promised that those who keep asking in prayer will be heard (Matthew 7:7–12). In this and other ways he spoke about faith as an insider, who knew what the life of faith was like and wanted to share it with others. His self-surrender to God showed itself in, and was fed by, the life of prayer he assiduously practised (e.g. Mark 1:35; 6:46; 14:12–26, 32–42). Praying like that expressed a deep sense of dependence and trust – in other words, an intimate relationship of faith in God. The hidden years at Nazareth brought Jesus to that uniquely robust faith which underpinned his ministry for the divine kingdom.[2]

Luke helps us further in our reflection on the hidden years in Nazareth through a story about Christ as a boy (visiting the Temple in Jerusalem) that the evangelist received and adapted (Luke 2:41–52).[3] We find the kernel of the tradition which Luke received in the question: 'Did you not know that I must be in my Father's house [or 'involved in my Father's affairs', or even 'among those belonging to my Father']?' From stage three (Luke) we can move back to stage two (a pre-Lukan tradition). But it is difficult to move further back to stage one, and hazard any guesses about what the twelve-year-old Jesus might have done and said. Such tests as multiple witness do not apply here; there is no comparable story, for instance, in Matthew. What we can be more confident about is seeing how Luke recognises that, already as a boy, Jesus was the Son of God, and wants to develop initially some redemptive themes.

First, the journey to Jerusalem for the Passover feast anticipates the later journey Jesus will make with his disciples to

Jerusalem (Luke 9:51–19:28). Luke presents Jesus as the Saviour on *pilgrimage* to the holy place. Second, Mary and Joseph find the boy Jesus among the teachers in the Temple, the sacred setting where Luke begins his Gospel (1:8–22) and the sacred setting where his Gospel will end. After Jesus has gone 'up to heaven', the disciples return to Jerusalem and spend time in the Temple praising God (24:52–53). Luke introduces a clear *inclusion* to suggest how Jerusalem and its Temple create the centre point in the whole history of salvation. Third, the story of the finding of the boy Jesus leads up to the 'punch line' in which Luke provides the first words spoken by Jesus. They take the form of a question: 'Did you not know that I must be in my Father's house?' It is no longer the angel Gabriel, old Simeon, or anyone else who pronounces on the *identity* of Jesus. He himself does so, and reveals an intimate relationship of obedience to 'my Father'. He says about himself what the heavenly voice will say at his baptism (Luke 3:22). For the first time Luke introduces *'dei* (must)', a Greek word which will turn up eighteen times in his Gospel and twenty-two times in Acts and which conveys a sense of events and persons being in conformity with the divine will. In the drama of human salvation, Jesus will show himself unreservedly at the disposal of God who is his Father. His visible obedience to Mary and Joseph (Luke 2:51) on their return to Nazareth symbolises his radical obedience to the invisible God.

A further way in which the Gospels, this time Matthew, Mark, and Luke, (unwittingly) fill in the years of preparation comes through their reports of the preaching of Jesus, which followed his baptism and time in the wilderness. The content of that preaching of the kingdom discloses something of what had been happening in the imagination, mind, and heart of Jesus during his hidden years in Nazareth. He had been building up a rich store of *images* and full-blown *parables* that were to characterise his vivid presentation of the saving reign and rule of God. His preaching of the kingdom took shape during the thirty or so years before Jesus began his public ministry. Joachim Jeremias hints at this when he writes: 'the pictorial element in the parables is drawn from the daily life of Palestine'.[4] If we were to gather all the images from the sayings and parables of Jesus and put them together, we would have a broad picture of daily life in ancient Galilee. As he was growing up, Jesus obviously had a keen eye for his environment. What he saw and heard spoke to him of God's kingdom and would feed into his preaching of the kingdom.

Jesus was to speak of stewards running large households for absentee landlords, burglars ransacking homes, judges administering the law, fishermen sorting out their catch, merchants in search of precious pearls, robbers beating up travellers on lonely roads, farmers harvesting their crops, sick beggars starving outside the houses of the rich, women mixing yeast into dough, young men leaving home and family for a more 'cheerful' life elsewhere, children playing games and sometimes quarrelling in the village squares, and neighbours looking for food when unexpected guests arrive late at night. Jesus had noticed women using the right kind of material when they mended torn clothes, rich people throwing big parties, businessmen unable to repay loans, landowners building bigger granaries to hold bumper harvests of grain, lilies growing in the fields, and young people playing their part when friends got married. He knew that sheep could easily stray into the wilderness, that farmers fatten calves for special feasts, and that donkeys and oxen should be taken every day to water. At times these animals would fall down wells and needed to be rescued at once, even on the Sabbath day. Jesus noted that cultivating the soil and adding fertiliser could revitalise barren fig trees. Farmers might buy up to five yoke of oxen. Gentile farmers kept pigs and fed them on pods. Jesus became familiar too with the market price of sparrows, the skins used for different brands of wine, the safe places above the flood-line for constructing large buildings, and with weather forecasting. Winds from the West blow off the Mediterranean and bring rain; those from the South come off the desert and will be hot and dry.

Certain of these images came from the rich storehouse of the Jewish Scriptures or had clear associations with them. For instance, the language of Jesus about vineyards, harvests, feasts, and a merchant in search of fine pearls had its Old Testament roots. He had prayed over such images himself and heard them read in the synagogue. That also tells us about what happened during the hidden years at Nazareth when he was preparing for his ministry. Yet he gave those inherited images his own special 'twist'. The pictures he was to add later illustrated how, as he grew to mature manhood, Jesus was deeply sensitive to the people and things around him – from kings going to war, farmers piling up manure heaps and growing mustard plants, right through to tiny sparrows falling dead to the ground. Everything spoke to him of God and what God wanted to do for human beings. His preaching and teaching during his public ministry revealed how responsive he had been to all that was taking place around him and how he saw it all as alive with God and the desire of God to share the fullness of life with us. Such commonplace scenes as farmers sowing seed in variable terrain had suggested to him God's coming close to human beings and the problems they meet in responding to the powerful presence of the One who is always actively and lovingly attentive to them. During the years in Nazareth Jesus had been intensely alive to his world and what was happening between human beings and their constantly loving God. When he began preaching, he wanted to infect others with that perspective on life, a perspective that could bring their conversion and open them to the grace of the divine kingdom.

The baptism of Jesus, with his anointing by the Holy Spirit, marks the transition from his hidden life to his public ministry for the kingdom. Although the other Gospels report the descent of the Holy Spirit at the baptism of Jesus, it is only John who writes of the Spirit descending and 'remaining' on Jesus (John 1:32–33). Jesus will then speak 'the words of God, for he [God] gives the Spirit without measure' (John 3:34). God gives this measureless gift of the Spirit, first to Jesus and, then, through him to others. Jesus is uniquely endowed with the Spirit and will be the source of the Spirit, the fountain from whom will flow 'rivers of living water' (John 7:37–39). John's Gospel understands Jesus' dispensing of the Spirit to be without parallel.

THE JOY OF THE KINGDOM

Jesus spent his brief ministry announcing the royal reign of God, both as already present (e.g. Matthew 12:28; Luke 17:20) and as coming in the future (e.g. Mark 1:15; Matthew 6:10). On the lips of Jesus, 'the kingdom' was tantamount to talking of God as the Lord of this world, whose decisive intervention would liberate sinful men and women from the grip of evil and give them a new, final, and lasting age of salvation. Jesus never stood back and clearly defined exactly what he meant by the central symbol he chose for his preaching. He let aspects of the kingdom emerge: for instance, the joy it brings.

By proclaiming the kingdom Jesus has introduced the joyful time of salvation, a kind of marriage feast at which he himself is the bridegroom. In his presence, sorrow, mourning, and fasting are simply out of place (Mark 2:18–20). The happiness of discovering the kingdom, he assures his hearers, turns life around and makes everything else seem unimportant. His parables of the treasure in the field and pearl of great price highlight the ecstatic joy experienced by those who come across such a once-in-a-lifetime 'godsend' (Matthew 13:44–46). These parables match the sheer delight of Levi, other tax collectors, and various public sinners when Jesus shares meals with them, forgives their sins, and calls them to become his disciples (Mark 2:13–17). The kingdom of God is a reign of merciful love. The boundless joy brought by God's compassionate love bursts through the Parable of the Prodigal Son to round off the first part of the story (Luke 15:24), and then again at the very end, when the father insists with his other son, 'we had to celebrate and rejoice, because this brother of yours was dead and has come to life; he was lost and has been found' (Luke 15:32). In this parable and elsewhere, Jesus has much to say about the way in which God's kingdom of love will surprise us with joy, both in this life and in the life to come.

Over and over again in his preaching Jesus brings in the image of a feast. He pictures our future life with God that way: 'Many will come from the east and the west and eat with Abraham and Isaac and Jacob in the kingdom of heaven' (Matthew 8:11). But such joyful feasting, as we have just seen, does not have to wait until the end, when human history finishes. Right now during his ministry Jesus happily eats with sinners and outcasts; he loves them and wants to bring them forgiveness and peace of heart. He is happy and at home with them. Luke appreciates how the joyful, forgiving love of the kingdom that the Parable of the Prodigal Son expresses serves to defend Jesus' own practice. Critics grumble and complain: 'This fellow welcomes sinners and eats with them' (Luke 15:2). But Jesus remains undeterred. His happiness seems unbounded when prodigal sons and daughters hear the message of the kingdom, come home, and accept the divine love.

Luke tells a classic story of such a prodigal son, Zacchaeus, a chief tax collector in Jericho, a town situated on a main trade route and an important customs centre. By taking a contract for collecting revenue in the district and by defrauding people, Zacchaeus had became rich. Despised by his fellow Jews for collaborating with the Roman authorities, he did not plan to meet Jesus, only to see him from a perch in a tree. But Jesus stopped, looked up, and addressed him by name: 'Zacchaeus,

hurry and come down, for I must stay at your house today.'
Zacchaeus rushed home and was delighted to welcome Jesus,
who was bent on 'seeking out and saving' such 'lost' sinners and
was obviously overjoyed at the wholehearted response of Zacchaeus to the message of salvation (Luke 19:1–10).
Even more than the other Gospel writers, Luke accentuates the
joy caused by the coming of God's kingdom. When a group of
seventy disciples return from a mission, they report to Jesus with
delight: 'Lord, in your name even the demons submit to us' (Luke
10:17). Although they have not been promised this power when
sent on their mission (Luke 10:1–12), they find themselves sharing
in Jesus' dominion over the forces of evil. Jesus alludes to this
victory over the demonic powers by replying: 'I watched Satan
fall from heaven like a flash of lightning' (Luke 10:18). The power
of Satan has been broken; by implication God's kingly power has
been established. The context in which Luke quotes this saying
from Jesus is suffused with a sense of joyful excitement. Jesus
rejoices in the Holy Spirit and says: 'I thank you Father, Lord of
heaven and earth, because you have hidden these things from
the wise and the intelligent, and have revealed them to infants.
Yes, Father, for such was your gracious will' (Luke 10:21).
Luke presses ahead in this section to underline further the
saving power of God that, to the delight of the disciples, is now
transforming the present situation. This group of ragtag Galilean
peasants is experiencing what great prophets and kings longed
to see and hear: the fulfilment of the divine promises of salvation. Jesus declares: 'blessed are the eyes that see what you see.
For I tell you that many prophets and kings desired to see what
you see, but did not see it, and to hear what you hear, but did not
hear it' (Luke 10:23–24). The disciples rejoice in seeing and
hearing what Jesus is doing and saying when proclaiming the
kingdom. They hear the teaching of Jesus and witness his
striking actions, which include not only his miracles but also
things that no prophet or rabbi had done: he accepts women
among his close followers (e.g. Luke 8:1–3; 10:38–42) and shares
meals with tax collectors and other notorious sinners. The Gospels make it clear how his fellowship with the outcasts of society
outraged 'good' people. To have women among his travelling
companions was a startling, even scandalous innovation.
We can put the finishing touches to this account of the marvellous joy brought by the kingdom if we recall an image Jesus
used of himself, that of a doctor with his patients. He defended
his loving concern for sinners by presenting himself as a doctor

totally dedicated to his sick patients: 'Those who are well have no need of a physician, but those who are sick do. I have come to call not the righteous but sinners' (Mark 2:17). The Gospels show how effective was this language (backed up by his practice of associating with sinners) in attracting to the person of Jesus all kinds of men and women ashamed of their sins and looking for forgiveness through him (e.g. Mark 2:15; Luke 7:36–50). The merciful Doctor put his words into action by joining at table the sinful sick; his language and presence transformed them (e.g. Luke 19:1–10). Augustine of Hippo treasured this image of Christ as the humble and loving Physician, and knew how well it worked in his own pastoral ministry. There are over fifty extant texts from Augustine which either allude to or elaborate on the healing and saving actions of Christ the Physician.[5]

Clearly the preaching of the kingdom triggered joyful delight among many who heard Jesus. The joy of the kingdom was inseparable from the person who proclaimed it. He made unprecedented claims about himself and his message. We must reconstruct those claims if we are to understand what his audience struggled with when they experienced him.

THE KINGDOM IN PERSON

In the third century Origen (c. 185–c. 254) packed a lot into a comment about Jesus as being 'the kingdom in person, *autobasileia*' (*In Matt.* 24.7; on Matthew 18:23). If we follow the Gospels, we cannot conceive of the kingdom detached from the person of Jesus. Both in his preaching and in his miraculous deeds, Jesus was inseparably connected with the arrival of the divine kingdom. Through his person and presence, God's rule had come and was coming. As speaker of the parables, for example, Jesus was identified with the kingdom and effected its powerful presence. Mark, followed by Matthew and Luke, clearly saw Jesus and his activity in that way. A saying about God's kingdom coming with power (Mark 9:1) could easily be applied to Jesus himself as the Son of Man coming in his kingdom (Matthew 16:28). High implications about Jesus' saving function and personal identity emerge from the ways in which the Synoptic Gospels portray his role for the kingdom. But how did Jesus think of himself and his mission?

At the very least, he seems to have conceived of his mission as that of one who had been sent by God (Mark 9:37; 12:6), to break

Satan's power (Luke 10:17–18) and to realise the final rule of God (Matthew 12:28). Despite evidence that Jesus distanced himself from talk of being 'the Messiah' or promised deliverer sent by God (e.g. Mark 8:27–31; 15:2), it is quite implausible to argue that Jesus was oblivious of performing a messianic mission. He gave some grounds for being perceived to have made such a claim (Mark 11:1–11). Otherwise it is very difficult to account both for the charge against him of being a messianic pretender (Mark 14:61; 15:2, 9, 18, 26, 32) and for the ease with which his followers began calling him 'the Christ' immediately after his death and resurrection. He had also disclosed messianic consciousness by a key saying about his miraculous activity (Matthew 11:2–6), and implied something about himself when contrasting 'mere' Davidic descent with the higher status of being the Messiah (Mark 12:35–37).

But there was more to his self-presentation than that. At times he went beyond a prophetic 'I was sent' to say 'I came' or 'I have come'. To be sure, we find the language of 'being sent' when Jesus described his mission. He was remembered as having taken a small child into this arms and saying: 'Whoever receives one such child in my name receives me, and whoever receives me receives not me but him who sent me' (Mark 9:36–37). In a parable about the wicked tenants of a vineyard, Jesus obliquely referred to himself as 'the Son' who had finally been 'sent' (Mark 12:6). He expressed the limits set to his mission as being 'sent only to the lost sheep of the house of Israel' (Matthew 15:24). Yet on other occasions he went beyond the normal prophetic 'I was sent' to affirm, 'I came': 'I came not to call the righteous but sinners' (Mark 2:17); 'I came to cast fire upon the earth. Would that it were already kindled!' (Luke 12:49).

The 'coming' language is also connected with a major self-designation used by Jesus: 'The Son of Man came not to be served but to serve' (Mark 10:45). Occasionally the language of 'coming' and of 'sending' is combined (e.g. Luke 13:34–35). Without insisting that every 'sending' and 'coming' saying derives from the historical Jesus, they are numerous and various enough to support the conclusion that he conceived of his mission both as one who came and as one who had been sent by the Father. The Old Testament prophets shared a radical sense of being sent by God, but never purported to come in their own name. Furthermore, they never presented themselves as 'sons of God', nor were they ever called that. In short, none of them ever laid claim to his personal initiative in the mission on which he was embarked by saying: 'I have come.'[6] Moreover, Jesus presented himself as something 'greater than' a prophet like Jonah, and, for that matter, as greater than the classically wise king, Solomon (Matthew 12:41–42).

Over and above any such sayings, Jesus so identified himself with the message of God's kingdom that those who responded positively to this message *committed themselves to him* as disciples. To accept the coming rule of God was to become a follower of Jesus. To be saved through the kingdom was to be saved through Jesus. With authority Jesus encouraged men and women to break normal family ties and join him in the service of the kingdom (Mark 10:7–31; Luke 8:1–3). By relativising in his own name family roles and relationships, Jesus was scandalously at odds with the expectations of his and other societies. All this raises the question: who did Jesus think he was if he made such personal claims?

The personal authority with which Jesus taught and performed miracles was blatant. Unlike normal miracle workers in Judaism, he did not first invoke the divine intervention, but simply went ahead in his own name to heal people or deliver them from diabolic possession. He likewise spoke with his own authority, prefacing his teaching with 'I say to you' (Matthew 5:21–44) and not with such prophetic rubrics as 'thus says the Lord' or 'oracle of the Lord'. It was above all the 'objects' over which he asserted authority that made such claims startling. Either by what he said or by what he did (or both), Jesus claimed authority over the observance of the Sabbath (Mark 2:23–28; 3:1–5), the Temple (Mark 11:15–17), and the Law – three divinely authorised channels of salvation. A unique sacredness attached to that day, place, and code. Let me briefly recall some aspects of the attitude towards the Law and the Temple that Jesus showed in his ministry.

He took it upon himself not only to criticise the *oral law* for running counter to basic human obligations (Mark 7:9–13) but also to set aside the *written law* on such matters as retribution, divorce, and food (Matthew 5:21–48; Mark 7:15, 19). This was to put himself on a par with the divine Lord who had prescribed these matters through Moses: 'Of old it was said to you by God speaking through Moses, but I say to you.' Apropos of the Temple-saying, it is admittedly hard to establish its original form (Mark 14:57–59; Acts 6:13–14). But it involved some claim that his mission was to bring a new relationship between God and the chosen people, which would supplant the central place of their current relationship, the Temple in Jerusalem.[7] His mission was to replace the Temple and its cult with something better ('not made by human hands').

Seemingly on a level with Jesus' astonishing assertion of personal rights over the day, place, and law of Jewish life was his willingness to dispense with the divinely established channels for the forgiveness of sins (sacrificial offerings in the Temple and the mediation of the priestly authorities) and to take on God's role by forgiving sins in his own name. He did this by word (Mark 2:1–11; Luke 7:47–49) and by table fellowship with sinners (Luke 15:1–2). Eating together is a means of communion between human beings – a kind of 'natural' sacrament. By sharing food and drink with sinners, Jesus conveyed to them divine pardon and loving acceptance. Doing that was tantamount to saying, 'I accept you, I love you.'

Apropos of the forgiveness of sins, even before Jesus began his ministry some challenge to the established provision for dealing with sins had already come from John the Baptist. He 'proclaimed a baptism of repentance for the forgiveness of sins' (Mark 1:4). Apparently John proposed his ritual as an alternative to what was done in the Temple, with baptism taking the place of a sin-offering. When Mark and the other evangelists report the practice of John, they give no indication that he required a sacrifice or some other act of atonement. But they do not indicate that he excluded any such ritual in the Temple. What was distinctive about John's ministry was that he immersed others and did so seemingly once and for all. He did not call for repeated, ritual purification of oneself, as was the case elsewhere – for instance, in the Essene community at Qumran. Essentially what John practised was a baptism through which people expressed repentance and sought the forgiveness of their sins. John did not, however, anticipate the authoritative practice of Jesus. Matthew seems sensitive to this issue by describing John's baptism simply as a baptism 'for forgiveness'. He postpones the reference to 'the forgiveness of sins' until the Last Supper, where he recognises that the forgiveness of sins comes through the pouring out of Jesus' blood (Matthew 26:28).[8]

Jesus' practice set him off from John the Baptist. It was much more than the fact that, unlike John, he did not belong to a priestly family. In his own name Jesus forgave sins against God, without prescribing baptism through which sinners could express repentance and seek for forgiveness from God. Jesus himself claimed, there and then, to mediate such forgiveness of sin.

Thus, in proclaiming salvation through the *present* divine rule, Jesus claimed or at least implied a personal authority that can be described as setting himself on a par with God. Since he gave such an impression during his ministry, one can understand members of the Sanhedrin charging Jesus with blasphemy. They feared that he was not merely a false prophet but was even usurping divine prerogatives (Mark 14:64).[9]

But what of Jesus and the *final* rule of God? Apparently he saw his ministry not only as embodying the climax of God's purposes for Israel (Mark 12:2–6) but also as involving his own uniquely authoritative role for bringing others to share in the final kingdom. He said to his core group of twelve disciples: 'I assign to you, as my Father assigned to me, a kingdom that you may eat and drink at my table in my kingdom, and sit on thrones judging the twelve tribes of Israel' (Luke 22:29–30). Here Jesus testified to himself as critically significant for the full message of the coming kingdom. His testimony to himself was an essential part of that message. Other such claims to be decisive for our final relationship with God got expressed in terms of his self-designation, 'the Son of Man': 'I tell you, every one who acknowledges me before men, the Son of Man will acknowledge before the angels of God. But he who denies me before men will be denied before the angels of God' (Luke 12:8–9). Jesus understood the full and final salvation of human beings to depend on their present relationship with him.[10]

Deliverance and the gift of life in abundance sum up much of what Jesus intended when proclaiming the saving kingdom of God. He understood that life to be mediated through the new family of God that he was establishing. Becoming, through dependence on Jesus, his brothers and sisters, men and women could accept a new relationship with God, even to the point of addressing God as their loving and merciful 'Abba (Father dear)' (Mark 3:31–35; Matthew 6:9 par.). Jesus himself seemed to be conscious of his unique divine sonship (Matthew 11:25–27), an intimate filial relationship with 'Abba' which gave him a unique right to invite others to enjoy the loving and life-giving fatherhood of God.[11] In other words, that relationship underpinned what we would call his role as the Revealer and the Saviour in creating this new family.

Knowing and naming God in a new way came through as a striking feature of Jesus' message of the kingdom. In the Old Testament Scriptures God was known through many names, above all the personal name of YHWH (e.g. Exodus 3:14; 6:6–8).

This, the most sacred of names, appears about 6,800 times in the Old Testament, both by itself and in compounds. In *God is King: Understanding an Israelite Metaphor*, Marc Zvi Brettler points out that 'God is King' is the 'predominant metaphor for God in the Old Testament, appearing much more frequently than metaphors such as "God is lover/husband" (e.g. Jeremiah 3, Ezekiel 16 and Hosea 2) or "God is father" (Deuteronomy 32:6; Isaiah 63:16; Jeremiah 3:19)'.[12] This last metaphor is certainly rare; it is hardly twenty times that God is named (or addressed) as 'Father' in the whole of the Old Testament.[13] Through the preaching of Jesus, this name moved into centre stage. 'King' dropped out entirely (except for Matthew 5:35, which echoes Psalm 48:1). Jesus preached the kingdom of God, but at the heart of that kingdom was the divine Father, not the King. At the core of Jesus' preaching of the kingdom was his intimate experience of God as the loving, trustworthy 'Abba' ('Father dear' or even 'Daddy').

THE TRINITARIAN FACE OF THE KINGDOM

From the account offered so far of what Jesus intended when preaching the kingdom, we have seen hints of how this story bore a trinitarian face. He lived in a human way his personal identity of being the Son in constant relationship to the Father and empowered by the Holy Spirit. Beyond question, we should not expect to find anything like a fully deployed doctrine of the Trinity in what the Gospels – and, in particular, the Synoptic Gospels – recall about Jesus. It would be wildly anachronistic to look for such a clear doctrine in the story of Jesus' ministry. Nevertheless, there are hints of God's tripersonal reality in that ministry, hints that provide the starting point for what councils of the Church were later to elaborate explicitly – above all, in the Nicene–Constantinopolitan Creed of 381 that all Christians use when celebrating the Eucharist. We begin with the point of departure for the public ministry of Jesus: his baptism, related by Mark 1:9–11 and, with some variations, by Matthew 3:13–17 and Luke 3:21–22. John 1:29–34 refers to the baptism but does not tell the story as such.

The baptism

More than twenty years ago, defying the oppressive heat and squadrons of flies, I joined a devout Arab Christian at a location on the River Jordan where tradition has placed the baptism of Jesus. 'Here', my old friend told me, 'the most Holy Trinity was revealed.' What do the Gospels say? Mark (followed by Matthew and Luke) recalls a kind of appearance of the Trinity at Jesus' baptism: in the voice of the Father, the obedience of the Son, and the descent of (and anointing by) the Holy Spirit.[14] The Spirit descended on him 'like a dove', and 'a voice came from heaven, "You are my Son, the Beloved; with you I am well pleased"' (Mark 1:10–11).

Even if, according to Mark and – somewhat less emphatically – Luke (Luke 3:22), but not according to Matthew (Matthew 3:17), the voice from heaven was directed to Jesus, these evangelists (and still less Matthew[15]) do not seem to be thinking of a divine call accompanied by visionary elements. Despite a few similarities, the episode at the Jordan does not follow the pattern found in the vocation of Moses (Exodus 3:1–4:27), Isaiah (Isaiah 6:1–13), Jeremiah (Jeremiah 1:4–19), or Ezekiel (Ezekiel 1:1–3:27). Jesus does not respond to the divine voice, as do Moses, Isaiah, and Jeremiah. Granted that Ezekiel, like Jesus, remains silent and does not reply to the voice from heaven, nevertheless, in the story of Jesus' baptism there is nothing remotely like the spectacular vision of the throne chariot recounted by Ezekiel (Ezekiel 1:4–28). The inaugural vision of Ezekiel takes place on the banks of a river (Kebar) with the heavens opening (Ezekiel 1:1), but the rest of that symbolic vision differs strikingly in its content and length from what we read in Mark 1:10–11. A close reading of the four prophetic callings shows up at once the serious differences between these stories and what the evangelists say about the baptism of Jesus. The Gospels do not encourage the conclusion that the voice from heaven conveyed to Jesus for the first time his divine commission.

Mark admittedly represents the episode as Jesus' own visionary experience and personal hearing of the heavenly voice. Perhaps he allows us to conclude that the voice strengthened Jesus' sense of communion with the Father and confirmed a vocation he had already accepted. Yet Mark, still less the other Gospels, does not want to probe and report the inner experience of Jesus. Like the other evangelists and unlike most modern readers, Mark has no particular interest in Jesus' consciousness as such, nor does Luke, even if he makes the baptism epiphany an experience of Jesus in prayer (Luke 3:21–22), as he will do with the transfiguration (Luke 9:29).

The story of the baptism, in particular the earliest version from

Mark, functioned to reveal the identity of Jesus (as approved from heaven in his state of being God's beloved Son), to tell of his consecration for his mission, to introduce his public activity, and to indicate the form that activity will take (as witnessing to the Father and being empowered by the Spirit). The revelatory opening of the heavens, the sound of the Father's voice, and the descent of the (creative and prophetic) Spirit disclosed that with Jesus, the bearer of God's Spirit, the final time of salvation was being inaugurated. Mark 1:10 writes of 'the heavens being torn apart'. The evangelist will use the same verb (*skizo*) about the curtain of the Temple being 'torn in two' – symbolising, among other things, the revelation of Jesus' identity to the centurion and through him to others (Mark 15:38). The baptism episode assures Mark's readers that Jesus was/is related to God in a special, filial way and would initiate a heaven-blessed ministry. John's Gospel, while not directly recounting Jesus' baptism, implies it, twice adding the detail that the Spirit not only descended on Jesus but also 'remained on him' (John 1:32–33). In the same passage John further presents Jesus as the One 'who baptises with the Holy Spirit', a theme that we find at an earlier stage in the other Gospels.

In Mark's narrative, John the Baptist says of the 'mightier one' coming after him: 'He will baptise you with the Holy Spirit' (Mark 1:8). When following Mark at this point, Matthew and Luke add a significant phrase: 'He will baptise you with the Holy Spirit *and with fire*' (Matthew 3:11; Luke 3:16).[16] In the event, neither Mark nor Matthew report any coming of the Holy Spirit, as does Luke (Luke 24:49; Acts 1:8; 2:1–4), who also includes a reference to the 'fiery' Spirit (Acts 2:3, 19). Matthew will include a mandate to baptise 'in the name of the Father, and of the Son, *and of the Holy Spirit*' (Matthew 28:19). Where Luke clearly refers being 'baptised with fire' to the fire of the Spirit at Pentecost, Matthew may understand this fire to be the judgement facing those who fail to respond appropriately to the call for repentance (Matthew 7:19; 13:40, 42, 50; 18:9) when the Son of Man comes to judge all people (Matthew 25:41). At all events, the three Synoptic Gospels all envision Jesus, after being baptised with the Holy Spirit at the outset of his ministry, to work as one empowered by God's Spirit. His baptism with the Holy Spirit signifies the arrival of the final age and the fulfilment of God's promise to pour out the divine Spirit (Isaiah 44:3; Ezekiel 39:29; Joel 2:28–29).

According to Mark, the Spirit who had come down on Jesus

'drove' him at once into the wilderness (Mark 1:12). Like Matthew (Matthew 4:1), Luke puts this more gently: Jesus 'was led by the Spirit' into the desert (Luke 4:1). For Luke, the earthly Jesus showed himself in his ministry of preaching and healing to be the paradigmatic Spirit-bearer (Luke 4:14, 18–21; 6:19). Here Luke approaches the conviction of John (John 1:32–33) that Jesus, like the Glory of the Lord on the Tent of the Meeting (Numbers 14:10), possessed the Spirit permanently and was the source of the Spirit. Unlike Matthew (Matthew 11:25), Luke introduces Jesus' prayer of thanksgiving to the 'Father, Lord of heaven and earth' by representing Jesus as 'rejoicing in the Holy Spirit' (Luke 10:21–24). He depicts Jesus as delighting, under the influence of the Spirit, in his relationship to God acknowledged as Father.

We have just been looking at the way in which the evangelists depict the start of Jesus' ministry in trinitarian terms. But what of Jesus himself and, in particular, his consciousness of sonship and awareness of the Holy Spirit? As we have seen, the Gospel stories of Jesus' baptism, while coming from an historical episode (John did baptise Jesus), may not be used as ready sources of information about some deep experience Jesus himself underwent on that occasion. As John Meier convincingly argues, Jesus' consciousness of his sonship and of the Spirit could have 'crystallised' before, during, or even after the baptism. Although we may reasonably imagine that this consciousness developed and was confirmed through what he experienced at the Jordan, we cannot be 'more specific' about 'exactly when and how this happened'.[17] What can we say about Jesus' experience of the Spirit and consciousness of sonship during his ministry for the kingdom?

The Spirit

Apparently Jesus was aware of being empowered by the Spirit, and deplored the attitude of some of his critics. So far from acknowledging the divine Spirit as being at work in his ministry, they attributed Jesus' redeeming activity to Satan and so sinned against the Spirit (Mark 3:22–30). But Jesus never unambiguously pointed to his deeds as signs of the Spirit's power. Matthew has Jesus say, 'if by the Spirit of God I cast out demons, the kingdom of God has come upon you' (Matthew 12:28; see 12:18). But we may well be reading here an editorial modification introduced by the evangelist. Luke seems to provide the original version of the saying: 'if by the finger of God I cast out demons ...' (Luke 11:20).[18] Elsewhere, however, it is Luke who apparently introduces reference to the Spirit when developing the story of Jesus' rejection in Nazareth (Luke 4:18–21).

In what we glean from the Synoptic Gospels, Jesus is never credited with an awareness of the Spirit that had anything like the intensity of his consciousness of the God whom he called 'Abba'. He never, for instance, prayed to the Spirit: 'Holy Spirit, all things are possible to you, but not my will but yours be done.' Rather, he prayed in the Spirit or with the Spirit in him. As far as the evidence goes, Jesus apparently described and thought of the divine Spirit in a fairly normal prophetic way: the dynamic power of God reaching out to have its impact on Jesus and through him on others. It took Jesus' resurrection and exaltation to initiate a new, characteristically Christian manner of thinking about the Spirit and about the relationship of Jesus to the Spirit.

A much later 'spiritual' interpretation of the transfiguration (Mark 9:2–8 par.) understood the bright cloud to be not simply part of the general scenario for the divine presence and glory as in Old Testament language, but to be a particular image of the Holy Spirit. In the words of St Thomas Aquinas, 'the whole Trinity appeared: the Father in the voice, the Son in the man, and the Holy Spirit in the bright cloud'.[19] Such a trinitarian interpretation might have done better to associate the Spirit with Moses and Elijah, two heavenly figures in the transfiguration who had been especially gifted by the Spirit during their earthly activity. In any case a presence here of the Holy Spirit goes beyond what Matthew, Mark, and Luke intended when reporting this remarkable event. As at his baptism, Jesus said nothing, at least during the transfiguration itself; Elijah and Moses did the talking. Unlike the baptism, the episode took place privately and on a high mountain, the symbolic border between heaven and earth, and not down at a major river and on the location of a religious revival for the general public.[20]

The sonship of Jesus

It was Jesus' sonship rather than any theme connected with the Spirit that Mark and Matthew exploit to structure a 'christological inclusion' into their Gospels. Mark begins with a double announcement of Jesus as the Son of God in the context of his baptism (Mark 1:1, 11), and via the metaphorical sense of baptism as suffering (Mark 10:38) has the revelation of Jesus' sonship peak immediately after the crucifixion with the confession of the centurion: 'Indeed this man was Son of God' (Mark 15:39). Matthew uses a double christological frame: the theme of 'God with us' (Matthew 1:23; 28:20), and that of the obedient Son of God who is tried and tested at the beginning (Matthew 3:13–17; 4:1–11) and at the end (Matthew 27:39–54).

The evidence from the ministry makes it clear that Jesus himself understood his relationship to God as sonship. Because it was/is a relationship with God, this automatically means that we are dealing with some kind of divine sonship. But what kind of divine sonship did Jesus imply or even lay claim to? Merely a somewhat distinctive one, or a divine sonship intimate to the point of being qualitatively different and radically unique? To prevent things from becoming confused and confusing when examining the Synoptic Gospels, we must distinguish between what Jesus said (or seems to have said) about his divine sonship from anything others said about him in this connection. We come across Jesus speaking absolutely of 'the Son' but never of 'the Son of God'. In an important passage, Jesus refers to the Father, identified as 'Lord of heaven and earth' and claims that a unique and exclusive (salvific) knowledge of 'the Father' is possessed by 'the Son' who is tacitly identified with 'me': 'All things have been delivered to me by my Father; and no one knows the Son except the Father, and no one knows the Father except the Son and anyone to whom the Son chooses to reveal him' (Matthew 11:25–30). This is to affirm a unique mutual knowledge and relationship of Jesus precisely as the Son to the Father, a mutual relationship out of which Jesus reveals, not a previously unknown God, but the God whom he alone knows fully and really. A distinctively new feature in Father/Son talk had emerged here.[21]

Then Mark 13:32 (followed probably by Matthew 24:36) also has Jesus referring in an unqualified way to 'the Son' and, with respect to the end of the age, (implicitly) acknowledging the limits of his knowledge over against 'the Father': 'Of that day and of that hour no one knows, not even the angels in heaven, nor the Son, but only the Father.'

Third, the Parable of the Vineyard and the Wicked Tenants reaches its climax with the owner sending to the tenants 'my son' and their killing this 'beloved/only son' (Mark 12:1–12). Mark or the pre-Markan tradition has apparently added 'beloved/only' and almost certainly the tacit reference to the resurrection at the end. But the substance of the parable, with its allegorical allusion to his own violent death (which says nothing about its expiatory value and its actual mode – by crucifixion), seems to derive from Jesus. A son could act as his father's legal representative in a way that slaves or servants could not; in the parable, this differentiates the son from the previous messengers. It seems that Jesus intended his audience to identify him with the son in the story – the only parable in which he gave himself a part.[22] Yet neither here nor elsewhere in the Synoptic Gospels does Jesus ever come out in the open and say: 'I am the Son of God.' (See, however, Matthew 27:43, where those who taunt him during the crucifixion recall, 'He said, "I am the Son of God,"' even though Matthew's Gospel has never previously represented Jesus as saying just that.)

Three times the Synoptic Gospels report Jesus as referring to the divine sonship enjoyed by others here and hereafter (Matthew 5:9; Luke 6:35; 20:36). All in all, even if every one of the references to his own unique divine sonship or the 'participated' sonship of others comes from the earthly Jesus himself, we are faced with much less use of this theme than we find in the Old Testament. In a fairly widespread way those Scriptures name the whole people (e.g. Hosea 11:1), the Davidic king (e.g. Psalm 2:7), and righteous individuals (e.g. Wisdom 2:13, 18) as children/sons/daughters of God. The situation is the opposite with God as Father. The Old Testament rarely calls God 'Father' and hardly ever does so in any prayers addressed to God.[23] Jesus changed that situation, spending his public ministry in dialogue with 'Abba' and humanly aware of his oneness-in-distinction with the Father.

Mark's Gospel at least five times calls God 'Father' – most strikingly in Jesus' prayer in Gethsemane: 'Abba, Father, all things are possible to you; take this cup from me. Yet not my will but yours be done' (Mark 14:36). Even if 'Abba' was not merely a child's address to its male parent,[24] Jesus evidently spoke of and with God as his Father in a direct, familial way that was unique, or at least highly unusual, in Palestinian Judaism. 'Abba' was a characteristic and distinctive feature of Jesus' prayer life. In several passages in Matthew (e.g. Matthew 6:9; 11:25–26; 16:17), in one passage at least in Luke (Luke 11:2), and perhaps in other passages found in these two Gospels, 'Father' stands for the original 'Abba'.[25] The example of Jesus, at least in the early days of Christianity, led his followers to pray to God in that familiar way – even as far away as Rome (Romans 8:15; Galatians 4:6). As

James Dunn points out, 'the clear implication of these passages is that Paul regarded the 'Abba' prayer as something distinctive to those who had received the eschatological Spirit' – in other words, 'as a distinguishing mark of those who shared the Spirit of Jesus' sonship, of an inheritance shared with Christ'.[26]

Altogether in the Synoptic Gospels (excluding simply parallel cases), Jesus speaks of God as 'Father', 'my heavenly Father', 'your (heavenly) Father', or 'our Father' 51 times. Sometimes we deal with a Father-saying which has been drawn from Q, or a source ('Quelle' in German) containing sayings of Jesus used by Matthew and Luke (e.g. Matthew 11:25–27; Luke 10:21–22). Or else we find a Father-saying which, while attested by Matthew alone (e.g. Matthew 16:17) or by Luke alone (e.g. Luke 22:29), seems to go back to Jesus. Matthew shows a liking for 'heavenly' and at various points may have added the adjective to sayings that originally spoke only of 'your Father' or 'my Father' (e.g. Matthew 6:32). The same evangelist may at times have inserted 'Father' into his sources (e.g. Matthew 6:26; 10:29, 32–33). Even discounting a number of such cases as not directly derived from Jesus himself, it remains clear that he spoke fairly frequently of God as 'Father'.

Further, Jesus called those who did God's will 'my brother, and sister, and mother' but not 'my father' (Mark 3:31–35). He invited his hearers to accept God as their loving, merciful Father. He worked towards mediating to them a new relationship with God, even to the point that they too could use 'Abba' when addressing God in prayer. However, being his brothers and sisters did not put others on the same level with him as sons and daughters of God. Jesus distinguished between 'my' Father and 'your' Father. He did not invite his disciples to share with him an identical relationship of sonship. No saying has been preserved in which Jesus linked the disciples with himself so that together they could say, 'Our Father'. When he encouraged the disciples to pray to God as Father, the wording 'Our Father' (Matthew 6:9, unlike Luke 11:2 where there is no 'our') was for the disciples only.[27] If Jesus did say 'Our Father', it was in a prayer he proposed for others ('Pray then like this' – Matthew 6:9). When he invited his hearers to accept a new relationship with God as Father, it was a relationship that depended on his (Luke 22:29–30) and differed from his. That brings us to the key question: In speaking of 'my Father', was he conscious of being 'Son' in some kind of distinctive way, or was he even aware of possessing a unique divine sonship vis-à-vis 'Abba'?

At least we can say this: Jesus applied the language of divine sonship individually (to himself), filling it with a meaning that lifted 'Son (of God)' beyond the level of his merely being either a man made like Adam in the divine image (Luke 3:38), or someone perfectly sensitive to the Holy Spirit (Luke 4:1, 14, 18), or someone bringing God's peace (Luke 2:14; 10:5–6) albeit in his own way (Matthew 10:34), or even a/the Davidic king (Luke 1:32) who would in some way restore the kingdom of Israel. We do not have to argue simply from the fact that Jesus referred to himself (obliquely) as 'the Son' and to God as 'my Father'. He not only spoke like 'the Son' but also acted like 'the Son' in knowing and revealing the truth about God, in changing the divine law, in forgiving sins (outside the normal channels of sacrifices in the Temple and the ministry of the levitical priesthood), in being the one through whom others could become children of God, and in acting with total obedience as *the* agent for God's final kingdom. All this clarifies the charge of blasphemy brought against Jesus at the end (Mark 14:64); he had given the impression of claiming to stand on a level with God. Jesus had come across as expressing a unique filial consciousness and as laying claim to a unique filial relationship with the God whom in a startling way he addressed as 'Abba'.[28]

Even if historically he never called himself the only Son of God (see John 1:14, 18; 3:16, 18), Jesus presented himself as *Son* (upper case) and not just as one who was the divinely appointed Messiah and in that sense *son* (lower case) of God.[29] He made himself out to be more than simply someone chosen and anointed as divine representative to fulfil an eschatological role in and for the kingdom. Implicitly, Jesus claimed a personal relationship of sonship toward God that provided the grounds for his functions as revealer, lawgiver, forgiver of sins, and agent of the final kingdom. Those functions (his 'doing') depended upon his identity as Son of God in relationship with the Father (his 'being').

Inasmuch as Jesus experienced and expressed himself as the Son, that means that the YHWH of the Old Testament was now known to be Father. The revelation of *the* Son necessarily implied the revelation of the Father.

The highpoint of this chapter has been establishing the 'trinitarian' face of the kingdom that Jesus preached and inaugurated. Once again I should warn against being anachronistic and finding too easily the doctrine of Trinity in the story of his ministry. Nevertheless, the ministry of Jesus exhibits him living out in a human way his filial relationship and mission as One sent/coming from the Father in the power of the Holy Spirit.

There remain further key aspects of the ministry to explore which will fill out our portrait of Jesus and his work for the kingdom: for instance, his miracles and parables. But before doing so, it seems important to stand back and reflect on what we have already gleaned about his being divine and being human.

Chapter 3

◆

DIVINE AND HUN

Roses are reddish, and violets are blueish.
If it wasn't for Christmas, we would all be Jewish.

Rabbi Lionel Blue

Live life, welcome Jesus!

slogan on a T-shirt

THE LAST CHAPTER MAY have prompted for some readers the question: What would be lost if we were to read the Gospels, or at least the Synoptic Gospels, and conclude that the historical Jesus was merely an outstanding Spirit-filled prophet, a charismatic preacher who made God very real for others but who was not personally divine? Certainly John (even more than Matthew – e.g. Matthew 1:23) presents him as God-with-us, the Son sent to save the world by the Father (e.g. John 3:16). But did the earliest Christians (after the resurrection) or even the first followers of Jesus (during his lifetime) think that way about Jesus? Should we agree with those who hold the divinity of Christ to be the central theme of the New Testament?[1] In particular, did I exaggerate in drawing that picture of Jesus out of Matthew, Mark, and Luke (who all wrote later than Paul but who all recorded very early, pre-Pauline, oral and written traditions coming from eyewitnesses)?

What would we lose if we did everything we could to play down the high claims made by Jesus and then deny any qualitative difference between the divine presence in him and the divine presence through grace in other human beings, or at least in those of heroic, shining virtue? Some Christians rightly point out the practical consequences of this procedure. If we insist on making Jesus no different in *kind* (even if perhaps somewhat different in *degree*) from outstanding holy men and women who reveal God and contribute to the salvation of others, could we stake our lives on our personal relationship to him? Would we be justified in giving him the unqualified allegiance that we see him asking from his disciples, an allegiance that costs nothing less than everything (e.g. Mark 8:34–38; 10:21)? After all, only God may make such unqualified claims on us. It matters profoundly for the conduct of our lives what answer we give to the question: 'Who do you say that I am?' (Mark 8:29).

This chapter aims to ponder the implications of recognising in Jesus of Nazareth someone who was not only an extraordinary, even uniquely extraordinary, human being but also someone who was and is personally divine. His human life was the human life of the Son of God, or God's human way of being and acting. To reach back to the language used in Chapter One, Jesus was the beautiful, human face of God.

BEING DIVINE

'Soft' accounts of the identity and function of Jesus assert that in a new and final way God was disclosed in Jesus. When Jesus preached the kingdom, he decisively opened the way to God and focused the challenge of faith in God more than anyone had so far done or would ever do. Such accounts 'reduce' Jesus to being God's fully empowered representative, who 'embodied' the divine purpose and plan for human salvation. The choice then becomes: Was and is Jesus only a fully empowered representative who tells us about God, or was and is he God's self-gift? Is he merely a window on God (or, to change the metaphor, someone who mirrors God perfectly), or is he the reality of God? Does he simply reveal God and 'embody' the divine purposes (as a leader of a nation might reveal his/her people and embody their highest ideals), or is he the divine Mystery that is 'beyond' our world but comes from 'the beyond' to be with us and for us, as the divine Gift-in-person within our world?

Such 'soft' accounts of Jesus must face the questions: Could Jesus fully and finally reveal God to us without being himself a 'divine Insider'? Would we be able to find in him the absolute representative of God, someone in whom we can know, experience, and meet God, without his being personally divine? Would we be right to acknowledge in him the Saviour for all human beings, who makes them God's adopted sons and daughters and 'divinises' them through grace (to use the language of the Greek Fathers of the Church), without also acknowledging in him characteristics that identify God? Could he, to adapt a key theme from those writers, promise and give us eternal life without being personally eternal? An affirmative answer to such questions would, in effect, ask us to accept a Jesus who functions for us as God, but without actually being God. This position seems at least as strange as asking others to accept someone who acts in every way as the President of the United States without actually being the American President.

Years ago in my own country (Australia) I heard the American evangelist and itinerant preacher Billy Graham preach one of his Jesus-centred missions to the public. When he came to his punch line, he reached for a text from St John: 'God so loved the world that he sent his only begotten Son' (John 3:16). Graham's punch line would have sounded very flat, if John had supplied him with a different text: 'God so loved the world that he sent another prophet.' We would not have been much more impressed if John had written: 'God so loved the world that he sent a fully empowered representative.' Sending a representative or a prophet would have 'cost' God nothing personally, as the Parable of the Vineyard and the Wicked Tenants implies (Mark 12:1–12). Sending his only son cost the owner of the vineyard everything. By recognising the divine identity of Jesus, Christians are justified in drawing a consoling conclusion: God so valued and cherished us and our world, that the Son of God in person entered this unjust and violent world and let himself become humanly vulnerable, even to the point of dying on a cross. By assuming a human existence, the second person of the Trinity showed how much we meant and mean to God. The alternative, a Jesus who is not truly divine, suggests that God was not really willing to become human and did not after all set such a value on us. Someone else (who was not divine) was sent to do the job of mediating to us final revelation and salvation.

Whenever I read Matthew's words about Jesus being 'Emmanuel' or 'God with us' (Matthew 1:23), I think of a friend who years ago was complaining to me about what he took to be the poor state of Roman Catholicism in France. His voice faltered and he summed things up: 'The French went in for Catholic Action. Then they pushed the line of *témoignage* or witness. Now they are satisfied with mere presence.' To be sure, we can reduce 'presence' to something insignificant, a weak excuse for slothful detachment. But true personal presence is the very antithesis of that. Every day of our lives we look for the presence of those whom we care for and whose care for us makes us live and grow. We cannot endure to leave friendship and love at a distance. We want to enjoy the personal presence of those who fill our minds and let us live in their hearts. We live in God's heart, and Matthew's name for Jesus ('God-with-us') should remind us that God did not want to live that love at a distance. Jesus is and gives us God's personal presence. This divine self-sharing and self-giving make God's love for us truly believable and powerfully effective. So far from being 'the child of a lesser god', someone who will grow up and become commissioned by God as another prophet, Jesus is God-come-to-be-with-us, the Emmanuel who wants to be always and everywhere present to us. So long live Emmanuel, who is the face of God's love present among us. Nothing can substitute for self-gift and presence-in-person. It is precisely such a divine self-gift and presence-in-person that John's Gospel wrote about, Billy Graham preached, and Christians acknowledge in Jesus.

One might take over from my old friend the three key terms and see a lovely sequence. In the creation of the world we can acknowledge God's *action*. The prophets brought the divine *witness*. With the coming of Jesus, God became *present* to us in person.

By acknowledging Jesus to be personally divine, Christians are justified in doing what the vast majority of them have done from the first century and continue to do today: namely, adore him and give him the worship appropriate only to God. The alternative view, espoused by some contemporary, reductionist views of Jesus, may try to explain away this worship as a mere, unfortunate 'mistake' which has persisted since the origins of Christianity. But the bulk of Christians would have been guilty of idolatry in the full sense of the word – by worshipping someone who was not and is not personally divine. For two thousand years such an appalling sin would have underpinned Christianity, or so the revisionists would lead us to believe.

Worship of Jesus began very early in Christianity. In a hymn that he probably took over from existing community worship, Paul named the crucified and exalted Jesus as receiving the adoration of the universe and the title of divine 'Lord' to 'the glory of God the Father' (Philippians 2:10–11). These and further passages show how the worship of Jesus and belief in his divine identity went back not merely to Paul himself but also to the pre-Pauline traditions and to Palestinian Christianity in the years following the crucifixion and resurrection.[2]

What of the Gospels and their accounts of belief in Jesus during his ministry? John's Gospel contains explicit confessions of Jesus that go beyond the merely human. Many Samaritans, after two days of listening to Jesus, concluded that he was truly 'the Saviour of the world' (John 4:42). Even before her brother was brought back to life, Martha made her 'high' confession to Jesus when he identified himself as 'the resurrection and the life': 'Yes, Lord, I believe that you are the Messiah, the Son of God, the one coming into the world' (John 11:25–27). After the resurrection, Thomas confessed the risen Christ as 'my Lord and my God' (John 20:28). In such passages and elsewhere, the Fourth Gospel reflects a situation of Christian faith towards the end of the first century.

The Synoptic Gospels suggest the conclusion that, during the public ministry of Jesus, some of his followers acknowledged him as the divinely authorised Messiah (e.g. Mark 8:29; 11:9–10) and/or prophet (Luke 24:19). Here and there Matthew and Luke also offer hints that the claims and deeds of Jesus were already pushing his disciples to 'upgrade' their belief in him, even to the point of offering him worship (e.g. Matthew 14:33) and recognising him as 'Lord' (e.g. Luke 7:13). But these are only hints, and sometimes we seem to deal with something added by one of the evangelists in the light of his Easter faith.[3] It took the resurrection and the coming of the Holy Spirit for the followers of Jesus to grasp the full force of the (largely implicit) claims to divine identity that they remembered from his ministry for the kingdom.

Jesus himself made the high, divine claims that we summarised in the last chapter. In doing so, he constantly connected himself to 'Abba'. The language of Jesus defined him in the relationship of Son to his loving Father. It was a relationship of total obedience in which without qualification he practised what he preached: 'losing' his life for the sake of the kingdom (Mark 8:35), through an utterly coherent policy of obedient 'self-emptying' (Philippians 2:6–8) rather than through a policy of self-actualisation and self-fulfilment.

During his lifetime Jesus persistently presented himself as 'the Son of Man', a title with a huge range of meaning.[4] It could simply be a circumlocution for the speaker: 'the Son of Man has nowhere to lay his head' (Matthew 8:20 par.) – in other words, 'I have nowhere to lay my head.' At the other end of the scale of possible meanings was the mysterious, heavenly figure, 'one like a son of man', to whom God gave universal and everlasting dominion (Daniel 7:13–14). Jesus himself used this title in such a 'high' sense when laying claim to the divine prerogatives of forgiving sins (Mark 2:10) and judging all people (Matthew 25:31–32). The intriguing range of possible meanings in this self-presentation could well have encouraged Jesus to insert it constantly into his teaching. His hearers were faced with the task of grappling with the mystery of his identity and of determining their personal attitudes towards him.

BEING HUMAN

The Gospels repeatedly testify to the genuine human life that the incarnate Son of God took on. Like any man or woman, he was born and, through his childhood and youth, grew to maturity – physically and intellectually. Unlike Adam and Eve (as they are pictured in the Genesis story), Jesus emerged as a tiny baby from his mother's womb, experienced the dependent life of an infant, and passed through the normal stages of physical and intellectual immaturity before becoming an adult. As with other human beings, there were all kinds of limits to what he could do and to what he could know (e.g. Mark 5:25–34; 13:32). Far from being embarrassing admissions, such limits in his human knowledge reflect the genuine status of his humanity. Like any human being, he felt weariness (John 4:6) and could be so tired that he could sleep through a storm at sea (Mark 4:37–38).

No cold 'extraterrestrial' who would never put his feelings on display, Jesus showed deep compassion for a leper (Mark 1:41), for hungry people (Mark 8:2), and for those who desperately needed his teaching (Mark 6:34). He looked with anger and deep grief at some hardhearted critics who disapproved of his doing good on a Sabbath by healing a man with a withered hand (Mark 3:1–6). He wept in painful frustration over the city of Jerusalem, since its inhabitants risked destruction by not recognising 'the things that make for peace' (Luke 19:41–42). When Lazarus died and left two sisters in deep grief, Jesus also wept at what death had done to a family he loved (John 11:35–37). Jesus looked lovingly at a rich man before inviting him to sell his possessions, give the proceeds to the poor, and join the ranks of Jesus' followers. At the end, in the Garden of Gethsemane Jesus became 'distressed', 'agitated', and 'deeply grieved' (Mark 14:33–34). He did not face his violent and terrifying death with impassive stoicism. Right through his ministry Jesus let his feelings show. One valuable but normally neglected aspect of Jesus' humanity comes from significant clues in the Synoptic Gospels that tell us something about the way his *imagination* worked. The language of life permeated his preaching. We can glean from those Gospels four features of his characteristic imagery.

Firstly, as we saw at the beginning of the last chapter, Jesus showed himself responsive to a broad range of human activity, suffering, and happiness. The pictures he used suggest an imagination that had scanned a great deal of normal human living. When we gather together all his images, we would have a reasonably detailed sketch of daily life in ancient Galilee.

The preaching of Jesus throws light on his imagination in a second way. His sensibility seems to have had certain preferences. Although he was described as a 'carpenter' (Mark 6:3) and the 'son of a carpenter' (Matthew 13:55), he used a large number of farming images. He characteristically drew his illustrations, not from carpentry, but from agriculture and the care of cattle. Piling up manure heaps, growing mulberry trees, harvesting crops from the fields, separating wheat from darnel, minding sheep, ploughing the land – references to these and other farming activities dot the preaching of Jesus. Early in Chapter Two we gathered further examples that illustrate how the activities of farmers caught his imagination.

For the most part, Jesus reveals an imagination that has grown to be sensitively aware of what is going on in the world around him. Nevertheless, there are some gaps in the picture. And this is my third point about his imagery. He delights in children, but he has next to nothing to say about the *mother–child relationship*. Occasionally he glances at the father–child relationship: 'What father among you, if his son asks him for a fish, will instead of a fish give him a serpent; or if he asks him for an egg will give him a scorpion?' (Luke 11:11–12). But Jesus somehow finds his way around the mother–child relationship almost without pausing to notice it. When his eye runs forward to coming tribulations, he grieves over the sufferings that will afflict pregnant women and nursing mothers: 'Alas for women with child in those days, and for those who have children at the breast' (Mark 13:17). Yet, except for one or two such tangential remarks, Jesus bypasses the mother–child relationship. Did he have such an untroubled relationship with his own mother that this intimate area of life produced nothing for his language? Does it take the 'grit' of tension in such area to produce imaginative pearls? Whatever the reason, his preaching does not draw imagery from the ties between mothers and children.

Almost as remarkable is the silence of Jesus about the *husband–wife relationship*. He defends married life by rejecting divorce, and insisting that even in their minds men should not go lusting after other men's wives. He speaks of marriage feasts, wedding guests, and the maidens who waited for the bridegroom to fetch his bride from her parents' home to his own. But there the imagery stops. Nothing survives from the preaching of Jesus about the loving and caring life together of married people. To illustrate the power of prayer, Jesus tells a story about disturbing one's neighbour late at night to borrow some food:

> Which of you who has a friend will go to him at midnight and say to him: 'Friend, lend me three loaves; for a friend of mine has arrived on a journey, and I have nothing to set before him'; and he will answer from within: 'Do not bother me; the door is now shut, and my children are with me in bed; I cannot get up and give you anything'? I tell you, though he will not get up and give him anything because he is his friend, yet because of his importunity he will rise and give him whatever he needs. (Luke 11:5–8)

We might have expected the story to run: 'Do not bother me. The door is now shut, and my wife and children are with me in bed.' But Jesus has the man say: 'My children are with me in bed.' Are we supposed to think of the man as a widower? Or does Jesus and his imagination work too delicately to picture a man in bed with his wife?

By not drawing images from the mother–child and husband–wife relationships, Jesus differs from the Scriptures he inherited. Isaiah and other Old Testament books made childbirth a common simile: 'Like a woman who writhes and cries out in her pangs, when she is near her time, so were we because of you, O Lord' (Isaiah 26:17). Such imagery moves with natural ease to depict nursing mothers and growing babies: 'Rejoice with Jerusalem, and be glad for her, all you who love her ... You shall suck, you shall be carried upon her hip, and dangled upon her knees. As one whom his mother comforts, so I will comfort you' (Isaiah 66:10–13). The husband–wife relationship likewise turns up frequently to focus the disobedience of God's people. Their idolatry and other sins grieved YHWH just as a wife's infidelities grieve her husband. The inspired writers also saw the positive possibilities in this comparison. Hosea celebrates God as the tender lover who longs to woo his people (Hosea 2:14–15). But none of this language turns up in the Gospel record about Jesus.

Besides the mother–child and husband–wife relationships, there are *other facets* of human life that fail to get reflected in the language and imagery of Jesus. He refers to the ravens and the lilies, goes into the wilderness to pray, and climbs mountains with his disciples. Nevertheless, his preaching reveals no delight in nature and natural beauty, and so does not anticipate a development in human sensibility that would come many centuries later. Furthermore, Jesus does not indulge any pathos at the transience of things – something already powerfully present in ancient literature. He is so busy urging his hearers to live like genuine children of God that he has no time to indulge wistful sadness at the world, still less disillusionment with it. He could never make Virgil's sentiment his own: 'there are tears for human affairs and mortal things affect the mind (*sunt lacrimae rerum et mentem mortalia tangunt)'*. Admittedly Jesus weeps over Jerusalem and shakes his head sadly: 'O Jerusalem, Jerusalem, killing the prophets and stoning those who are sent to you! How often would I have gathered your children together as a hen gathers her brood under her wings, and you would not' (Luke 13:34). But, by and large, Jesus says little about his own failures and perplexities.

Finally, images drawn from *history, current world affairs, and geography* hardly surface in the preaching of Jesus. There is a hereness and a nowness about his language, a concern with the scene right in front of him. He recalls, of course, a few episodes from biblical history or legends like the story of the flood and the destruction of Sodom. But Jesus betrays little interest in the past. He never mentions that founding event in Jewish history, the exodus from Egypt. The Maccabean revolt (which began in 167 BC), the Hasmonean period (134–63 BC), the capture of Jerusalem by Pompey in 63 BC, the switch of Jewish allegiance to Julius Caesar, the reign of Herod the Great (37–4 BC), and all the other crowded events of recent history never get a passing nod in the preaching of Jesus. That larger world of politics does not come into sight. Apart from a brief remark about paying taxes to Caesar (Mark 12:13–17) and a comment on some victims of Pilate's brutality (Luke 13:1–5), Jesus hardly even suggests that he is living in a province of the Roman Empire. Once he draws a lesson from a military build-up – the king with ten thousand troops deciding not to risk war against a king with twenty thousand troops (Luke 14:31–32). But Jesus names no specific king and no particular cold-war situation in the Mediterranean world of the first century. Another time he speaks vaguely of 'a nobleman' who 'went into a far country to receive kingly power and then return' (Luke 19:12). But he cites no specific historical figure as the peg on to which he hangs the Parable of the Pounds that follows. The mind and imagination of Jesus reach out to the *immediate situation here and now in front of him*. He neither scans history, not even the most recent history, nor lets his eye run around the Roman Empire for images and examples that he could press into service.

At times the message of Ezekiel and other classic prophets glances around the world of their day: Mesopotamia, Egypt, Cyprus, Greece, southern Russia, and other places. But the known geography of his day provides little or no imagery for Jesus. His preaching does not even suggest that he lived near the Mediterranean.

To sum up: there is a hereness and a nowness about the language of Jesus, a vivid concern with the people and the scene right in front of him. He responds to everything he sees and hears. He does not anticipate the rise of the romantic imagination that revels in ancient times and faraway places.

Fourth, we throw away any right to comment on the way Jesus perceived reality, if we ignore the *earthy particularity* of his language. Characteristically, he answered general questions like 'Who is my neighbour?' by telling a story (Luke 10:29–37). Of course, other rabbis did that – both before and after Jesus. But the fact that they displayed this habit did not make it any less his own. He thought from below, not by way of deduction from above. He offered cases from which his audience could draw general principles, if they wanted to. Even his generalising remarks stayed close to the earth: 'No one after drinking old wine desires new' (Luke 5:39). There was a common touch to the proverbial saying he cited: 'Doubtless you will quote to me this proverb: "Physician, heal yourself" ' (Luke 4:23). He invited his audience to attend to the particular things around them. His imagination was attuned to the earthy wisdom of ordinary people. All of this made him the supreme preacher with the common touch. He spoke with us and to us, not merely at us.

Let me draw matters together: the pictures and, in general, the language that Jesus used suggest at least four conclusions about the way his imagination worked:

1. A very wide range of things in his immediate environment caught his eye. If he was intensely aware of God, he also seems to have been intensely aware of what he experienced on the human scene.
2. Among the things he observed he had his preferences – notably for the activities of farmers.
3. In what he appeared to notice or at least in what he wanted to reflect on, there were some 'gaps' – for instance, the mother–child relationship and the larger world of politics.
4. His mind and imagination seem to have worked from below – from the concrete case. In his own special way he disclosed the earthy wisdom of ordinary people.

Examining in this fashion the imagery that Jesus employed, we can glimpse something of the way in which his (human) perception of the world worked. To move through his language to some insights into his imagination can only be a real gain.

THE SIGNIFICANCE OF JESUS' HUMANITY

Recognising Jesus to be truly and fully human is obviously utterly important for Christian faith. First, our world is no longer only the 'work' of the Son of God; he is now part of it. He no longer merely sees its life; he is caught up in it. He now experiences immediately our world of joy and sorrow, hunger, weariness, hatred, fear, and pain. When taking on the human condition, he claims no special exemption and treatment; he shares it all with us. He now knows at first hand what it is to be human – with all our limits, including the final limit of death. As one of us, he can experience and love us.

Second, he can represent human beings before/to God, since he belongs to us by completely sharing our condition both in life and in death. An 'alien' who does not authentically share as an insider in our condition could not appropriately represent us human beings. Third, by being truly and fully one of us, Jesus can communicate very concretely and show us how to act, suffer, and pray – in short, show us what a human life before God should really be.

A fourth issue has been sketched above. The fact that Christ has genuinely shared our experience from the inside can persuade us that God personally understands and loves us. Thus we can be convinced that we are uniquely worthwhile and loveable. By taking on the full human condition, the Son of God assures us of this in a way that no amount of messages from and about God could, so long as God remains personally an outsider. Fifth, we can lovingly identify with and follow Christ in faithful discipleship because we know that he shares our human condition.

Sixth, if his genuine humanity brings the effective revelation of God, it likewise indicates something about the nature of our redemption. God also heals and saves us from the inside and not simply by a divine action from the outside. Our Saviour is also one of us. The Fathers of the Church were classical champions of the conviction that Christ must be truly human and truly divine if he is to function as our effective Redeemer.[5] To mediate revelation and salvation, Christ needs, so to speak, a foot in both camps.

DIVINE AND HUMAN

Right from the outset Christians had to struggle with the two sides of their basic faith in Jesus: his being simultaneously divine *and* human. In his Letter to the Galatians, written around AD 55 and so more than ten years before Mark composed his Gospel, St Paul expressed the 'double' aspect of his faith. Christ was both the Son 'sent by the Father' in 'fullness of time' and the Jewish child born of 'a woman' (Galatians 4:4). A few years later the Apostle expressed the same two aspects in the opening words of his Letter to the Romans. Christ was both physically 'descended from David' on the human side and Son of God manifested and installed as such through his resurrection from the dead (Romans 1:3–4).

The challenge has been to hold together this double affirmation. By the end of the first century two opposite false tendencies had already emerged, to mark out for all time the possible extreme positions. On the one hand, Ebionities, an umbrella name for various groups of Jewish Christians, considered Jesus to be no more than the human son of Mary and Joseph, a mere man on whom the Spirit descended at baptism. This was to assimilate Christ so much to us that he too would need redemption, and so could not function as 'the Saviour of the world' (John 4:42). On the other hand, the early heresy of

Docetism held that the Son of God merely appeared to be a human being. Christ's corporeal reality was considered 'heavenly' or else a body only in appearance, with someone else, such as Simon of Cyrene, suffering and dying in his place. The Docetic heresy, to the extent that it separated Christ from the human race, made him irrelevant for our salvation. The Johannine literature insisted against Docetic tendencies that Christ had truly 'come in the flesh' (1 John 4:1–3; 2 John 7) and against any Ebionite tendencies that he was truly divine Lord (John 1:1; 20:28).

During the ministry of Jesus, his genuine humanity was blatantly clear to all, friends and foes alike. But was he more than merely human? An affirmative answer had to wait until after his resurrection from the dead and the coming of the Holy Spirit. Even in St John's Gospel it was only in that post-Easter situation that Thomas confessed 'My Lord and my God'.

In the light of Easter faith one can reflect on the miraculous activity that marked the ministry of Jesus. To be sure, inasmuch as these deeds required special activity on the part of God, they went beyond the merely human. At the same time, they involved human gestures and words from Jesus. Before healing a leper, he reached out his hand and touched him (Mark 1:41). When bringing the daughter of Jairus back to life, he took her hand and said, 'Little girl, get up' (Mark 5:41). The miraculous deeds of Jesus involved him in being both divine and human. They are the theme of our next chapter.

Chapter 4

JESUS THE HEALER

Go and tell John what you hear and see: the blind receive their sight, the lame walk, the lepers are cleansed, the deaf hear, the dead are raised, and the poor have the good news brought to them.

Matthew 11:4–5

Jesus went about doing good and curing all who had fallen into the power of the devil.

Acts 10:38

IN ACTS 10:38, LUKE sums up Jesus' activity for the kingdom as 'doing good and curing' people who were afflicted by disease and demonic powers. A few chapters earlier, Luke has already called him by a lovely title, 'the Author of life' (Acts 3:15). Jesus had healed people and restored them to fresh life, because he was supremely good and powerful. In his compassion, he gave them back their full humanity.

The last chapter recalled the *compassion* that Jesus showed to all kinds of people and in all kinds of ways. A leper asked for a cure, but Jesus would not heal him without first compassionately reaching out and touching him – presumably on his ravaged face (Mark 1:40–42). Shunned and excluded from society, the leper was now restored to normal human living. Mark writes of Jesus 'being deeply moved' at the sight of the leper, and will use the same verb (*splanchnizomai*) to describe the reaction of Jesus when he saw a crowd of people waiting for him 'like sheep without a shepherd'.[1] As the Revised English Bible translates the phrase, 'his heart went out to them'. Jesus taught them and then miraculously fed them

(Mark 6:30–44). The same verb turns up in the Lukan story of the widow of Nain who had lost her only son (Luke 7:11–17). Jesus was moved with compassion for her ('his heart went out to her', REB) and he brought her dead son back to life.

Compassion so defined the miraculous deeds of Jesus that at least once Matthew added the relevant verb when recounting a miraculous cure. Mark had described how on leaving Jericho Jesus cured the blind Bartimaeus (Mark 10:46–52). Matthew picks up the same story, has Jesus cure two (unnamed) blind men, and adds that he did so because 'his heart went out to them' (REB).[2]

The verses from Matthew, cited above and paralleled in Luke 7:22, lists five types of miracles that characterised Jesus' ministry of healing: the blind saw, the lame walked, lepers were cleansed, the deaf heard, and the dead were brought back to life. Part of this list harks back to the promise that God would deliver Israel and do marvellous things in the age to come: 'then the eyes of the blind will be opened, and the ears of the deaf unstopped. Then the lame will leap like deer, and the tongue of the speechless sing for joy' (Isaiah 35:5–6; see 29:18–19). The saying from Jesus quoted by Matthew and Luke intriguingly does not reach its climax with the startling reference to the raising of the dead. It moves on to add the final sign of the messianic age and an unusual beatitude: 'the poor have the good news proclaimed to them. And blessed is anyone who takes no offence at me' (Matthew 11:5–6; parallel in Luke 7:22–23).

Mark includes many stories of Jesus' miracles, which he obviously believes to belong integrally to the preaching of the kingdom. The other evangelists add accounts of a few further miracles. When we reconstruct the miraculous activity of Jesus, we see him doing good to all: to those who asked for his help and those who did not, to the grateful and the ungrateful (or the merely unresponsive). We also see him doing good in situations where it was dangerous for him to do so.

When exploring the miracles of Jesus,[3] it can be helpful to take two examples from one or other of the classes listed by Jesus in his response to the disciples of John. We can begin with a case from Mark and a similar (but not identical) one from John about men who were in some way paralysed or lame.

TWO PARALYSED MEN

Mark includes a remarkable story about the tenacity of four friends (or relatives?) who are so intent on bringing to Jesus a paralysed man that they climb up on top of a house, dig a hole through the clay roof, and lower their friend down on his stretcher right in front of Jesus (Mark 2:1–12).[4] In the course of the story some scribes say in their hearts, 'this fellow [Jesus] blasphemes', while all those who witness the cure of the paralytic glorify God, saying, 'We have never seen anything like this.' But the four men who have brought the paralytic into the presence of Jesus do not speak. Jesus 'sees their faith', but they do not have a word to say – to express that faith or anything else, for that matter. Nor does the paralytic himself have anything to say. He simply lies there in front of Jesus and, when told to do so, picks up his stretcher and walks out with it. Obviously he has agreed to be carried into the presence of Jesus, and his four friends do just that for him. Yet right through the story these five men remain silent. They all get themselves into the presence of Jesus, which is the only thing that seems to matter to them. Somewhat surprisingly none of them respond with gratitude to what Jesus does for the paralytic, unless we are meant to understand that the four friends should be included among 'all of them' who are 'amazed and glorify God'.

This story from Mark sets what is visible over against what is invisible: the visible power exercised by Jesus in curing the paralytic as evidence for his invisible power to forgive sins. Some link seems to be implied between sin and physical suffering. What the sins of the paralytic were is never specified, nor are we told how long he has been in that miserable condition.

John's Gospel also describes the healing of a lame man, and this time on the Sabbath (John 5:1–10).[5] In that story too Jesus draws some connection between the handicap from which the man suffers and his sins: 'See, you have been made well! Do not sin any more, so that nothing worse happens to you.' Yet there are major differences between the two stories.

Mark does not tell us how long the paralysed man has been in that state and where he lives. John is specific: the lame man has been an invalid for thirty-eight years and lies on a mat near the pool of Beth-zatha. Unlike Mark's paralytic, he receives no assistance from friends, who might have helped him into the pool at the times when, through intermittent movements, the water is believed to possess healing powers. Mark's paralytic is cured because the four friends show a faith that overcomes serious obstacles in bringing the poor man to Jesus and hoping for cure. With the lame man lying next to the pool, Jesus himself takes the initiative by asking: 'Do you want to be made well?' Yet the man responds, not by seeking a cure, but by excusing himself. Since he lacks friends, he has not been able to take advantage of the times when the pool of Beth-zatha might have remedied his condition.

The spontaneous act of Jesus in forgiving the sins of the paralytic ('Son, your sins are forgiven') stands at the heart of the story in Mark. In John's story, however, the link between the lame man's physical suffering and sin comes in only some time later. Jesus finds the man in the Temple and warns him not to sin any more, lest something worse happen to him. (There are even worse things than being a helpless invalid for thirty-eight years: in particular, sin and its results.) But in both stories ominous threats are unleashed, by what Jesus says (in forgiving the sins of the paralytic before healing him) and does (healing the lame man on a Sabbath day). In the former case some scribes are scandalised ('This fellow [Jesus] blasphemes. Who can forgive sins but God alone?'). In the latter case some Jewish authorities start persecuting Jesus, because in their eyes his healing act has broken regulations for the Sabbath.

In the two cases the reactions to the cure differ. In Mark's story the healing of the paralytic prompts those present to break into general praise of God. In John's story, however, the man who has been cured never bothers to express any gratitude for what Jesus has done – either at the time of the healing or when Jesus subsequently meets him in the Temple. Instead, he compliantly reports to some Jewish authorities that it was Jesus who healed him on the Sabbath, and thus prompts their menacing threats against the life of Jesus. The man's behaviour has prompted some commentators to see in him a kind of anticipation of the traitor Judas.

By comparing and contrasting the stories of these two cures, we can glimpse their individual profile and avoid the temptation to take them as simply two versions of one tradition. Moreover, such detailed examination can bring out the vivid, specific, and seemingly eyewitness quality of the accounts.[6] In both cases, albeit differently, the good that Jesus does prompts opposition, even murderous opposition. Dark shadows fall over his loving activity for others.

TWO HEALINGS IN SYNAGOGUES

We take up another story from Mark about Jesus curing a man with a physical handicap, but pair it this time with a similar (but not identical) story about a woman, found only in Luke. These two healings (Mark 3:1–6; Luke 13:10–17)[7] both take place in a synagogue and on a Sabbath day. In neither case are we told why the man and the woman are present in the synagogue. Has someone (a friend or relative?) brought them there? Do the handicapped persons secretly hope to be healed? At all events neither the man in Mark 3 nor the woman in Luke 13 request a cure. In both cases it is Jesus who takes the initiative by calling them forward and healing them with a word of command. For him the welfare of a human being takes precedence over such religious obligations as observing the Sabbath.

There are differences and vividly particular features of each story to be noted:

1. Mark neither mentions how long the man has suffered from his withered hand, nor does he associate this condition with any sin or with the influence of any demonic powers. Luke explains that the woman has been 'bent over' and 'quite unable to stand up straight' for eighteen years – a way of stressing the severity and incurable nature of her infirmity. Moreover, her condition has been due to 'a spirit that has crippled her', or, as Jesus says, she has been 'bound' by Satan for 'eighteen years'. It is not simply that she has been tied up like an animal for all those years. The evil that has afflicted the poor woman is worse than bonds tethering animals to troughs. The cure that Jesus *instantly* works stands in contrast with the eighteen *long years* of her infirmity.

2. It is the word of Jesus alone ('stretch out your hand') that cures the man with the withered limb. But a prophetic, 'sacramental' gesture is also involved in the healing of the woman. Jesus first says, 'Woman, you are set free from your ailment,' and then lays his hands on her. It is only then that she stands up straight and is cured.

3. A third significant difference concerns the reaction to what Jesus does by healing someone in a synagogue on the Sabbath. The woman responds by praising God at once. Even if the ruler of the synagogue and others with him are indignant at what they take to be a violation of the Sabbath, 'the entire crowd' present 'rejoices at all the wonderful things' that

Jesus is doing. This reaction puts to shame the opponents of Jesus. By contrast, the atmosphere in Mark's story is unrelievedly threatening. The man who has been cured expresses no gratitude. There is no positive response from anyone, and no one speaks up for Jesus. The episode begins with some anonymous hostile people 'watching' Jesus to see whether he will work a miracle on the Sabbath. He looks around with anger and sorrow at their hardhearted and stubborn stupidity. The situation is one of real conflict. When Jesus cures the handicapped man, his critics, now identified as some Pharisees, leave immediately and begin plotting with 'the Herodians' to destroy Jesus. In the event, neither group will be involved in the death of Jesus when Mark comes to tell the story of the passion. But Mark places the threat of death early in his narrative of the life-giving ministry of Jesus.

The question that Jesus asks before healing the man in Mark 3 ('Is it lawful to do good or to do harm on the Sabbath, to save life or to kill?') sets life over against death. Jesus saves a life by healing a man's crippled hand – a symbol of the fullness of life that Jesus proclaims and brings. Right from his prologue, John will take up the theme of life, as a *leitmotif* for his Gospel. Jesus is not merely the life-giver *par excellence*; he is Life itself. Yet, just as in Mark 3, John will set Jesus the Author of life over against the forces of death.

Luke's story of the healing of a crippled woman is one of the few miracle stories that the evangelist introduces in a long section about Jesus on his pilgrimage to Jerusalem (9:51–19:28). The story shows Jesus conquering evil on that journey up to Jerusalem where he will personally face evil in another form. Delivering the woman from bondage belongs to the divine plan of salvation that 'must (*dei*)' (Luke 13:16) work itself out in the ministry of Jesus. Setting her free from bondage symbolises the full work of deliverance on which Jesus is intent.

TWO HEALINGS OF LEPERS

We can now pass to another class of miraculous deeds listed by Matthew 11:5, of which only two examples are recorded: the cure of one leper (Mark 1:42–45)[8] and that of ten lepers (Luke 17:11–19).[9] In the first case, the leper boldly ignores the law about maintaining his distance from others. He seeks Jesus out, falls on his knees, and asks to be healed ('If you choose, you can make me clean'). Jesus shows his own (compassionate) boldness by touching the man's ravaged face before curing him ('I do choose. Be made clean').

The ten lepers in Luke's story observed the law by keeping their distance, when they cried out in a less specific request for help: 'Jesus, Master, have mercy on us.' Jesus performed a miracle of healing at a distance, but did so by testing the lepers' trust in his power to cure them. 'Go and show yourselves to the priests,' he said. 'And as they went, they were made clean.' With that they were healed and incorporated again into 'normal' human society. But nine of them failed to return and did not express their gratitude to Jesus. They received only a physical healing, and that was their loss. They missed the greatest chance in their lives.

A Samaritan outsider who had been a companion in misery with the other nine lepers (presumably Jewish) 'saw that he was healed and turned back, praising God with a loud voice'. The language is laced with implications. He 'saw' with the eyes of faith what had happened to him, and therefore he 'turned' around or was 'converted', when he returned to Jesus and glorified God. In his case a physical healing symbolised a spiritual conversion. The initial cry in which he joined ('Jesus, Master, have mercy on us') ended with his conversion to God and the divine agent, Jesus. Recognising the identity of Jesus, he 'prostrated himself at the feet of Jesus and thanked him'. It is only here in the Gospels (and also only here in the whole of the New Testament) that thanks are expressed to Jesus; elsewhere they are expressed to God.[10]

The story closes with Jesus declaring to the man at his feet: 'your faith has made you well'. Only the grateful Samaritan is described as having faith, and Jesus declares that his faith has brought him not only physical healing but also salvation in the full sense. He has been cleansed of leprosy and, what is much more important, his eyes of faith have been opened. Such saving faith presupposes and responds to the saving activity of God operating in Jesus. It calls a human being to praise God with gratitude and turn towards Jesus with reverent homage. Thus the story of the Samaritan enters essentially into a vital motif of Luke's Gospel: the saving activity of Jesus, announced at the nativity by an angel of the Lord ('to you is born this day in the city of David a Saviour, who is Christ the Lord') and deployed in the public ministry of Jesus – not least, through his miracles of healing.

'THE DEAD ARE RAISED'

When Luke quotes the words of Jesus to the disciples of John, 'the dead are raised' (Luke 7:22), his Gospel has already provided an example of such a remarkable deed (the raising of the widow's son in Luke 7:11–17) and will provide another example (the raising of the daughter of Jairus in Luke 8:40–56).[11] Let us take up the two stories and then compare and contrast them.

Before he recounts what happened at Nain, Luke has already demonstrated the merciful, saving action of God at work in Jesus. In particular, the episode that immediately precedes the raising of the widow's only son involves the healing at a distance of the slave or servant of a centurion in Capernaum (Luke 7:1–10), to which we return below. After showing his power on behalf of a gravely ill person, Jesus reveals that saving power on behalf of a person who is dead and about to be buried. He brings the dead man back to life simply with the words: 'Young man, I say to you, rise!' For the first time in a narrative section Jesus is called 'Lord' in a way that suggests more than human status.[12] 'When the Lord saw her [the widowed mother]', Luke writes, 'he had compassion for her and said to her, "Do not weep".'[13] Then he comes forward and raises her son from the dead. Clearly Luke has placed this story and that of the healing of the centurion's servant who had been not only ill but 'close to death' immediately before the visit of John's disciples who ask Jesus: 'Are you the one who is to come, or are we to wait for another?' (Luke 7:19–20). The stories about Jesus' power over death provide a clear basis for the reply: 'the dead are raised'. Jesus has already revealed his power as Lord of life and death.

Unlike the story from Nain, which is found only in Luke's Gospel, the raising of Jairus' daughter has been taken over from an earlier Gospel (Mark 5:21–43). In telling how the little girl was brought back to life, Luke adds something significant by calling her Jairus' 'only' daughter. Luke's desire for parallelism and pathos is clear. Just as the dead young man was the 'only' son of the widow at Nain, so the little girl who died was the 'only' daughter of Jairus.

Apart from this detail, there are at least six other similarities in the way Luke tells the two stories: (1) Unlike the case of Lazarus

(John 11:1–44), Jesus had seemingly never previously met either the young man or the little girl. Their first meeting face to face with Jesus came with their being brought back to life. (2) As we recalled above, Jesus told the widow at Nain not to weep. Before raising the little daughter of Jairus, he told those who were mourning, 'Do not weep', and this time added an explanation: 'for she is not dead but sleeping'. (3) When Jesus raised the young man at Nain, he did this in the presence not only of the young man's mother but also of his own disciples and 'a large crowd' of others. In the case of the little girl, Jesus brought her back to life in the presence of her parents, three disciples (Peter, James, and John), and some anonymous mourners whom he met inside the house of Jairus. (4) The widow took no initiative in asking Jesus to do something for herself and her dead son. Likewise, when news arrived that the little girl had died, Jairus did not make any request to Jesus. The friends (or relatives?) of Jairus told him: 'do not trouble the teacher any more'. No one thought of asking or dared to ask Jesus to do the seemingly impossible: restore the dead to life. It was Jesus who took the initiative by continuing to move towards the home of Jairus and saying: 'Do not fear. Only believe, and she will be saved.' (5) Jesus raised the young man by saying: 'Young man, I say to you, rise!' This matched what he would say to the dead daughter of Jairus: 'Child, get up!' (6) The young man showed, visibly and audibly, that he was alive again: 'The dead man sat up and began to speak, and Jesus gave him to his mother.' Something similar happened in the case of the small girl: 'her spirit returned and she got up at once. Then he [Jesus] directed them to give her something to eat.'

The last paragraph has listed the similarities between the two stories Luke provides about dead people being raised by Jesus. What of the dissimilarities? (1) First of all, the mother of the dead young man at Nain remains anonymous. Apparently the tradition or eyewitness drawn on by Luke supplied the location of the miracle (Nain) but no name for the widow, and the evangelist did not feel free to invent one for her. In the other story the father of the little girl is named in the eyewitness tradition used by Mark, from whom Luke took the story: Jairus. (2) There is no indication that the widow at Nain knew who Jesus was. She did not make any petition, and there is no reference to any faith on her part. Jairus, however, asked Jesus to come home with him since his small daughter was desperately ill. This ruler of a synagogue showed some faith when 'he fell at the feet of Jesus and begged him to come to his house'. (3) The narrative in Luke does not follow the widow's son as he moved from health, through sickness, and on to death. The story begins after he had already died. In the case of Jairus, the story opens with his daughter gravely ill; it is only in the course of the story that she died. (4) There were different reactions to Jesus and what he did. At Nain, struck with reverent awe, the crowd 'glorified God' and said: 'A great prophet has risen among us; God has visited his people.' News of what Jesus had done 'spread throughout Judea and the surrounding country'. Obviously Luke does not think that 'a great prophet' adequately describes someone who raises the dead; hence he adds 'God has visited his people'. He echoes here the *Benedictus*: '[God] has visited and wrought redemption for his people' (Luke 1:68). A few verses later in the same prayer we read: 'the rising sun will visit us from on high, to shine on those who sit in darkness and the shadow of death' (Luke 1:78–79). That was exactly what happened in the miracle at Nain: God visited those (the widow and her dead son) who were 'in darkness and the shadow of death'. The reaction to Jesus in the story of the raising of the little girl was very different. The mourners 'laughed' at Jesus when he said: 'she is not dead but sleeping'. They knew that 'she was dead', and did not (could not) appreciate that Jesus was saying to them that her death, like sleep, was limited in time. After he had brought the little girl back to life, Jesus told the witnesses to maintain secrecy: 'he ordered them to tell no one what had happened'. This attempt to curb intense public interest contrasted sharply with what happened at Nain, where Jesus never tried to check the news spreading about the miracle.

DOING GOOD TO GENTILES

The Gospels record further episodes in which Jesus responded to the needs of non-Jews: both specific individuals and groups. In Capernaum a centurion, a non-Jewish military officer in command of 50 to 100 soldiers, appealed to Jesus when his son (*'pais'* which could also be translated 'servant') fell desperately ill (Matthew 8:5–13).[14] Apparently the centurion knew that, as a Jew, Jesus should not enter the house of a Gentile. In his initial petition he said nothing about Jesus visiting his home. That proposal was raised by Jesus himself, when he offered to come and cure the boy. But the officer was willing to settle for less than

Jesus offered. He was convinced that a word of command from Jesus, even at a distance, would be enough, since diseases obeyed Jesus just as soldiers obeyed their officers. So he humbly waived the favour Jesus had proposed: 'Lord, I am not worthy to have you come under my roof, but only speak the word, and my boy will be healed.' Jesus was astonished at the way the centurion trusted his (Jesus') power to work the cure: 'Truly I tell you, in no one in Israel have I found such faith.' The faith of this Gentile put Israel to shame, in the sense that his faith went beyond anything Jesus had so far experienced in his ministry to Jews.

In response to the centurion's faith, Jesus healed someone at a distance. It is only in two cases that the Gospels record the healing of a person who was out of sight. The other case was that of the Syro-Phoenician woman, a Gentile woman living in Gentile territory; she asked help for her daughter who was tormented by an evil spirit. While Jesus took his mission of salvation primarily to his fellow Jews, he was ready to respond to faith wherever he found it, and he healed the woman's daughter instantly (Mark 7:24–30).[15] The story of the Syro-Phoenician woman stands apart as being the only example in all four Gospels of an exorcism that takes place at a distance and, for that matter, the only example of someone who wins an argument with Jesus.

In that section of Mark's story, many people joined Jesus on his journey through the predominantly Gentile area of Decapolis (Mark 7:31). The crowds who followed Jesus were with him for three days and faced a long trek home. Jesus miraculously multiplied some loaves and fishes to feed them (Mark 8:1–10). Earlier Jesus had miraculously fed 5,000 fellow Jews (Mark 6:36–44). Now, in a separate episode in Mark's story, he provided an abundance of food for a crowd who seem to have been Gentiles. The second feeding substantially parallels the first, and shows Jesus providing plenty to eat for a large group of Gentiles, after having done the same earlier for Jews.[16]

EXORCISMS

The last two examples of Jesus' wonder-working activity present us with cases that might have featured along with the other five categories in Jesus' response to the disciples of John. He might have added: 'the hungry are fed, and the possessed are delivered'. Our next chapter will attend to the former; here let us add something about the latter.

Deliverance from evil spirits features prominently in the account that Mark offers of the ministry of Jesus. When Jesus began his activity in Galilee, his very first remarkable deed was an exorcism. In a synagogue at Capernaum he delivered a man from an 'unclean' spirit, a demon which separated him from worshipping God and from those concerned with ritual purity. People were astonished at the authoritative teaching of Jesus and his power over evil spirits (Mark 1:21–28). Mark, Matthew, and Luke reflect a widespread dread of demons, a great sense of helplessness in the face of demonic activity, and an astonished joy at the power of Jesus over Satan and his forces.

But how should we interpret this activity of Jesus in opposition to Satan and his forces? Should we simply translate the New Testament language in terms of various forms of bondage which afflict human beings and from which they need deliverance, for instance, those obsessions, compulsions, and mental ailments that hold people helplessly captive? Two recurrent experiences encourage me to continue thinking that Jesus was engaged against personal powers of evil from which we need deliverance. First, the massively destructive and self-destructive folly of savage conflicts continues to hint at the existence and influence of invisible satanic evil that inspires the visible, human protagonists. In an article published at the start of the recent wars in the Balkans,[17] Bernard Levin remarked, 'We don't believe in the devil. But the trouble is that the devil does believe in us.' The murderous determination to kill other people has, Levin argued, 'nothing to do with recognisable and logical explanations'. There was, he suggested, 'a powerful scent of brimstone that fills the air'. At that point he anticipated 'the imminent death of twenty thousand' people; in fact around 200,000 died in the four cruel years of the death throes of Yugoslavia. A brilliant, secular journalist, Levin made a good case for attributing to a personal power of evil the blatant insanity and mutual destructiveness of so many wars.

Second, in 1942 C. S. Lewis published *The Screwtape Letters,* supposedly a collection of letters from a senior devil to his nephew, a junior devil, which wittily express what experts on 'the spiritual life' had taught from the time of early Christianity about the activity of evil spirits in tempting human beings. What Lewis and the long tradition behind him had to say about 'good people' being led astray rings true in my own experience. Such people, with the best of intentions, can be mysteriously led astray into doing things that are in fact evil, or at least into failing to do the great things that they might or should have done for the good of others. Obviously, there is very much more to be said about interpreting the New Testament and what it proposes about satanic powers. But those two experiences boost my sense that we should not rush into removing the personal reference when the Gospels report Jesus' activity in overcoming demonic powers.

That activity provoked sharp conflict with some scribes from Jerusalem; they admitted that Jesus performed exorcisms but attributed these acts to demonic powers. They even alleged that Jesus was possessed by Beelzebul, a pagan deity whom they identified with Satan himself. Jesus vigorously rejected their argument. Such divisions between the satanic powers would be unthinkable, as being mutually destructive: 'if Satan has risen up against himself and is divided, he cannot stand, but his end has come.' Jesus pictured himself as a powerful super-bandit who had entered the strong man's house, tied him up, and was 'plundering' his property (Mark 3:22–30).

The most dramatic exorcism in the ministry of Jesus delivered a demoniac who seems to have been a Gentile (Mark 5:1–20).[18] Even if textual variants do not allow us to pinpoint the precise locality (Gerasa or Gadara), the area (the Decapolis) was Gentile. The non-Jewish identity of the possessed man is also 'suggested by the presence of a herd of swine into which the demons flee'.[19] The man has behaved in a violent, antisocial, and self-destructive manner. He lives among the tombs and so belongs, as it were, to the abode of the dead. He is an outcast, excluded from the community, someone with whom no one dares to live. The people of the neighbouring town do not speak with him, let alone love him. He is one of the living dead, an exiled non-person who is cut off from society, feared, and despised. In the words of Mark: 'He lived among the tombs, and no one could restrain him any more, even with a chain. For he had often been restrained with shackles and chains, but the chains he wrenched apart and the shackles he broke in pieces. No one had the strength to subdue him. Night and day among the tombs and on the mountains, he was always howling and bruising himself with stones.' But with a word Jesus overcomes those who torment the poor man, the demonic forces who call themselves 'Legion'. These many demons are then deprived of any place to stay in this world. They are given permission by Jesus to enter a great herd of swine. As swine were unclean animals, it seems fitting for unclean spirits to enter into them. The story then moves, to borrow a phrase from a friend of mine (Peter Steele), to 'the theatre of the diabolical'. Suddenly the two thousand swine stampede, hurl themselves off a cliff, and are drowned in the sea. Without being asked to deliver the demoniac, Jesus sets him free, restores his human dignity, and reintegrates him into the community of men and women. When people come out of the nearby town, they find the demoniac clothed, in his right mind, and sitting peacefully near Jesus. The demons who have tormented the demoniac are gone and have seemingly perished with the pigs. For the first time in years, he enjoys peace of mind and has been led back into the life of human society. The people who have come to see what has happened are no longer terrorised by the former demoniac. But they are 'afraid' and beg Jesus to leave their district. Do these Gentiles fear that, after the suicidal stampede of the swine, they might suffer further loss of livestock? Or is their reaction something deeper, a fear of the numinous power that Jesus has just shown?

The reaction of the ex-demoniac himself is very different. He wants to stay with Jesus, who has proved himself more powerful than a 'legion' of demons. Does the man fear a relapse, once Jesus is gone? Or, as seems more likely, has his deliverance from the forces of evil given rise to a desire to follow Jesus as a disciple? However, Jesus says to him: 'Go home to your friends and tell them how much *the Lord* has done for you, and what mercy he has shown you.' The man obeys and begins to 'proclaim in the Decapolis how much Jesus had done for him'. The evangelist Mark seems to hint at an equivalence between 'the Lord' and 'Jesus', and clearly portrays the ex-demoniac as the first missionary for Jesus. He proclaims Jesus not simply to his 'own people', but also in the whole Decapolis, a collection of ten cities in eastern Palestine.

This chapter has sampled something of the miraculous activity of Jesus. All four Gospels present that activity as a vital motif in his ministry. Any portrait of Jesus would be drastically diminished if it ignored his miracles. But what did they mean and what do they mean in the big picture? To that we turn in the next chapter.

Chapter 5

♦

THE MEANINGS OF THE MIRACLES

Then the eyes of the blind will be opened, and the ears of the deaf unstopped.

Isaiah 35:5

He [Jesus] has done everything well; he even makes the deaf to hear and the mute to speak.

Mark 7:37

SEVERAL WORDS GATHER TOGETHER motifs that shaped the ways in which the Gospels portrayed Jesus' miracles: deliverance, forgiveness of sins, light, and life. Privileged interpreters of his story, the evangelists, who were steeped in the story of Jesus and the testimony to which it had given rise, expounded the import of his miraculous activity in these ways. They understood the miracles to be prophetic gestures that prefigured the sacraments of the Church – above all, the light and life communicated by baptism and the Eucharist, respectively.

DELIVERANCE

We find vivid examples of the effective power over demonic forces exercised by Jesus in the exorcisms. The Gospels viewed human existence as a battlefield dominated by one or other supernatural force: God or Satan. Right from his baptism, Jesus was aware of struggling with the devil in what was and is the end-time of history. He exerted the divine power to liberate people enslaved by demonic forces.

During the ministry of Jesus, someone under the control of evil spirits was at times present when Jesus was teaching (e.g. Mark 1:21–28). The encounter, which ended with Jesus driving out the evil spirit, could almost seem to have happened by accident. At other times, relatives or friends sought Jesus out and implored his help, as did the Syro-Phoenician woman whose daughter was possessed (Mark 7:24–30). In all cases the power of Jesus was very apparent in his exorcisms. He did not begin by laying on hands, using incantations, or appealing in prayer to God for the expulsion of demons. He simply rebuked them, commanded them, and cast them out. The story of the Gerasene demoniac provides the classic example of Jesus delivering someone from the power of the evil one, especially in the long, vividly dramatic form supplied by Mark (Mark 5:1–20).

The closing petition of the Lord's Prayer corresponds to this first meaning of the miracles that Jesus worked. Found in Matthew's longer version of the Lord's Prayer (Matthew 6:13) but not in Luke's (Luke 11:2–4), it has been normally rendered 'deliver us from evil'. But it seems more accurate to translate the petition as 'deliver us from the evil one'. In Matthew's version of the Lord's Prayer, the evil one ('*ho ponêros*') is the same evil one who will be mentioned when the Parable of the Sower is explained. The evil one comes and snatches away 'the word of the kingdom' which is sown in human hearts (Matthew 13:19). But Jesus is stronger, and strikingly overcomes the demonic powers through his exorcisms. No other episode in any of the four Gospels comments more eloquently on the plea 'deliver us from the evil one' than Mark's lengthy story of Jesus delivering the Gerasene demoniac from the grip of a 'legion' of evil spirits.

As was pointed out in the Preface, John, unlike the other Gospels, includes no accounts of demons being expelled by Jesus. Yet Satan is far from absent in the Fourth Gospel. Jesus uses vigorous language about him when confronting critics: 'you are from your father, the devil ... He was a murderer from the beginning and does not stand in the truth, because there is no truth in him ... He is a liar and the father of lies' (John 8:44). Thus John fills out what human beings wish to be delivered from when they pray, 'deliver us from the evil one'. No less than in the other Gospels, the Jesus of the Fourth Gospel is in the business of delivering people from lies and death by giving them the truth and the fullness of life.

Not only the exorcisms but also other miracles worked by Jesus are victories over evil. In their various ways they can all be seen as acts of deliverance that contribute to the liberation of human beings and their world. Who is truly free? All find themselves in some kind of bondage.

FORGIVENESS OF SINS

The Markan story of the healing of the paralytic is laced with implications about the connection between a miraculous healing and the forgiveness of sins (Mark 2:1–12). Jesus first forgives the sins of the silent man, and then proceeds to heal him of his physical ailment. We might apply to this case a phrase from an alternative prayer proposed for priests in the Latin rite before receiving Holy Communion. The paralytic receives a double blessing, 'health in mind and body'.

In this case it was the person healed who also received forgiveness for his own sins. His visibly handicapped condition reflected and symbolised something invisibly wrong with him in his relationship with God. Jesus dealt with the visible *and* the invisible handicap. On other occasions someone was physically healed (e.g. a man with a withered hand) and nothing was said about his spiritual condition, while others who were present and witnessed the miracle (some hostile Pharisees) needed to be healed spiritually. Their hard, hostile hearts called out for divine healing and forgiveness (Mark 3:1–6).

Perhaps more than the other evangelists, Luke takes up the link between miracles of healing and the miracle of forgiveness. He follows Mark in reporting the healing of the paralytic (Luke 5:17–26), and then presses on to develop the connection Jesus had made between bodily healing and forgiveness. For Luke the forgiveness of sins is the spiritual equivalent of healing the sick and the raising of the dead. Both belong to that fullness of salvation which Jesus brings. The link emerges beautifully in Chapter 7 of Luke's Gospel and does so in three stages. First, the evangelist pictures Jesus bringing 'physical' salvation in Capernaum to the slave of the centurion and in Nain to the widow who has lost her only son. Second, the evangelist comments on the ordinary people and the tax-collectors who had been willing to confess their sins and receive baptism from John – unlike Pharisees and scribes (experts in Jewish law) who refused to be baptised by John and so 'rejected God's purpose for themselves' – their spiritual salvation (Luke 7:29–30). Third, an anonymous sinful woman turned up at a dinner to which Jesus had been invited. He unlocked her pent-up feelings of repentance: 'She stood behind his feet, weeping, and then began to bathe his feet with her tears and to dry them with her hair. She continued kissing his feet and anointing them with ointment' from an alabaster jar (Luke 7:36–38). In defending the woman's conduct, Jesus underlined her 'great love' which showed that her many sins had been forgiven. The whole episode ended with Jesus saying to her: 'your faith has saved you; go in peace' (Luke 7:47–50).

There is no other scene in the Gospels which suggests more poignantly the exchange between a reputedly sinful woman (Grushenka) and a young monk (Alyosha) in Fyodor Dostoyevsky's *The Brothers Karamazov*: 'She fell on her knees before him as though in a sudden frenzy. "I've been waiting all my life for someone like you. I knew that someone like you would come and forgive me. I believed that nasty as I am, someone would really love me, not only with a shameful love." '[1] These could have been the words or the thoughts of the anonymous woman in Luke 7. The story of her being 'saved' draws together in one divine drama of salvation the spiritual miracle of repentance with the physical miracles of healing the sick and raising the dead. With her, Luke closes the circle of Chapter 7 in his Gospel.

LIGHT FOR THE BLIND

In reply to the disciples of John the Baptist, Jesus names as the first example of his messianic deeds 'the blind see'; 'the deaf hear' comes in fourth place (Matthew 11:5). In the event the Gospels report only a few specific examples of such miracles, but the cases brilliantly suggest the redemptive activity of Jesus. One can reasonably suppose that he knew what immediately followed the first Servant Song in Isaiah and understood his mission accordingly: 'I am the Lord, I have called you in righteousness ... I have given you as a covenant to the people, a light to the nations, to open the eyes of the blind, to bring out the prisoners from the dungeon, from the prison those who sit in darkness' (Isaiah 42:6–7). Let us examine how two evangelists, Mark and John, develop this meaning conveyed by 'opening the eyes of the blind'.

Several chapters in Mark picture Jesus as struggling to bring spiritual insight to his obtuse disciples. Earlier, Jesus adapts two verses from Isaiah 6:9–10 to express the insensitive state of 'those outside'; they lack the spiritual capacity to see and hear what Jesus and his message are offering them (Mark 4:11–12). But such comments are soon applied to the disciples themselves. After multiplying five loaves and two fish to feed five thousand hungry people, Jesus made the disciples take a boat across the Lake of Galilee while he went up a mountain to pray. When he came to them, walking on the water, they 'were utterly astounded, for they did not understand about loaves, but their hearts were hardened' (Mark 6:51–52). The Gospel begins here to use about 'insiders' the language already applied to 'those outside'.

Mark's narrative then supplies two similar miracles, which symbolise Jesus' desire to heal the spiritual blindness and deafness of his disciples. The healing of a deaf-mute in the Decapolis (Mark 7:31–37) is paired with the healing of a blind man at Bethsaida (Mark 8:22–26). Jesus wanted to empower his followers to hear and see what they were encountering in him and his activity. This would take time, and come about only through a miracle of enlightenment.

Immediately before the cure of the blind man at Bethsaida, we find Jesus in a boat with his disciples, who fail to appreciate what Jesus is saying to them and what he has done in feeding the five thousand and subsequently in feeding the four thousand. He sternly reproaches them in words that he has used about the spiritual insensitivity of outsiders: 'Do you still not perceive or understand? Are your hearts hardened? Do you have eyes and fail to see? Do you have ears and fail to hear?' (Mark 8:14–21).

Immediately after the cure of the blind man, the scene switches to the far north and Caesarea Philippi. There, Jesus puts to the disciples the question: 'Who do you say that I am?' When Peter replies, 'You are the Messiah', Jesus makes the first prediction of his coming passion, death, and resurrection. Peter reacts by 'rebuking' Jesus. But Jesus takes nothing back; in fact he sees in the words of Peter a continuation of Satan's temptation (Mark 1:13): 'Get behind me, Satan! You are entertaining the thoughts not of God but of human beings.' Jesus then goes further, by insisting on the cost of discipleship: 'if any want to become my followers, let them deny themselves and take up their cross and follow me' (Mark 8:27–38).

In Chapters 8–10, Mark recounts various sayings and doings of the historical Jesus and weaves them together in order to drive home the lesson which also stems from Jesus himself: unless divine grace opens the eyes of his followers, they will not be able to follow in the footsteps of a suffering Messiah. This spiritual enlightenment may come in stages, just as the blind man at Bethsaida was not healed at once. His healing came through successive acts of Jesus who twice laid hands on his eyes. At Caesarea Philippi, Peter has seen something and presumably the other members of the core group of disciples agree with him in recognising Jesus as the hoped-for Messiah. But they have not seen everything – either about the identity of Jesus himself or about the nature and cost of discipleship.

Mark constructs his spirituality of the cross around a pilgrimage of Jesus and his disciples involving three 'stations of the cross': from Caesarea Philippi, 'through Galilee' (Mark 9:30), and on to 'the region of Judea' and 'the road going up to Jerusalem' (Mark 10:32). This pilgrimage to Calvary is punctuated by two further predictions of the passion – in Galilee and Judea, respectively (Mark 9:30–32; 10:32–34). The disciples do not understand what Jesus is saying, and are even afraid to ask (Mark 9:32). They continue to show themselves dull-witted about such matters as real leadership and the right to do deeds in the name of Jesus (Mark 9:33–41). In response to his third prediction of his passion, James and John ask for places of special honour, but they still have much to learn about the destiny of Jesus and themselves. So too have the other ten apostles, who are angered by what the two brothers presume to ask (Mark 10:35–45).

This whole section in Mark's Gospel begins with the healing of a blind man (Mark 8:22–26). Very significantly it ends with a similar miracle when Jesus gives sight to Bartimaeus, a blind beggar sitting by the roadside at the gates of Jericho (Mark 10:46–52). In the Synoptic Gospels this is the only case of someone who is healed by Jesus and named, but only by Mark. The account given by Luke 18:35–43 drops his name, whereas that in Matthew 20:29–34 not only drops his name but reports the cure of two blind beggars.[2] Both Luke and Matthew write of the blind man who has been healed (or in Matthew's case of the two blind men) 'following' Jesus. Mark meaningfully states that Bartimaeus 'followed' Jesus 'on the way'. A few verses earlier this 'way' has been identified as 'the way going up to Jerusalem' (Mark 10:32).[3] The implication seems patent: without being healed and empowered by God, people will not have the spiritual insight to follow Jesus on the way of the cross. The words Jesus addresses to Bartimaeus ('your faith has made you well') imply both physical and spiritual healing.

John's Gospel dedicates a whole chapter to the link between

physical and spiritual 'enlightenment'. The disciples are with him when Jesus meets a man blind from birth (John 9:1–41). They see the poor man sitting there and begging, but show themselves quite blind to his misery and also to the power of Jesus. They do not ask their master to do anything. Rather, they treat the blind beggar as a good occasion for a theological discussion: 'Rabbi, who sinned, this man or his parents, that he was born blind?' The question is somewhat inane, even for those who (wrongly) understand physical ailments to be a divine punishment for sin. How could the man have sinned before birth and so be punished by being born blind?

The blind man does not say anything, let alone ask for a cure. Somehow he already knows Jesus' name (John 9:11), and presumably is heartened by what he hears Jesus say: 'It was not that this man sinned, or his parents, but that the works of God might be made manifest in him. We must work the works of him who sent me, while it is day; night comes, when no one can work. As long as I am in the world, I am the light of the world.' Then Jesus takes the initiative and anoints the blind man's eyes with clay. Now the blind man has something to do. He must go and wash his eyes in the pool of Siloam. He does that and comes back seeing for the first time in his life.

At this point Jesus has left the stage, so to speak. In the Fourth Gospel there is no other passage in which he is so long off the stage (John 9:7b-34). But the man who now sees fills the scene as he starts to speak and act with simple vigour. He begins also to suffer in new ways.

Encountering Jesus has brought pain as well as healing. The man born blind would presumably have learned to cope with his situation. Then Jesus comes along not only to heal him and reconstruct his world, but also to disturb his relationship with his parents and bring him into conflict with the religious authorities (John 9:13–34).

Yet the man born blind moves from truth to truth. He first recognises 'the man called Jesus' as 'a prophet' and 'from God'. Finally, he worships Jesus and expresses his faith: 'Lord, I believe.' His encounter with Jesus has moved steadily to that climax. What leads him there is his willingness *to trust and integrate his own experience.* The religious authorities badger him and in the name of God's sacred laws try to force him to agree that Jesus is a sinner. After all, the work of healing (like the episodes in Mark 3:1–6 and Luke 13:10–17 that we saw above in Chapter Four) has taken place on the Sabbath. But the man stands his ground and insists on what he has experienced: 'Whether he is a sinner I do not know; one thing I know, that though I was blind, now I see.' Further reflection on this experience makes him realise the startling nature of what has happened: 'Never since the world began has it been heard that anyone opened the eyes of a man born blind. If this man were not from God, he could do nothing.' When Jesus returns to search for him, the man born blind is ready to confess his faith.

Chapter 9 of John's Gospel presents a scene of universal blindness, of human beings born into world of spiritual darkness. There is the man born blind himself. The disciples of Jesus do not see the truth (John 9:1–2). Some Pharisees are likewise spiritually blind (John 9:39–41). At the level of language the chapter is dominated by words for blindness, eyes, and sight. Among all those terms one recurrent phrase, 'to open the eyes' (John 9:10, 14, 17, 21, 26, 30, 32), points ahead most clearly to the great conclusion. We can think that we see, by presuming ourselves to have spiritual insight. But it is only when we acknowledge that we are spiritually blind and ask for help that our eyes will be opened by Jesus, who is the Light of the whole world.

LIFE

Even more than Mark and the other Synoptic evangelists, John expounds the deeper meaning of what Jesus did when opening the eyes of the blind. John likewise goes beyond Mark, Matthew, and Luke in elaborating the nurturing, life-giving significance of Jesus' miracles.

As we recalled in the last chapter, Jesus (according to Mark 3:1–6) defends healing someone on the Sabbath because it means 'saving life'. Matthew 12:9–14 takes over the story but omits the question from Mark ('is it lawful to save life or to kill?'). Luke 6:6–11, however, maintains the reference to life.[4] Then we should recall that the four Gospels tell the story of how Jesus 'saved life' by feeding five thousand hungry people – the only miracle reported by all the Gospels. The Synoptic evangelists use language that evokes the Eucharist when telling the story: '*Taking* the five loaves and two fish, he [Jesus] *looked up to heaven*, and *blessed* (*eulogêsen*) and *broke* the loaves and *gave* them to his disciples to set before the people' (e.g. Mark 6:41). John makes the connection with the Eucharist even clearer by substituting 'gave thanks (*eucharistêsas*)' for 'blessed', and then by letting the story of that miracle introduce a long discourse on Jesus as 'the bread of life' (John 6:22–71). Jesus not only works miracles which bring and enhance life, but he is also life itself. The climax of the discourse comes when Jesus declares: 'I am the living bread that came down from heaven. Whoever eats of this bread will live forever, and the bread that I will give is my flesh for the life of the world' (John 6:51). The life-giving force of Jesus' miracles leads to the conclusion that Jesus himself is divine Life in person (John 11:25; 14:6).

We can draw clear from the miraculous activity of Jesus at least four major themes: deliverance, forgiveness of sins, light, and life. But it is the last which seems to resonate most in human experience and still communicates best. Let me blend in two homilies on life to illustrate this claim and the range of possible re-interpretations and applications.

PREACHING LIFE

Mark 5:21–43

This Gospel passage reports how Jesus healed two women. Those two women and their stories differ in various ways. One was a mature, grown woman; the other a little girl of twelve. One had become poor; she had spent all her savings in an attempt to be cured from the persistent haemorrhaging from which she suffered. The other, the daughter of Jairus, obviously belonged to a well-to-do family.

Then the problems of the two women differed. The grown woman had suffered for twelve years from haemorrhages. Her condition was unpleasant, debilitating, but not lethal. A problem that a good gynaecologist could fix today, it left her in a constant state of religious impurity. The problem for the daughter of Jairus was, to put it mildly, extreme. She became seriously ill and then died. Not even the greatest doctor today can bring back to life someone who truly died.

The two women differed also in the way they came in contact with Jesus. The grown woman encountered him because she went looking for him. She pushed her way through the crowd and touched his clothing. The little daughter of Jairus could not go looking for Jesus, because first she became seriously ill and then died. She came into contact with Jesus, because he walked into her home and entered the room where she was laid out in death.

The way the miracles took place also differed. When Jesus brought the young girl back to life, he did so in a way which seems appropriate. He took hold of her dead hand and said, 'Little girl, I say to you, get up.' His powerful word of command raised her from the dead. In the case of the woman who suffered from haemorrhages, the way in which the healing took place can leave us uncomfortable. Healing power went out of Jesus, but he did not know who had touched his clothing. It can all seem a little magical. Over the centuries some Christians have been bothered by the fact that Jesus did not know at once who had benefited from his healing power.

In short, the two women and the stories of what Jesus did for them differed quite a lot. They varied in age and social status. Their problems were very different. The way they met Jesus and the way he helped them did not coincide. But behind all these differences there is a deep unity between the two stories. In both cases Jesus met the person concerned. He wished to identify the person who had touched his garment and been blessed by his saving power. He wanted to say to her, 'Daughter, go in peace.' He wanted to change a somewhat impersonal encounter into a thoroughly personal encounter. Then, in the case of the daughter of Jairus, he went to her bedside, took her by the hand, and said: 'Little girl, I say to you, get up.' He was not going to bring her back to life without meeting her personally.

In both cases Jesus was there, giving *life* and restoring *life*. The woman's life was draining away through her recurrent haemorrhages. The little girl had lost her life. In both cases Jesus came on the scene as the life-healer and the life-giver.

John 6:41–51

For a long time, I have been fascinated by the way modern advertising uses the language of 'life'. So much advertising promises to improve and enhance our life. One brand of Parmesan cheese on sale in Italy offered to help customers to 'live in good form and live better'. I remember a huge advertisement for milk, which guaranteed to bring serious milk-drinkers towards 'a better life'. A sharp after-dinner drink joked about its name ('Amaro') to assure prospective drinkers that it would 'make life less bitter'. In the campaign leading up to an election some years ago, one Italian political party popularised the slogan 'more life, less bureaucracy'. Not unexpectedly *Playboy* magazine used to sell itself with the caption, 'all the pleasures of life'. When I returned to England early in the new millennium and went up to Oxford, I bought a book in one of the world's legendary bookstores, Blackwell's. When the shop assistant handed me the bag, I was delighted to read the message, 'live life, buy the book'.

All that publicity for food, drink, political votes, uncommitted sex, and new books promises customers a richer, more satisfying life. Whatever the real value of the particular items being promoted, the advertisements all converged on one magic word: life. They all undertook to improve and enrich our living. Eat this cheese and drink this liqueur, or somehow fail to live. Be a consumer, or miss out on what matters. Be a playboy, or be nothing.

The truth is that we all have hungry hearts. We want to escape from all that is deadly, and find a life that is fuller and more satisfying. My faith and my personal experience tell me where to look. Look for Jesus. Welcome Jesus and you will be welcoming someone who gives us real life, the fullness of life. He is *the* Lifegiver, the supreme Life-giver. It wouldn't be a bad idea to have T-shirts with the message: 'Live life, welcome Jesus'. If we open our arms to Jesus and let him into our little world, we will live life, the only life that truly fills our hearts and will continue forever.

Modern advertising can offer products that provide passing relief for our hungry hearts, and make life for a time a little bit sweeter and richer. But those products can never fully satisfy our hungry hearts. Only Jesus can do that. Life is a magic word; it is something everyone hungers for. But genuine life is not there for the taking, as *Playboy* magazine and so much modern advertising would have it – in the spirit of 'here's life, help yourself'. We cannot truly live by helping ourselves and by exploiting others – sexually or in other ways.

Real life does not come by taking it for ourselves, but by receiving it from Jesus and sharing it with others. Only Jesus is the supreme Life-giver, the utterly satisfying Life-giver, who offers us life, now and forever. So, live life. Welcome Jesus.

THE HISTORICAL STATUS OF THE MIRACLES

I have dedicated two chapters to exploring the miracles of Jesus, what they mean, and how they might be preached today.

Normally, one faces questions of fact (did the miracles happen?) before tackling questions of meaning (what did/do they mean?). I have reversed the usual procedure, because, in my experience, many reject the factuality of the miracles because they are baffled about their possible meaning. Those who begin to appreciate something of the significance of Jesus' miraculous deeds will have less trouble with their historical status. Nevertheless, this neuralgic question must be faced.

Some dismiss the miracle stories as a secondary accretion, an unfortunate product of the fervid imagination of the first Christians. Those early believers worshipped Jesus as their risen Lord. What could be more natural and inevitable than that they should have looked back through the golden haze of Easter and glorified his human life by attributing to him all kinds of wonderful deeds? Was this not, after all, standard practice in those ancient times? Legends of healing and other miracles gathered quickly around the names of great religious leaders. In any case some of the alleged miracles have magical overtones: the healing of the deaf-mute in the Decapolis (Mark 7:31–37) and the healing of the blind man at Bethsaida (Mark 8:22–26). In both cases the saliva of Jesus functions to heal an infirmity. Can we attribute some of his alleged miracles to his powers of suggestion, which had strikingly visible effects on some people who were physically handicapped or mentally disturbed?

This part of the record about Jesus' ministry cannot be repudiated as easily as that. To begin with, in Mark's Gospel almost half of the treatment given to Jesus' public life is concerned with miracles. Many of the miracle stories are inextricably bound up with other elements in the narrative. In particular, they are remembered as essentially linked to Jesus' forceful preaching of the kingdom. These deeds of power anticipated the full divine rule and complete salvation of God's coming kingdom. If the miracle stories were to be removed from Mark's account of Jesus' ministry, a great deal would have to be ripped away with them. To say the least, it would be very difficult to take all the miracle stories out of Mark and still recognise that Gospel as a substantially reliable guide to the history of the ministry. Either we accept Mark and his miracle stories or we dismiss the book as an unsound source for the activity of Jesus.

Second, here if anywhere, the criterion of *multiple (independent) witness* applies. Besides the actual miracle stories themselves, Mark also records sayings concerned with one class of extraordinary deeds, the exorcisms (Mark 3:14–15, 22–27; 6:7). Then

Matthew and Luke add material from Q (their common source for sayings), which attests that the earthly Jesus worked miracles (Matthew 11:5; Luke 7:22). An interesting pointer supplied by Q concerns the 'woes' pronounced against certain Galilean towns: 'Woe to you, Chorazin! Woe to you, Bethsaida! For if the mighty works done in you had been done in Tyre and Sidon, they would have repented long ago in sackcloth and ashes' (Matthew 11:21; Luke 10:13). Here Jesus speaks of miracles done in two towns, but while the Gospels report his miraculous activity in Bethsaida (Mark 8:22–26; Luke 9:10–11), they have nothing to report from Chorazin. Thus we have a Q *saying* about miracles in Chorazin but no matching story or stories. It appears that this saying came from the earthly Jesus and that the Gospels and/or their sources did not feel free to invent stories about miracles worked in Chorazin or to locate in that town unattached miracles found in the tradition. Further, Luke includes a warning against Herod Antipas which is generally agreed to come from Jesus and which affirms that he worked miracles: 'Go and tell that fox for me, "Listen, I am casting out demons and performing cures today and tomorrow, and on the third day [not to be taken literally but meaning 'in a limited time'] I finish my work"' (Luke 13:32). Jesus insists that no threats from 'that fox' will cut his miraculous activity short. Finally, summary accounts of Jesus' activity include his miracles (e.g. Matthew 4:23; Acts 2:22). Thus at least six different sources witness to the miraculous activity of Jesus. If we wish to widen the application of the criterion of multiple witness, we could also point to ancient Jewish sources. They accepted the fact that Jesus worked miracles but explained it all as sorcery.

As regards the view that in the first century believers were prone to make up miracles and attribute them to religious heroes, we should remind ourselves of John the Baptist. The four Gospels have much to say about the forerunner of Jesus. This great prophet had played a pre-eminent role in preparing the people for the ministry of Jesus, and later he was remembered with honour in the emerging Church. The Baptist had been 'there' as the trailblazer when the Christian movement began. And yet no miracles were attributed to him – a point which John's Gospel explicitly notes (John 10:41). The case of the Baptist establishes that, at least in first-century Palestine, it was by no means inevitable that as a way of enhancing their memory, traditions of supposed miracles would gather around John, Jesus, or any other religious leader.

To sum up: there exists no convincing evidence for the case that Jesus was remembered first as a preacher, and that only later a miracle-tradition was attached to his name. Here we might recall the historical conclusion of Rudolf Bultmann (1884–1976) about the miracles of Jesus: 'Undoubtedly he healed the sick and cast out demons.'[5] Later on, Bultmann argued that miracles are offensive and inconceivable to 'modern' persons.[6] But that is another question. In any case, disparaging remarks about first-century people often suggest or imply that they were uniformly gullible and credulous, and persistently ignore all the elements of sophisticated (and sceptical) culture that had built up for centuries around the ancient Mediterranean world – not to mention elsewhere. Moreover, Bultmann's claim about 'modern' persons ignores, of course, those millions among his and our contemporaries who do not find miracles offensive and inconceivable.

Very often the challenge to the miracles of Jesus comes in the name of *historical method, scientific knowledge,* or *theological conviction.* Cherished principles in the areas of history, science, or theology are invoked to rule out the very possibility of such special divine acts.

It is claimed that historians must deal with human history as a closed system of empirically verifiable causes and effects, in which they should expect things to follow similar patterns (the principle of analogy) and exclude the possibility of religious 'wonders' caused by special divine causality. To maintain that human history is such a closed system is to endorse a pre-supposition – prior to any particular historical investigation – and to assert something that can never as such be proved historically. But one continues to hear this assertion, not least in television programmes about the origins of Christianity in which talking heads from some universities continue to maintain that about the miracles of Jesus and his post-resurrection appearances, 'as an historian this is all that I can say'. Furthermore, analogy means some degree of similarity, but not identity. So, far from ruling out different, even strikingly different, events, the principle of analogy rules them in, inasmuch as it entails both likeness *and difference.* A miracle, in fact, manifests a likeness both to other (ordinary) religious events and a difference (in being a religious 'marvel' that reveals God's special activity in suspending or overriding 'normal' causality). So, far from flouting the historical principle of analogy, a genuinely miraculous event would endorse it.

Science, in general, has become rather more open to the possibility of miracles, in that it has come to allow for what is unexpected and downright extraordinary. While science seeks at every level to describe and explain the phenomena of our world, it has relinquished something of that former rigidity which dismissed the miraculous as impossible. Here, however, one point should be added. A miracle differs from an event that appears to be scientifically unusual, indeterminate, and arbitrary. A miracle is not, so to speak, a 'marvel' which, for instance, baffles the research scientists at the European Laboratory for Particle Physics (CERN, near Geneva), but an event which stunningly conveys God's loving mercy and invites the appropriate human response.

Theologically (or should we say philosophically?) some exclude miracles in principle because they believe that God operates and is revealed only through normal, everyday events. This is to rule out in principle any *special* divine acts, including any miraculous events. Such a position has implications far beyond the particular issue of miracles. The objections to special divine activity that have been repeated or have come up for the first time in the late twentieth century are summarised, classified, and – I believe – satisfactorily answered by Paul Gwynne, who concludes that the concept of special divine action 'emerges somewhat battered but intact. It seems to be far from collapsing and there are good reasons for affirming its coherence and credibility.'[7]

Let us return in conclusion to the Gospel record of Jesus' miracles. I continue to suspect that it is the significance rather than the fact of these miracles which poses a problem for some or even many people. Not only the evangelists but also Jesus himself shunned any exhibitionism. As a saying preserved by Q shows, Jesus understood the preaching of the good news to the poor as the climax of his miraculous deeds (Matthew 11:5; Luke 7:22). When pressed to do so, Jesus refused to legitimate his claims by some 'sign from heaven' (Mark 8:11–12). Even though the words are found only in Luke, what Jesus is reported as saying to 'the seventy' disciples on their return from a trial mission coheres perfectly with his reluctance, attested elsewhere, to exaggerate the importance of miraculous deeds: 'I have given you authority to tread upon serpents and scorpions, and over all the power of the enemy; and nothing shall hurt you. Nevertheless, do not rejoice in this, that the spirits are subject to you. But rejoice that your names are written in heaven' (Luke 10:19–20).

At least something is clear about the way Jesus himself and the evangelists thought his miracles functioned. They were not overwhelming arguments which should *force* people to believe that he was the Messiah and the Son of God. It remained open to his audience to disqualify these deeds as evidence by attributing them to demonic influence (Mark 3:22). Those who refused to be touched in the depths of their existence by Jesus' words were not going to be persuaded by his miraculous deeds.

Positively, Jesus seems to have understood his miracles as deeds of power that expressed and proclaimed the way in which anti-God forces were being overcome. The divine power was finally and effectively saving human beings in their whole physical and spiritual reality: 'If it is by the finger of God that I cast out demons, then the kingdom of God has come upon you' (Luke 11:20). Over and over again Jesus associated his miraculous deeds with his call to a faith that would believe in his authority to forgive human sin and save people from the forces that afflicted them. No less than his preaching, his miracles manifested the reign of God and the divine promise to deliver sick and sinful human beings from the grip of evil.

The stories of Jesus' miracles disclose permanent possibilities of revelation and redemption – *both* meaning and truth *and* new life through liberation from evil and the forgiveness of sins.

Chapter 6

♦

JESUS THE STORY-TELLER

The kingdom of heaven is like yeast that a woman took
and mixed in with three measures of flour until all of it
was leavened.

Matthew 13:33

Then Jesus said, 'there was a man who had two sons ...'

Luke 15:11

THE PARABLES THAT JESUS told and the images he used let us
into his mind and heart.[1] They let us see what he prayed and
thought about, and what he wanted to share with us. They
convey his vision of the world and of all that God offers us. They
show us how he saw reality and what he truly treasured. Above
all, they disclose his deepest and richest answers to the questions: What is God like? What is God doing for us?

Jesus generated his parables and images by noticing a wide
range of human experiences and activities and reflectively presenting them in the light of the reign of God. He told of things
that happened frequently or at least every now and then. There
was no gap to close between his parables and everyday life. He
showed constant insight into and empathy with the ordinary
things of life: sons leaving home to live elsewhere; workers
hired, even towards the end of the day; farmers sowing seed;
hidden treasures being discovered; money being offered for
investment by high-risk speculators; managers being accused of
dishonesty; people running up huge debts; travellers beaten and
robbed on lonely roads; men using fresh wineskins for new
wine; judges lazily neglecting their duties; owners of big estates

going away for shorter or longer periods; farmers thrilled by bumper harvests. Jesus experienced all these things, and they spoke to him of 'Abba', his loving Father, of what 'Abba' was doing in and for the world, and of what 'Abba' expected from human beings. The parables and images Jesus used open a window on what he perceived and remembered – how he saw everything in the light of God, and how he longed to coax us into giving ourselves to God's final rule over our lives.

Some parables have no Old Testament background and seem original to Jesus: for instance, the Lost Coin (Luke 15:8–10) and the Dishonest Manager (Luke 16:1–9). Others have partial precedents: the Parables of the Widow and the Unjust Judge (Luke 18:2–8) recalls, for instance, Old Testament figures of defenceless widows to whom justice may be denied (e.g. Psalm 68:5; Ruth 1:20–21). The Parable of the Prodigal Son (Luke 15:11–32) may bring to mind younger sons like Jacob (who tricks his way into securing the inheritance in place of his brother Esau) and Joseph (sold into slavery by his older brothers). Even then, Jesus gives these figures his own special twist. His widow nags her way towards securing justice from a bone-idle judge; his younger son leaves home freely and manages to dissipate an inheritance with sex workers and dissolute friends.

The original hearers and those close to them treasured the parables they had heard from Jesus and handed them on faithfully, very occasionally adding their own explanations (e.g. Mark 4:14–20). The actual order in which Jesus originally preached his parables has been lost forever. The evangelists often group the parables and/or insert them into the story according to the way in which they want to present the teaching of Jesus in their overall narrative. Their example encourages me to suggest a fresh arrangement of the parables, this time as replies to four questions: What is God's initiative towards us? How should we receive the divine kingdom? How should we live under the divine rule? How should we wait for the end – our own end and the end of all things? This arrangement sets the parables out in a scheme based on divine offer and human acceptance.

This chapter will take up some of Jesus' parables to demonstrate the value in this manner of arranging them. I postpone until the next chapter the Parable of the Prodigal Son, the most sublime of the parables, which has been rightly called the heart of the Third Gospel. It divulges God's love and mercy towards sinful human beings and the call to repentance and conversion.

GOD'S INITIATIVE TOWARDS US

Growth and life

Several parables of growth presented the kingdom of God as thriving steadily, quietly, and powerfully in our world. The growth of crops provided Jesus with such a picture: 'The kingdom of God is like someone scattering seed on the earth; he then sleeps at night and gets up by day. Meanwhile, the seed sprouts and grows, he does not know how. The earth produces of itself, first the stalk, then the head, then the full grain in the head. When the grain is ripe, at once he starts reaping because the harvest has come' (Mark 4:26–29). Jesus brought in the mustard seed as another parable to display how from apparently tiny beginnings God's rule grows dynamically: 'when sown in the ground, it [the mustard seed] is smaller than any seed. Yet once sown it grows up and becomes the greatest of all plants. It puts forth large branches, so that the birds of the air can perch in its shade' (Mark 4:31–32).[2]

One of life's special blessings for me was the chance of growing up on a small farm. Those years taught me to marvel at the mystery of new life: fluffy chickens darting ahead of the hens, white rings of flowers appearing on the pear trees, wild rabbits enjoying the grass on an early summer's evening. I still feel a thrill of wonder when I remember all that growth: cows licking their new-born calves, sharp-eyed magpies strutting around with their young, and – not least – peas and beans shooting up through the soil where I had planted seeds in the vegetable garden.

Once I started to read the Gospels seriously, it made me happy to find how often Jesus took his images from the world of farming and agriculture. The marvel of seeds that send up shoots and, slowly but surely, produce crops and trees caught his eye. He drew on this experience to make up parables that speak to us of God's powerful rule establishing itself in our world. Jesus' parables of growth encourage an utter confidence in God's power to bring about the new and wonderful life of the final kingdom. Many good things of the kingdom are happening right now, and many more are on the way. The kingdom of God will carry all before it.

There is a lovely homeliness in these parables of growth. Where the Old Testament knew God to be even more powerful than the majestic cedars of Lebanon (Isaiah 2:13), Jesus brings divine things right down to earth: to grains of wheat and tiny mustard seeds. It is all rather like what he does by turning eagles into barnyard hens. The Old Testament compared God's care for the chosen people to the majestic flight of an eagle carrying her young (Deuteronomy 32:11). Jesus knows these images but prefers to picture himself as a barnyard hen with her chickens. 'How often,' he exclaims, 'have I desired to gather your children together as a hen gathers her brood under her wings, but you would not let me' (Luke 13:34). Just as God nurtures and protects us in homely ways, so the divine power works in all the growth and life that surrounds us. Jesus wants us to look at our gardens, our orchards, and our fields. Quietly but powerfully God makes everything grow, bloom, and ripen – a plain and unpretentious picture of how he wants to share with everyone life in lasting abundance.

Thus some of Jesus' most unforgettable parables took up very ordinary farming experiences and invited us to think about God's power in bringing life and growth. 'Be a member of this new reign of God,' he was implying, 'or miss out on what really matters and fail to live. Be part of this final kingdom or be nothing.' When they experienced the risen Jesus and his Spirit, early Christians knew him to be Life itself. Jesus had preached his message of the new life of the divine kingdom; now they knew him to be that Life in person. The First Letter of John opened by saying: 'We declare to you what was from the beginning, what we have heard, what we have seen with our eyes, we have looked at and touched with our hands, concerning the *Word of Life* – this *Life* was disclosed, and we have seen it and witness to it, and declare to you the *eternal Life* that was with the Father and was disclosed to us' (1 John 1:1–2). Many scholars have accurately expressed the shift from the period of Jesus' own preaching to the time of the emerging Church by declaring: 'the Preacher became the One who was preached'. To say the least, the Preacher of life and growth came to be known and followed as the very source of growth, even Life itself.

John's Gospel, while including hardly any of the parables that Jesus preached,[3] vigorously puts across their meaning for those who join the Church as the first century moves on. This Gospel does just that for the parables of growth by identifying the risen Christ as Life itself. This theme runs from John's prologue, 'in him was life' (John 1:4), through the promise, 'I came that they may have life and have it abundantly' (John 10:10), and on to the staggering self-description that comes from Jesus: 'I am the resurrection and the life' (John 11:25) and 'I am the way, the truth and the life' (John 14:6). Just in case any reader may have read the text but missed the meaning, the Gospel ends by clearly stating its intention: 'These things have been written so that you may come to believe that Jesus is the Messiah, the Son of God, and that through believing you may have *life* in his name (John 20:31).

As regards 'life', English, Italian, German, and a number of other modern languages have only one word: life, *vita*, *Leben*, and so forth. The New Testament, however, was written in Greek and has two words: *zöe* (which is connected with zoology or the scientific study of animals) and *bios* (which we find taken into current English words like biochemistry, bio-ethics, and biology or the science of living organisms). John's Gospel and the First Letter of John use *zöe* in the passages quoted above. Jesus promises *zöe* and not *bios*; he identifies himself with *zöe* and not with *bios*. What is the difference between the two words? What is so special about *zöe* or life in St John's sense?

One should admit that life in any sense is marvellous, elusive, and impossible to pin down and define totally. To be sure, scientists have discovered an enormous amount about matters biological and zoological. Yet there is still much more to know. It is still anybody's guess how terrestrial life first appeared, let alone whether there is life elsewhere in the universe. But St John talks not of life which comes through things when the conditions are right, but of the life that we experience and receive through persons – the *zöe* or life for ever that faith in Jesus brings. It is no accident that the First Letter of John begins by witnessing to experience: to the One who has been heard, seen, looked upon, and touched. It is personal experience of Jesus that proves life-giving. To experience Jesus is to experience the One who gives life 'abundantly' and proves himself to be the very 'bread of life'.

When preaching his parables and even more when risen from the dead, Jesus was and is well within reach – for us to experience him in common and accept him together. During his earthly ministry Jesus preached publicly; his parables encouraged all his hearers to let the power of God's kingdom bring them growth. After the resurrection the First Letter of John testified to what 'we' have experienced and continue to experience together. Accepting the crucified and risen Jesus means passing from 'death to life' (1 John 3:14). The *zöe*, to which this letter and John's Gospel witnessed, is an amazing new life in common: a life to be experienced, shared, and proclaimed together.

This growth and life come not only in the company of others but also through death. Dying is the way to this new living. John's Gospel may well be echoing and developing Jesus' parables about growing seeds when we hear Jesus say: 'unless a grain of wheat falls into the earth and dies, it remains just a single grain. But if it dies, it produces much fruit' (John 12:24). Jesus saw the power of God's coming kingdom in the seed that is buried in the ground and sends fresh life sprouting up. The preacher of the seed dramatised his own parable by dying and being buried to bring forth the richest of harvests.

Repeatedly, John's Gospel indicates such death as the way to life. When Jesus promises life 'abundantly', the very next verse identifies him as the 'good/beautiful shepherd' who dies for his sheep (John 10:10–11). In proving himself 'the resurrection and the life' by raising Lazarus from the dead, Jesus provokes his enemies into plotting his death (John 11:45–53). When he calls himself 'the way, the truth and the life', Jesus is spending his last evening with the core group of his friends. Over and over again in his final discourse (John 13–17), we read of the death which Jesus is ready to face – for them and for all of us. To be a life-giver and a harvest-maker, he will become like a grain of wheat falling into the ground and dying. At the end Jesus will act out what he has preached in his parables about the seed being sown.

The parables Jesus draws from seeds of grain and mustard seed are stories of a growth that is beyond our understanding and control. These stories coax us into opening our eyes to the divine energy that is at work in our world. They take me back to my childhood when I would dart out in the freshness of the morning to find that shoots were sprouting through the soil where I had planted seeds in the vegetable garden. Some days later, rows of beans and peas stood up cheerfully in the sunlight. Vital energy was at work, even though I did not know how. God was already teaching me that the growth and fruitful increase of the divine kingdom go beyond our understanding and control.

Through his parables of growth Jesus gently encourages us to realise a startling contrast in the history of God's kingdom: between its small and unpromising beginning and its huge outcome in the future. A minute mustard seed, the size of a pinhead, seems only a tiny, inconspicuous start. Yet the mys-terious, dynamic power at work will bring a great and glorious ending, imaged forth by a mustard tree, which is large enough to shelter the nests of birds. Overwhelming results will arise from a humble start. Jesus sets himself to open up a vision of the divine force unleashed in the world; he knows with utter assurance that a wonderful, enormous ending will come.

The Scriptures that Jesus prayed over use the image of a sheltering tree. Ezekiel, for instance, imagines God taking 'a sprig from the lofty top of a cedar' and planting it 'on a high and lofty mountain' where it will become 'a noble cedar'. Then 'under it every kind of bird will live; in the shelter of its branches will nest winged creatures of every kind' (Ezekiel 17:22–23). By contrast, Jesus' picture is modest and homely: a tiny mustard seed that will become a bushy, welcoming shrub at the bottom of the garden.

Once again we profit by observing how Jesus himself acted out his own parables. He was and is the divine kingdom in person. Dying and being buried in the ground like a tiny mustard seed, *he* rose from the dead to trigger the startling growth of a world-wide community and to touch the lives of millions who have joined that community through baptism. The tree of the cross, as many believers have imaginatively grasped, became a living tree with branches large enough to shelter the whole human race. The crucified and risen Jesus himself is the tiny mustard seed that has grown to welcome and shelter the world.

The Book of Daniel portrays an immense world-tree that stands at the centre of the earth, reaches to the heavens, and shelters all life: 'There was a tree at the centre of the earth, and its height was great. The tree grew great and strong, its top reached to heaven, and it was visible to the ends of the whole earth. Its foliage was beautiful, its fruit abundant, and it provided food for all. The animals of the field found shade under it, the birds of the air nested in its branches, and from it all living beings were fed' (Daniel 4:10–12). But in the prophetic vision this world-tree was cut down, its branches chopped off, and its foliage stripped away. The tragic tree symbolised the unfortunate king of Babylon, Nebuchadnezzar (Daniel 4:22). Where he failed to become a lasting haven even for his own people, the cross of Jesus would give shelter and life to all human beings.

The hidden yeast

Jesus used the image of yeast that leavens bread for a further parable expressing the powerful growth of God's rule: 'the kingdom of heaven is like the yeast that a woman took and mixed in with three measures of flour until all of it was leavened'

(Matthew 13:33).[4] In the Old Testament leaven symbolised the corrupting influence of evil and had to be removed from Israelite households at the time of Passover (Exodus 12:15, 19). It could also be presented in a good light: for instance, in Leviticus 23:17. There it was a question of the loaves to be baked for the Festival of the Weeks, celebrated at the time of the wheat harvest (the festival which came to be called Pentecost since it was celebrated fifty days after the festival of unleavened bread). Yet this Leviticus passage does not mention women baking the bread as does Jesus in his brief parable.

This parable lets us spot an image that came right out of the experience of Jesus. From his childhood he had innumerable chances of watching women, presumably also his mother, doing just what he said: mixing the right amount of yeast in the flour they were kneading for the oven. He had seen for himself the power of a little yeast to affect a whole lump of dough. What happened from adding the yeast followed with certainty: the flour rose, and a fragrant loaf appeared on the table. That elementary, domestic experience entered the way Jesus thought and spoke about the growth of the divine kingdom. The dynamic power of the hidden yeast enjoyed an inevitable, astonishing impact upon the whole batch of dough. Unimpressive and apparently insignificant at the start, the yeast had an effect out of all proportion to what one might have expected. In the parable Jesus spoke of a large amount of dough, three measures of flour which produced around fifty pounds weight of bread.

Jesus introduced a homely example to picture the growth of the kingdom. God could be seen to be like a woman doing such an ordinary thing as baking bread. Like yeast, the divine power was hidden, but it would certainly leaven everything. Immense and wonderful results were sure to come. We will eat bread together in the future kingdom. God wants to feed the whole world and the hearts of everyone.

The Labourers in the Vineyard

Before leaving the ways Jesus initiated his hearers into the mystery of God and the divine initiative, I should add something about a remarkable parable which we find only in Matthew, but which forms a partial diptych with the Parable of the Prodigal Son (found only in Luke). The Labourers in the Vineyard (Matthew 20:1–15)[5] shows God to be very different from the scrupulously 'fair' and quite predictable God we might otherwise expect. Jesus divulges an incredibly large-minded God, a most generous God of surprises.

In this parable the landowner seems deliberately provocative, both with his first decision to put at the head of the pay queue those hired last, and even more with his second decision to be outrageously generous with those who have worked for the shortest amount of time. The second decision is simply bewildering. He challenges normal views about proper rights and rewards. His selective generosity undermines our usual human system of just rewards. To put it mildly, Jesus' story challenges our customary notions of fairness.

Those who have worked in the vineyard all day long bring to mind everyone who sees life as a competition and moves forward in the spirit of 'if they win, I lose'. Such a competitive spirit fosters the constant need to compare ourselves with 'those others', especially with those 'undeserving' others. My successes and failures over against 'them' provide the basis for my self-evaluation and self-image. Like the elder brother in the Parable of the Prodigal Son and the labourers who have worked right through the day, we can too easily take life as a contest in which we fail or succeed. Do I feel myself a failed competitor whenever others are treated with extraordinary generosity?

Jesus puts his finger squarely on a pervasive meanness of spirit that is not limited to workers who do not like seeing others treated with special benevolence. The indignation of the men in the parable calls to mind what the elder brother of the prodigal son says in complaint: 'I have worked well and faithfully all these years. And look at what this disgraceful son of yours has got up to in his life of dissipation!' The labourers in the vineyard grumble, precisely because they 'have borne the burden of the day and the scorching heat', and not because the latecomers have proved themselves incompetent slackers or have been stealing on the job. This is to forget the misery of those who have waited desperately all day long for the chance of making a little money from some casual work. In their own way, the men hired late in the afternoon have been bearing the burden of the day and the scorching heat before they surprisingly get the chance of earning something.[6] Those who have worked right through the day ignore all that, just as the elder son fails to think of the suffering his sinful younger brother has been through. Those who complain in these two parables show the same ungenerous spirit, an insistence on matters of justice and principle that cannot cope with acts of extraordinary magnanimity shown by the owner of the vineyard and the father, respectively.

Jesus' God is fair to all, just as the vineyard owner does no one any wrong but pays everyone the proper daily wage they had agreed to. God certainly does no one any wrong, and yet is not equal with all, inasmuch as God is utterly free, creative, and unimaginably kind. God is never unjust and yet treats everyone in an unpredictable, endlessly variable range of ways, because God takes each of us as uniquely special and irreplaceably valuable individuals. Whether or not we complain and grumble, God calls each of us 'my friend' (Matthew 20:13).

Jesus does his best in this parable to convince us that we should not judge our lives or the lives of others in terms of performance. Ultimately it does not make any difference whether we work through a complete daytime or lifetime of public success, or simply get taken on at five o'clock in the afternoon. What matters for all of us is the reckless generosity and exuberant kindness of God.

We have taken up three parables through which Jesus wished to initiate his hearers into the mystery of God and the divine kingdom. These were parables in which he highlighted God's attitudes and initiatives. How should human beings respond to God's offer? The divine kingdom has gone on the market. What should our reaction be to this wonderful offer?

RECEIVING THE KINGDOM

The Treasure in a Field

Jesus suggested the right reaction to the message of the kingdom in a number of parables, one of which was very short: 'the kingdom of heaven is like treasure hidden in a field which someone found and hid. Then in his joy he goes and sells all that he has and buys that field' (Matthew 13:44).[7] The treasure hidden in a field evokes a gamut of feelings and insights. Despite warnings from some 'rigid' scholars that Jesus intended his parables to make only one point, those who prayerfully mull over this story which is only one verse in length will sense the rich range of meanings that Jesus conveyed.

First, the parable speaks of the immeasurable value of something which comes as pure gift, not something the finder (conceivably a poor labourer) had ever worked for and expected. The divine kingdom has an incalculable worth like some magnificent hoard of gold buried years before out in a field, perhaps when an invading army threatened to overrun the land and plunder everything within sight. The treasure which God offers is colossal, and yet totally free and not needing to be earned.

Second, suddenly blundering on the treasure changes the whole world for the fortunate finder. This totally unexpected stroke of good fortune turns life around for the finder and fills him with ecstatic joy. 'All things have been made new' (Revelation 21:5) for the lucky man.

Third, the finder must take the plunge and sacrifice everything if he is going to gain the precious treasure. He needs to 'sell all that he has', if he wants to buy the field which hides the immensely valuable prize that he has stumbled on. The treasure is there for the having, and the field is apparently up for sale. But first the lucky finder must convert into cash the small amount of property he currently owns. He needs to sell everything, if he is going to secure everything and more than everything.

Fourth, it goes without saying that the chance of gaining such a treasure turns up only once in a lifetime, if that. Finding a hidden hoard of gold gives us a chance that may never come again. Those who find such caches must instantly take advantage of their opportunity. They have to trust their quick judgement that the treasure is worth gaining at any cost and by any means. Immediately risking all and giving up all will make it possible to enjoy something that is truly a unique 'godsend'.

As much as in any of his parables, Jesus brings out here how the kingdom is something that comes to us from God and yet is also an adventure we must boldly embrace. The kingdom is an incredible godsend, something that is totally, completely, and entirely God's work. And yet, at the same time, we must realise that it is also our affair, *the* good thing that turns up on our road through life and for which we must be ready to give up all – here and now.

The Gospels themselves offer lovely examples that match the story of the treasure in the field: for instance, in the calling of two sets of brothers, Simon Peter and Andrew, and James and John: 'As Jesus passed along the sea of Galilee, he saw Simon and his brother Andrew casting a net into the sea – for they were fishermen. And Jesus said to them: "Follow me and I will make you fish for human beings." And immediately they left their nets and followed him. As he went a little farther, he saw James son of Zebedee and his brother John, who were in their boat mending their nets. Immediately he called them; and they left their father

Zebedee in the boat with the hired hands, and followed him' (Mark 1:17–20). The two sets of brothers provide us with a wonderful instance of what the treasure in the field can mean to individuals.

They have come across someone of immeasurable, incalculable worth, Jesus himself. Suddenly Peter, Andrew, James, and John are offered a magnificent treasure. It is totally free; they do not have to work for it. Like the man who comes across the hidden treasure, the two sets of brothers run into something, or rather someone, who changes their whole world for them. Of course, they have to give up something if they are going to gain the treasure. The man in the parable sells everything he has in order to buy the field and win the hidden hoard. Peter, Andrew, James, and John must leave behind their boats, their fishing nets, and their families, if they are going to gain the colossal treasure, which is Jesus in person. Finding a treasure like that is a 'godsend' that turns up once in a lifetime, if that. Coming across the hidden pot of gold gives the man in the parable a chance that may never repeat itself. He must trust his quick judgement, and take advantage at once of his opportunity. Jesus is the incredible 'godsend' for Peter, Andrew, James, and John, a chance that has turned up and may never come again. They must trust their judgement and risk everything to follow Jesus. He is worth gaining at any cost, and will bring them wonderful lasting joy. He is the utterly priceless gift that could change their life forever.

Those who come across the treasure will remember the time and the place for the rest of their lives. At the birth of Christianity two sets of brothers found their treasure by the Sea of Galilee. Many centuries later, Paul Claudel (1868–1955), a French writer and diplomat, praised the moment during the singing of the office in the Cathedral of Notre Dame in Paris when his heart was suddenly touched and he believed. It was Christmas Day 1886, and in the crowded congregation he was standing near the second pillar, at the entrance to the choir, on the right, on the same side as the sacristy. It was a moment of light and conversion that Claudel located very precisely and remembered for ever. He came across the treasure at that time and in that place. No one could ever forget such a moment of discovery.

The Pearl of Great Price

Jesus appears to have thought up the parable of the hidden treasure for himself. At best the Book of Proverbs might have supplied him with a slight pointer, when it spoke of searching for wisdom 'as for a hidden treasure' (Proverbs 2:4). But in Jesus' story the lucky finder seems to run across the concealed hoard and not to have been out looking for what he might find. Here the finder differs from the merchant who travels in deliberate search of fine pearls: 'the kingdom of heaven is like a merchant in search of beautiful pearls; on finding one pearl of great value, he went and sold all that he had and bought it' (Matthew 13:45–46).[8] When he has come across the kind of magnificent pearl he has long dreamed about, the merchant acts instantly. He seizes the chance that may never come again, and buys that gleaming pearl.

This parable calls to mind various passages in wisdom literature, above all those that encourage the search for wisdom (e.g. Proverbs 2:1–4; Wisdom 7:1–8:21). Yet Jesus took up this theme of search in his own way and did not merely borrow from the Scriptures he had inherited. What we read there, among other things, are poetical descriptions of Solomon's desire to have wisdom as his bride (Wisdom 8:2, 9, 16). Solomon values her more than 'any precious gem', not to mention an abundance of gold and silver (Wisdom 7:9; see Job 28:1–19). Yet the theme Jesus chose for his brief parable about the travelling merchant was the search for a priceless gem, not the search for the perfect bride (see Proverbs 18:22; 31:10). Dare we hazard a guess about his choice and the motives for his choice?

Could it be that he did not feel attracted to the image of a man travelling around the world in search of the perfect bride? Despite its positive possibilities, this image might demean women and reduce them to the object of a male search. Whatever the reason, Jesus preferred to use the image of a merchant searching for fine pearls and not that of some latter-day Solomon out and about checking the marriage-market.

The parable of the treasure and of the precious pearl highlight both the priceless value of what someone has come across and the right reaction on the part of the finder. To possess the glittering prize, a wise person would instantly surrender everything. Such a chance of a lifetime rules out half measures and any delay.

In his *preaching* Jesus transposed the two parables into peremptory claims he made on those who responded favourably to the call of the kingdom but were not yet inclined to take instant action. 'To another Jesus said, "Follow me." But he said, "Lord, first let me go and bury my father." But Jesus said to him, "Let the dead bury their own dead. But as for you, go and proclaim the kingdom of God." Another said, "I will follow you, Lord, but first let me say goodbye to those at my home." Jesus said to him, "No one who puts his hand to the plough and looks back is fit for the kingdom of God" ' (Luke 9:59–62). Obedience to the call and the gift of the kingdom, according to Jesus, must take precedence over every other duty. He specified here what finding the treasure and the precious pearl could entail. One should instantly decide to 'sell all that one has' and at once secure the unique gift of the kingdom. Not even the most sacred family ties and duties should stand in the way. Others who were not alive to the higher demands of the kingdom – the spiritually dead, as Jesus called them – would have to take care of their own affairs.

Thus, in the eyes of Jesus, the magnificent treasure of the kingdom could carry a most painful price-tag. It might involve not only leaving cherished people behind but even finding oneself in distressing conflict with one's nearest and dearest: 'Do not think that I have come to bring peace to the earth; I have not come to bring peace but a sword. For I have come to set a man against his father, and a daughter against her mother, and a daughter-in-law against her mother-in-law, and one's enemies will be members of one's own household' (Matthew 10:34–36). In this passage the repeated 'I have come' makes it clear that Jesus himself was and is the kingdom in person. Deciding for or against the kingdom meant deciding for or against Jesus. He was the treasure hidden in the field and the pearl of great price. Jesus himself was and is immeasurably valuable, someone who could joyfully turn our lives around, the unique 'godsend' from whom we would receive everything if we were ready to lose everything.

We rightly interpret these two parables in terms of the very person of Jesus, who can reshape the whole world for each of us. We may also interpret the parables as *autobiographical*, expressions of what Jesus himself based his own life on. For him God's will and the task of bringing us the divine kingdom were the treasure in the field and the priceless pearl for which he gave everything. He said farewell to those at home, and never looked back. He gave his all to the task of proclaiming the kingdom. He had found God's kingdom, he lived for it and made it accessible to others. He sacrificed everything for this task; at the end it would bring him to a violent death, because he had given his heart to his utterly precious mission for us.

The Dishonest Manager

Jesus and his presence offered a graced time and a special chance. But human beings needed to get moving quickly; the divine bargains would last for only a limited season. Hence Jesus introduced some 'parables of crisis' (or perhaps better entitled 'parables of critical situations') to fill out his teaching on the need for wise and rapid reaction to the coming of the kingdom. It is very likely that Jesus had heard a number of stories about managers running big estates in the Galilean countryside for absentee landlords. From them he fashioned the figure of the Dishonest Manager (Luke 16:1–13), a parable about a superbly clever rascal who seizes his opportunity before time runs out on him.[9] Faced with a dramatic crisis in his life, the crooked manager knows how to deal with it quickly. The slyness of such a person can teach everyone how to behave in a world plunged into an emergency as God comes on the scene with power. One must decide in favour of Jesus' message and act fast; any moment might be too late.

To illuminate the crisis of our times, Jesus does not limit himself to good characters like the father of the prodigal son or neutral figures like the merchant in search of fine pearls. The behaviour of smart crooks, who feather their own nests or at least ensure themselves a happy future, can serve to challenge those faced with God's final offer to us. Even dishonest administrators may have a lesson for those disposed to learn from Jesus' parables.

Mismanagement and wasteful practices create a desperate crisis for a rich man's manager. Has he been using funds from the estate to hold lavish parties and live it up? Or perhaps the hostile charges brought against the manager are untrue and no more than false smears coming from unfriendly locals. Either way the owner is convinced that mismanagement, if not worse, has been taking place, and decides to dismiss his administrator. Whatever the truth of the accusations and no matter what the manager produces in his final accounts, in a short time it is certain that he will become redundant. Apparently he has no savings to fall back on. Physically he is not strong enough to take on work as a labourer. Psychologically he cannot face cadging off people; he is too proud to beg. But as the old saying puts it, when the going gets tough, the tough get going. The manager who has so far probably been guilty only of squandering the owner's property, now comes up with a dishonest scheme which will retrieve the situation and secure him a comfortable future after he loses his job.

Reading the story today we may think that the manager was encouraging straight theft, and covering his tracks by having his master's debtors change the contracts in their own handwriting. But we need to remember the commercial system of Jesus' time to have a more accurate view of what was going on. When making the contracts for olive oil and wheat on behalf of the landowner, the administrator would add an extortionate rate of interest and put everything down in one lump sum. Thus one debtor in the story had received only 450 gallons of olive oil. But, with interest being charged at 100 per cent, 100 jars or the equivalent of 900 gallons were written on the contract. The manager's job was to make as much money as possible for his master; the extra 50 jars of oil went to the landowner and did not finish up as commission in a manager's pocket. Apparently the interest on wheat was lower: only 20 per cent. The cunning manager had the second debtor eliminate that interest as well, by cancelling what would be today around 220 bushels of wheat. In both cases the manager told the debtors to strike out the interest that should have been paid to the landowner.

The picture then is this. The administrator settles his grudge against his accusers and his boss by eliminating any profit for the landowner who is about to sack him. At the same time, the debtors will be more than happy at the cancelling of the interest. They are sure to repay the helpful manager by their hospitality and support. They will 'welcome him into their homes'. He has proved himself a real 'friend' when he summons the debtors. In their turn they are sure to take care of him when he loses his job.

The rich landowner, perhaps as much a rogue as the manager, somehow comes to hear about the interest being eliminated. Amazingly, instead of punishing the rascal, he commends him for having acted so shrewdly when caught in an emergency. It is an astounding conclusion to the story Jesus tells.

In prayerfully reading through the story, we must not miss the unusual soliloquy, which Jesus sets at the heart of it all. When the manager walks away from the interview with his boss knowing that he is to be dismissed from his job, he does not indulge in self-pity and start complaining to others that he has been wrongly treated. Instead he talks to himself, and quickly assesses the situation and his future prospects. At once he thinks of a way ahead and acts decisively. He moves rapidly from asking himself, 'What will I do?', to a firm decision: 'I know what

I shall do.' By introducing this brief soliloquy, Jesus invites us to identify with the manager caught in a critical predicament and, like him, to think things through quickly.

In effect, Jesus says to his hearers: 'Don't dilly dally and waver. You hear my message of God's kingdom. Time is running out on you. Respond to my message quickly and shrewdly. Can't you let the smart decision of the dishonest manager inspire you? Why don't you learn from him and show just a little heavenly wisdom? The stakes are much higher for you than for him. He secured hospitality for some years or maybe for the rest of his life – in the homes of his former master's debtors. You are facing a decision that will determine your eternal home.' In short, Jesus is appealing to his audience to show some enlightened common sense, and to do so instantly.

Settling out of Court

The Parable of the Dishonest Manager presses the need to decide quickly and wisely. Faced with Jesus and his message, we cannot take our time. The example that Jesus develops comes from business administration and the running of large estates of landowners who were often away. Jesus takes up other images when urging us to decide rapidly in favour of the good news. One comes from contemporary court procedures, the Parable about Settling out of Court (Matthew 5:25–26).[10] Jesus knows, perhaps from the experience of relatives and friends, that it is wise to avoid appearing before a judge, especially if one knows that the accuser is bringing a just case before the court and can prove it. Jesus' advice is: 'Settle with him at once before you both come before the judge; otherwise you may well be jailed and have a very unpleasant time of it.' Both then and now a timely reconciliation with the other party is often the most prudent thing to do.

Once again Jesus draws on the society of his day, this time not telling a particular story about some specific, if unnamed, individual but reflecting rather on what happens frequently enough in the administration of justice. Someone who knows that he is in the wrong refuses to settle at once with his opponent, tries to bluff his way through the court, and fails to get away with it. Then he will have to put up with a very distressing outcome. In its own wonderful way, Jesus points out, the coming of God's kingdom puts us up against it. We have little time to make up our minds. We must come to terms at once with the astonishing chance God gives us through Jesus.

LIVING THE KINGDOM

How does Jesus expect his hearers to behave towards one another and towards God, once they have received the uniquely precious gift of the kingdom? Jesus' primary directive was nothing if not clear: 'Be merciful, just as your Father is merciful' (Luke 6:36). A command of this importance simply had to make its way into the parables. Hence Jesus gave us the remarkable Parable of the Unforgiving Servant or the Merciless Debtor (Matthew 18:23–35).[11]

The Unforgiving Debtor

A servant owes his king a mind-boggling sum: in current terms around £2,250,000,000 or well over $4,000,000,000 (US). How has he managed to borrow so much or get so far into debt? Maybe he is the governor of a large province and the tax has not been paid for several years. Perhaps he has lost the money on huge projects which collapsed. We are not told; Jesus simply presents us with an utterly desperate debt, one that obviously could not be paid off even by selling into slavery the defaulting debtor along with his family and by liquidating all his property. The debt comes across as breathtaking; and so too does the amazing act of generosity on the part of the king. He goes far beyond what the debtor asks. At his wits' end, the servant falls on his knees and pleads frantically for some more time, without specifying how much. 'Out of pity', the king turns around and cancels the whole debt – an act of unbelievable magnanimity.

If Jesus were to stop his parable at that point, we would be left with a striking picture of the divine mercy. We are impossibly indebted to God. But this does not make our situation hopeless. Our God shows amazing mercy towards us. The divine forgiveness goes far beyond anything we might imagine and even ask for.

However, the parable presses on relentlessly. The forgiven debtor leaves the presence of the king and immediately runs into someone who owes him a relatively small amount: around £6,000 or over $11,000 (US), maybe a loan made out of the huge sum owed to the king. This debt seems a trifle compared with the debt the king has cancelled a few moments before. But the story goes ahead – not with a happy replay of what we have just read – but with a depressingly mean-minded outcome. The servant who has been forgiven the enormous debt now finds himself in the role of creditor, and he is asked for an extension of time in the very words that he himself has used with the king: 'Have patience with me, and I will pay you.' But with an extraordinary lack of compassion, he brutally seizes his debtor 'by the throat'. Even worse, he refuses to allow the unfortunate man any further time but has him flung straightaway into prison.

The king, when he learns of this cruel and merciless incident, summons the unforgiving servant and angrily revokes the pardon that has been granted. The servant will now be tortured until he repays the entire gigantic debt he has incurred. Remembering the astronomical amount he owes, we may well ask ourselves: No matter how the torture drives him to search out some solution, when will he ever be able to pay back what he owes?

To bring out the wonderfully tender love of God, Jesus tells us the story of the compassionate father of the prodigal son. But the same Jesus also portrays his and our heavenly Father as a powerful king who demands that we forgive our brothers and sisters from our heart. It is with utter seriousness that Jesus proposes the Parable of the Unforgiving Servant when urging us to show mercy to those who sin against us. God sets an astounding standard of compassion and expects us to follow this example in our own lives.

The unforgiving servant fails to marvel at the extraordinary generosity with which the king treats him. Here this ungrateful person shows himself staggeringly different from a chief tax collector in Luke's Gospel. Zacchaeus behaves in the way the servant should have behaved. Overcome by the generous forgiveness he has received, Zacchaeus tells Jesus: 'Half of my possessions, Lord, I will give to the poor; and if I have defrauded anyone of anything, I will pay back four times as much' (Luke 19:8).

The Good Samaritan

The Parable of the Unforgiving Servant bears on something that can be a challenge day by day: the call by Jesus to show at home, at our workplace, and everywhere a patient, merciful spirit. The second story we examine on the theme of living the kingdom proposes an emergency situation. In ancient Palestine and in most countries it was and is not a daily occurrence to come across a wounded man who has been robbed and left half-naked at the side of the road. It does happen, but fortunately in most places it is not a regular, daily event (Luke 10:29–37).[12]

The naming of the parable is also unusual. After all, the lawyer whose question prompts Jesus into telling the story asks about the object of his and our loving concern: 'Who is my neighbour?' Instead of being called 'the Parable of the Wounded Traveller' after someone who is obviously a striking case of a neighbour desperately needing help, the story has become known in terms of the Samaritan, the outsider whose generous involvement turns him into the central character.

This somewhat unexpected naming of the parable corresponds, of course, to the unexpected way in which Jesus develops the story. Instead of concentrating on someone who cries out for help, Jesus in a surprising way speaks about the agent of neighbourly love towards someone in a critical situation who needs intensive care. Jesus not only switches from the object to the agent of love, but he also gets in a strong plug against religious and racial discrimination.

Like so many of the parables, this story does not explicitly introduce God. It looks thoroughly secular and this-worldly. At most, the mention of a priest and a Levite, both connected with the divine service in the Temple in Jerusalem, hints at God and the other world. But, unlike what he does in all the parables we have so far looked at, Jesus does not talk vaguely of a farmer sowing seed, a woman mixing yeast in flour, a large vineyard situated somewhere or another, and a treasure that turns up in some field. In the case of the Parable of the Good Samaritan, Jesus locates his story very precisely: on the road from Jerusalem to Jericho.

Jesus draws his story right out of Palestinian Jewish society. Presumably the unfortunate traveller who is leaving the heights of Jerusalem for the plains of Jericho and on the way runs into a bunch of bandits is a Jew. One may also presume that the priest has been serving in the Temple and is returning to his wife and family. The Levite is likewise hurrying home, after assisting the priests at worship and attending to other services in the Temple. Yet the story catches us – and we can imagine – Jesus' original audience off guard.

Obviously there is nothing surprising about adopting the

traditional scheme of three characters. Yet one might expect Jesus to name as 'neighbours' three different people who live nearby: a person right next door, someone who lives down the road, and then someone who works in the same rural area. He could have said: 'You must show love to the woman in the next house who shouts at her children, to the wretched tax collector who works for Herod Antipas and the Roman authorities, and to the man who owns the vineyard next to your one.' Instead, Jesus takes his audience right out of their town or village, and invites them to think of people travelling along a dangerous country road. He jolts his audience further, as we saw above, by introducing not three objects of our neighbourly love but three people who are abruptly faced with a situation in which they might exercise such love.

Jesus, without any doubt, must have taken aback his first audience (and not just the lawyer who was speaking with him) even more by bringing on a priest, a Levite, *and a Samaritan*. We should recall that Jesus had not been born into a priestly family. In the eyes of the public, Jesus was a layman, known to be somewhat 'anticlerical'. Despite their privileged and respected status, he had so far never given anyone from the religious establishment a role in any of his extraordinary stories. He preferred to talk about farmers and their family, agricultural labourers, housewives, shepherds, servants working for rich folk, kings, managers of estates, merchants on journeys, widows, and judges. So Jesus' audience may not have been flabbergasted to find that, when he did something exceptional and gave a 'walk-on' role to two men from the religious classes, he put them in a bad light. But many in that audience must have expected that a kindly Jewish layman would have been the third to come down the road from Jerusalem and then take care of the wounded traveller. 'We knew that he was going to say that,' they would then have said to themselves. Instead, they were dumbfounded to hear Jesus send a Samaritan down the road.

It is all so improbable. What is a hated Samaritan doing travelling (apparently) alone in Judea? In today's terms, it sounds like one of the Taleban driving along a road near Kabul and stopping to take loving care of an injured British soldier. But, to everyone's astonishment, Jesus names a Samaritan as the person who 'came near' to the wounded man and 'was moved to pity'.

Far from even coming near, let alone being moved to pity, both the priest and the Levite pass by quickly 'on the other side'. Jesus probably does not need to explain the motivation behind the failure in neighbourly love on the part of those two. The robbers have left the wounded man naked, and unconscious, or perhaps semi-conscious. He cannot even cry out for help; to anyone who is going by hurriedly, he looks like a corpse. Contact with a dead body will defile the priest and Levite. They cannot afford to let themselves become unclean and so unfit for the holy service of God. They feel obliged to head off as fast as possible.

It is left to the Samaritan outsider, whom no one would expect to stop for a wounded Jew, to provide the intensive care desperately needed by someone who would otherwise die. He is 'moved with pity', just as Jesus was when he saw a leper (Mark 1:41) and a great crowd who seemed to be 'sheep without a shepherd' (Mark 6:34). The Samaritan personally looks after the wounded traveller. Conceivably he might have rushed on down the hill to the inn and told the innkeeper: 'Look, there's a chap lying badly wounded on the roadside up there. Here's some money to get him picked up and taken care of.' Instead, the Samaritan himself provides the 'ambulance service'.

The Samaritan is carrying some oil and wine – one supposes for snacks along the way. But now they serve to clean and soothe the wounds of the man victimised by the robbers. The Samaritan uses some cloth to make bandages. Does he tear up a change of clothing he is carrying in his baggage? Having done the best he can at the side of the road, he heaves the wounded man onto the pack animal and walks along with him to the next inn. He has brought the injured traveller to a secure place. In the story, the inn naturally stands for safety, shelter, and further care.

What some readers of the parable consider surprising is the way the Samaritan is trusted. He spends the night with the wounded man. Before leaving on the following morning, he tells the Judean innkeeper: 'Take care of him; and when I come back, I will repay you whatever more you spend.' The innkeeper finds himself dealing with a despised and even hated outsider, a Samaritan. But he behaves with the hospitality and openness characteristic of good innkeepers everywhere and at all times. On the scale of human kindness towards those in great distress, the innkeeper belongs towards one end, not too far behind the Good Samaritan himself. Even if we cannot say that he displays the same extraordinary generosity as the Samaritan, the innkeeper does well to welcome the wounded man and trust that the Samaritan will return and pay for any further expenses.

Jesus ends the parable by asking the lawyer whose question has occasioned the telling of the story: 'Who was a neighbour to the man who fell into the hands of the robbers?' It is a vivid and plausible touch when the Jewish lawyer avoids replying 'the Samaritan'. He cannot bring himself to name one of those 'horrible' religious schismatics and social outcasts, but simply answers: 'the one who showed him mercy'. Delicious irony peeps through. On the one hand, because of Jesus' story a precise expression, 'the Good Samaritan', will enter as such into world history and various languages to describe for all time anyone who shows remarkable benevolence to those in terrible trouble. The 'good Samaritan' of the parable creates the role and becomes a household word. On the other hand, the Jewish lawyer himself unwittingly begins the very process of generalising the point of the parable. Whether they are Samaritans, Jews, Koreans, Afghans, Scots, Italians, Nigerians, or of any other nationality, neighbours are those who 'show mercy' towards people in awful distress. Neighbours are those who go beyond the boundaries of their ethnic or religious groups to care for any suffering persons they meet on their journey through life.

Before leaving this parable, we should note how personal cost and personal risk belong right in the story that Jesus told. The Samaritan's kindness cost him some oil, wine, clothing, and money, as well as the loss of time caused by the unforeseen break in his journey. We should not miss also the slight whiff of danger. If one traveller had been victimised, bandits could still be prowling around to attack and rob others. On that stretch of the road they could easily appear again – over the next hill or around the next corner. It was dangerous to stop at the side of the road and then move ahead slowly, all the time intent on keeping the wounded man from falling off his seat on the pack animal. The bandits could have come for the Samaritan as well. In the parable that Jesus told no such attack came. But Jesus lived out that story, and paid the price for the risk he took.

Once again, one of Jesus' parables turns out to be implicitly autobiographical.[13] The life of Jesus would dramatise his story. At his own personal cost and risk, he stopped to save wounded human beings who had been robbed and stripped. In his case, however, love for his neighbours cost much more than possessions, money, and time. As he went down the road, 'they' did come for him. He was stripped and wounded, and not just left for dead but deliberately killed. Jesus the Good Samaritan would turn into Jesus the Victimised Traveller, not rescued but left to die on the cross.

The Rich Man and Lazarus

The case of the Good Samaritan confronts us with an emergency situation; it is not every day that we run into a desperately wounded person whose life depends on our compassionate concern. The story of the Rich Man and Lazarus (Luke 16:19–31)[14] opens, however, with a scene still repeated day by day in many cities around the world: wealthy, well-dressed people dining lavishly in their grand homes and apartments, while beggars lie outside in the streets with rags covering their ulcerated bodies. In his parable about the Rich Man and Lazarus, Jesus brought up a challenge that recurs constantly. As Jesus said in another context, 'You always have the poor with you and you can show kindness to them whenever you wish' (Mark 14:7). The words should sting our consciences. How often do we show them kindness? What stops us from wishing to do that and then going into action?

The parables of the Good Samaritan and of the Rich Man and Lazarus envisage different circumstances but converge in driving home the same basic programme of behaviour. Those who accept Jesus' message of the kingdom must actively reach out to their brothers and sisters in need. The two stories join in providing terrifying insight into a deep tendency of human beings to indulge and even justify selfish unconcern.

The two stories move apart, however, through their geography and their protagonists. The Good Samaritan story takes place very much in this world – in fact, along a road used by thousands of people right down to the present day. The story of the Rich Man and Lazarus begins in some unnamed town and then moves off into the other world, with Lazarus being 'carried away by the angels' and 'receiving good things' at the side of Abraham, and the rich man being 'tormented' in Hades. We shift from a street on this earth to the world of the angels and Abraham, a world that looks across 'a great chasm' to the 'place of torment'.

The characters Jesus puts into the Good Samaritan story belong very much to the sphere of daily experience: an unfortunate traveller, some robbers, a priest, a minor cleric, another traveller, and an innkeeper. The Parable of the Rich Man and Lazarus brings in angels and Abraham as protagonists. The angels may have, so to speak, only 'fly-on' parts, but Abraham has a notable speaking role in the dialogue that makes up almost half the story. In fact, this is the longest dialogue in any of Jesus' parables. In other stories such as those of the Prodigal Son and the Labourers in the Vineyard, Jesus injects some striking dialogue. But nowhere else does such dialogue include any otherworldly figures, let alone the patriarch Abraham who was called with his wife Sarah to initiate the saving history of God's chosen people.

This parable makes not the slightest suggestion that the rich man has gained his wealth by immoral or even criminal practices. He is not pictured as engaged in shady deals like the dishonest manager (see above). The rich man's sin is one of omission: although he has the money to be elegantly dressed and extremely well fed every day, he ignores a destitute person who would have been satisfied to eat the leftovers from the lavish feasts. He fails by the standards Jesus spells out elsewhere: 'I was hungry and you gave me food; I was naked and you gave me clothing' (Matthew 25:35–36).

Jesus portrays a painful contrast. The rich man dresses in the most expensive clothing and presumably has many friends, as well as his five brothers and other relatives, to gorge themselves at his table. Lazarus is 'dressed' in his sores. No one comes to do anything for him but some dogs. Where human beings fail in their duty of loving concern, the animals at least do what they can. By licking the sores of Lazarus, they give him some relief. The rich man enjoys nothing but 'good things', whereas Lazarus has almost nothing but 'evil things'.

The dreadful contrast continues after death, but now in a strikingly reversed shape. The poor, hungry Lazarus is carried away by angels to be 'comforted' in Abraham's bosom: that is to say, in the life to come he enjoys a choice position at the heavenly, messianic banquet. The rich, well-fed man dies and is 'buried', an ominous word that receives immediate clarification: he has gone down to be tormented in the underworld. When he looks up, he sees Lazarus at the side of Abraham. In his tragic situation the rich man now needs a little help from Lazarus, the very person he cruelly neglected during life on earth. He pleads piteously with Abraham: 'send Lazarus to dip the tip of his finger in water and cool my tongue, for I am in agony in these flames.'

But, as Abraham stresses, Lazarus and the rich man are now separated. During their earthly existence, they lived a very short distance from each other. The rich man could very easily and quickly have brought or sent some food, clothing, and medicine to Lazarus. Now, however, 'a great chasm' keeps the two men apart. It is impossible for them to meet. Even if Lazarus wants to perform some tiny act of kindness for the tormented rich man, a huge gulf separates them. It is not possible to cross from one side to the other.

In his dreadful misery, the rich man asks Abraham to send Lazarus back to his home and family. The rich man's five brothers will surely listen to someone risen from the dead, repent of their selfish life, and, presumably, begin to use their wealth to assist the utterly destitute. They will stop living in a callous, self-centred way and think of others who desperately need their help.

But Abraham sweeps aside the idea. The five brothers have the guidance and motivation provided by their religion: in particular, their Scriptures offer a strong message from Moses and the prophets about one's duty towards those in terrible deprivation. If they fail to hear that message, they will not pay attention to someone who comes to them from beyond the grave. The five brothers do not lack abundant spiritual direction and help. Will even the striking sign of a resurrection from the dead shake them out of their decadent and self-absorbed style of living?

Active, loving concern towards the impoverished and the afflicted belongs up front in Jesus' programme for those who accept his message of the divine kingdom. He depicts two men faced with persons in dreadful distress. The Samaritan seems moderately well off. He may be travelling alone and without any servants, but he has a pack animal. (Or perhaps he is riding an animal, a donkey or a horse?) He has brought some provisions and has at least a little spare cash. He does everything he can for the wounded victim of robbers. The wealthy man seems very affluent, but he does nothing for the starving Lazarus, who is lying not some distance away down the road but right there at the entrance to the rich man's house.

Why does the Samaritan act and the rich man remain coolly indifferent? Perhaps the latter's extraordinary opulence has corrupted him. Or is the rich man a professionally religious person who uses the 'right' words but fails to live out his faith? Three times he uses such 'right' words in his dialogue with Abraham, calling him 'Father Abraham', 'Father' and 'Father Abraham'. What Jesus says here may remind us of John the Baptist's stinging rebuke to those who boasted about having Abraham for their father: 'Bear fruits worthy of repentance' (Luke 3:8). The story of Lazarus and the Rich Man can highlight the fact that mere religious words to Abraham and about faith will not be enough. Those who hear the message of the kingdom must be known by their 'fruits' (Matthew 7:20). The story of the Good Samaritan says nothing about the religious profession and practice of the central protagonist. The only words he speaks concern arrangements he makes with the innkeeper to help the wounded person: 'Take care of him, and when I come back, I will repay you whatever more you spend.' To be sure, that story does not deny the Samaritan's faith in God, let alone represent him as being a first-century atheist or agnostic. A loving relationship with God should obviously be presumed by the opening exchange between Jesus and the lawyer – an exchange that puts right up front loving God with all one's heart. But in the parable itself the Samaritan acts instantly and with spectacular generosity when he finds himself faced with a near-fatal emergency. He acts rather than indulging some empty professions of faith in God.

WAITING FOR THE END

Jesus told a number of parables about his followers needing to show vigilance and faithfulness as they waited for the end: for instance, the Watchful Servants (Luke 12:35–38), the Wise and Foolish Bridesmaids (Matthew 25:1–13), the Watchful Householder (Luke 12:39–40), and the Rich Fool (Luke 12:16–21). Let us reflect on the last of these parables.[15]

Where the Parable of the Watchful Servants encouraged and illustrated the expectation of the Lord's coming appropriately shared by the community, with the story of the Rich Fool the focus shifted to an individual. Jesus invited his audience to overhear the rich man's soliloquy, when he 'thinks to himself' and 'speaks to his soul'. The situation changes abruptly when God addresses him, and it is a sobering message: 'You fool! This very night your life is demanded of you.' Instead of enjoying 'many years' of comfortable living and cheerful feasting, the rich man must face death that very night. He has been mistaken in the way he presumes to control his life and prepare his future: building larger barns and storing up all his goods will not guarantee his lasting future. Others will inherit his property and he himself will go empty-handed to meet God.

The story gives no hint that this rich man has gained his wealth through illegal activities. He is not to be compared with modern tycoons whose dishonest dealings can yield incredible profits. Slumps in the market may destroy their opulent lifestyle, and their financial failure often brings ruin to many others. In the Parable of the Rich Fool the man has become very affluent through the fertility of his land. God has blessed him with good seasons and abundant harvests. Perhaps he uses superior farming techniques. At all events he enjoys bumper crops – in fact, enormous crops. The sudden death of the rich man will not ruin anyone. Others, one presumes members of his family, will inherit all this wealth.

What has gone wrong then? The rich man has failed to acknowledge that he holds his life and property on loan from God. He has forgotten that it is not possessions but God who gives life, real life. The landowner has forgotten that he should behave like God's good steward with all that wealth. It does not occur to him to praise and thank God for the abundance of blessings he has received. As the parable puts it, he is not 'rich' towards God. Rather, he sets about planning his future in a completely self-sufficient way: 'I will do this; I will pull down my barns and build larger ones, and there I will store up my grain and my goods.' The rich man fails because he suffers from 'me-ism' and from over-planning. Let me explain.

'Me-ism' is the habit of referring everything to oneself, to 'me'. Certainly a great deal of 'me-ism' comes through the way the landowner thinks: he never mentions anyone else, but ten times brings up 'I' and 'mine'. He does not spare a thought for God, his own family, his friends, or the poorer people he might help. The landowner comes across as a serious case of 'me-ism'. He also deludes himself by imagining that he can control his own life and organise for himself an affluent future 'for many years'. In this parable Jesus warns against over-planning or thinking that we can assume complete control of our own lives. It takes only a sudden heart attack or an unexpected stroke to put an abrupt end to the landowner's self-centred plans for an opulent future.

The parable inevitably recalls that of the Rich Man and Lazarus. In both cases we hear the voice of some heavenly figure delivering a warning about the need to repent in time. Yet we should not miss the difference. In that other story it is Abraham who speaks, even if one admits that he does so with divine authority and in a position to share divine blessings. Being at Abraham's side in the other world brings Lazarus nothing less than the happiness of heaven. Nevertheless, in the Parable of the Rich Fool the solemn warning comes when God himself speaks to the rich man, and God's word of warning will certainly be fulfilled. That man will not live to enjoy another day; he will die during the night.

In the Parable of the Rich Man and Lazarus two people die, the poor man dying (probably of hunger) before the rich, well-fed one also passes away. But, after sketching the scene of famine and feast, the story makes no particular issue of how soon death comes to either of them. The timing of death, however, essentially shapes the story of the Rich Fool. The wealthy landowner plans 'many years' of comfortable living, but death comes for him the very next night after he has made those plans. A dramatic contrast is drawn between his long-term plans and their abrupt frustration.

The two stories also move apart somewhat by variations in religious directness. The Parable of the Rich Man and Lazarus tells of angels caring for the poor man after death, locates the second act in heaven and hell, engages Abraham in dialogue with the rich man, refers to Moses and the prophets, and alludes to the climax of divine revelation and salvation: the resurrection of Jesus from the dead. Nevertheless, this parable does not directly name God, still less put God on the stage. Here, the Parable of the Rich Fool differs strikingly. Its denouement comes when God himself speaks – the only time that God speaks in any of the parables that Jesus proposed. The story ends with the call to be 'rich towards God'. Human destiny finally depends on one's relationship with God.

In these two parables Jesus introduced the theme of death, but not to dwell on it morbidly, as if we might sum up his message of the kingdom as 'Prepare for death!' Instead he pushed at people the message, 'Practise true life!' We would be foolish, of course, to dismiss death from our mind and thoughts. But the Parable of the Rich Fool gives a special twist to remembering death (the *memento mori*). We have life on loan from God. Both here and hereafter our existence comes from God and is owed to God.

THE PARABLES AND JESUS

The New Testament (e.g. in the Book of Acts) reports how the followers of Jesus worked miracles. They began to do so even during his lifetime (e.g. Mark 6:13). But only Jesus told parables, well over thirty of them. He stood clearly apart from his disciples as a composer and teller of parables. The parables suggest the questions: How should we characterise someone who thought up and told stories like these? What kind of mind, imagination, and heart lay behind these very memorable stories? Something of his individual and even unique character traits are mirrored in the parables (e.g. his vivid attention to life around him, his deep concern for those who suffer, and his urgent commitment to the coming kingdom of God).

Earlier chapters have recalled how the evangelists, here and there, mentioned that Jesus showed such feelings as compassion, love, and anger. Yet they never stood back and attempted to describe directly his 'character', let alone try describing it fully. None of the evangelists wrote a formal character sketch of Jesus; they showed him in action. By reporting a rich variety of his words and deeds, they allow us to glimpse some of his distinctive characteristics and even construct something of his immensely attractive 'public personality'. The longest and most beautiful of his parables, the Parable of the Prodigal Son, opens a window on Jesus and his character in a remarkable way. Hence I dedicate a whole chapter to it.

Chapter 7

♦

THE PARABLE OF THE FATHER'S LOVE

Son, you are always with me, and all that is mine is yours.

Luke 15:31

Well into his Gospel Luke gathers together three parables that Jesus preached about loss: the first about a lost sheep (Luke 15:3–7), the second about a lost coin (Luke 15:8–10), and the third about a lost human being (Luke 15:11–32). Prayerfully contemplating passages in the Scriptures that compared God to a generously caring shepherd (e.g. Psalm 23:1–4), could have led Jesus to develop the Parable of the Lost Sheep. But there was nothing in the Scriptures that could have prompted – or at least prompted directly – the Parables of the Lost Coin and the Lost Son (*der verlorene Sohn*, as the parable is known in the German-speaking world).

The Parable of the Lost Coin, a story of a woman coping with a minor emergency, may well have come out of Jesus' own experience. Just as he saw women doing everyday things like baking bread and then produced the Parable of the Hidden Yeast, so he knew of women searching for lost property and he also drew a parable from that experience. Did he hear of a woman, perhaps one who lived nearby, who had lost a tiny silver coin, found it after searching carefully, and then shared her joy with friends and neighbours? Jesus himself could have been one of those neighbours.

111

THE LOST SHEEP AND THE LOST COIN

Before tackling the Parable of the Lost Son, we can introduce matters by comparing and contrasting the two, much shorter parables that precede it.[1] They differ, first of all, at the level of what is lost. A sheep that has strayed has little chance of finding its way back through the wilderness to the shepherd and the rest of the sheep. Yet that might happen; a frightened and dim-witted sheep could stumble on the right path. But a coin lost in a dusty corner of a badly lit house cannot do anything itself to be found again.[2] Its situation pictures perfectly the helplessness of human beings who must wait to be found again. But, Jesus insists, they will be found; God will seek them out with the diligence of a woman who has lost something valuable and will not give up until she has traced what is missing. In the parable, three actions call attention to the unwearied, unstinted efforts of the woman: 'she lights a lamp, sweeps the house, and searches carefully until she finds' the coin. The parable suggests that if a human being exerts such efforts to recover her property, how much more trouble will God take in seeking out and saving those who are morally and religiously lost.

The woman lost a 'drachma', which was worth about a day's wage for a labourer. It was not a great sum of money. Since, however, she possessed only ten drachmas, losing 10 per cent of what she had could hurt her. In any case, people in such circumstances are not consoled by the thought that they still have 90 per cent of their funds. The parable evokes the sense of loss and pain that the disappearance of even a small amount of money can cause and the joy felt when it is recovered.[3]

If the woman seems to be poor, the shepherd is presented as moderately well off; he has a flock of one hundred sheep. Although he loses only one sheep and still has 99 per cent of his flock, he feels the loss and makes enormous efforts to trace the lost sheep, and will not abandon the search until he finds it. His untiring search illustrates God's loving concern for all those who cannot find him; God will tirelessly seek them out.

The conclusions of the two parables resemble each other but also differ significantly. At the end of the Parable of the Lost Coin, Jesus moves from the exuberant joy of the woman who has recovered her missing drachma to remark: 'In the same way, I tell you, there is joy among the angels of God over one sinner who repents.' The conclusion to the Parable of the Lost Sheep uses the joy of the shepherd who has recovered the stray sheep to highlight the joy in heaven at the repentance of sinners, but adds something further. The repentance of a sinner is contrasted with the situation of the righteous: 'In the same way, I tell you, there will be *more joy* in heaven over *one sinner* who repents than over *ninety-nine righteous persons* who need no repentance.' Jesus may want to overstate matters to illustrate how God is delighted with repentant sinners, even if there are only a few of them when compared with those who do not need to repent. Another explanation, however, seems more likely. Faced with critics who have lined up against him for his compassion towards sinners, Jesus may be speaking with irony. Who, after all, is truly righteous? He may intend his hearers to understand the 'ninety-nine righteous persons' to be those who are only allegedly righteous. This issue emerges through the elder brother in the Parable of the Lost Son.

In the two parables about the straying sheep and the missing coin, Jesus talks of lost property and does so from the point of view of the human loser, not from that of the lost 'item' itself. He has nothing to say, for instance, about the experience of the sheep that goes astray. How does it feel when night falls and it cannot find its way back to the flock? Has it become terrified when it hears the barking of dogs and the howling of wild animals? The two stories, as we have just seen, close with references to repentance, but leave it unexplained. In any case, it makes little sense to attribute repentance to a lost sheep, still less to a lost coin. The Parable of the Father's Love tells, however, of the prodigal's experience when lost and of his repentance when found.

THE LOST SON[4]

Two of the three major protagonists in this parable are brothers: a younger brother and an elder brother. In a number of other parables Jesus drew contrasts between two individuals who function as representative types by acting and/or speaking in different and even opposite ways: for instance, the Two Builders (Matthew 7:24–27), the Two Creditors (Luke 7:41–43), and the Pharisee and the Tax Collector (Luke 18:9–14). Yet the central figure in the Parable of the Lost Son remains the father. The boundless, unconditioned love of the father means that the story could well be called the Parable of the Father's Love. He displays merciful love not only towards the repentant sinner but also towards his elder son, a self-righteous, uncomprehending critic of the sinner who returns. In its narrative way, the parable anticipates Paul's teaching about God loving all sinners while they are still sinners (Romans 5:8).

Jesus tells a story that takes place over and over again when dissatisfied young men and women want to break with their families and indulge their freedom. But Jesus gives the story an unusual twist: all too often when prodigals return home, they may not find much love and hardly, if ever, the astonishingly merciful and unconditional love with which the father of the prodigal son treats his sinful child. This story runs counter to what we might expect to happen when the young rascal trudges home.

The parable opens on a large estate, where the father did what Jewish customs allowed him to do: namely, dispose of his property during his own lifetime by making a gift to his children. In that culture, apparently, the firstborn son would receive twice the amount given to any other sons. So in this case we should surmise that the younger son received one third of the estate, while two thirds was to go later to the elder son. The younger son converted his inheritance into cash by selling his share of the property to purchasers who were to take possession of it only after the death of the father. Then the boy leaves for a distant country. Predatory 'friends' and high living eat up his money. The young man has run through his inheritance and is caught penniless when a severe famine hits the country.

Instead of doing what a practising Jew should do – namely, look for the nearest Jewish community where he could find work and help – the prodigal son attaches himself to a Gentile farmer. He is sent out into the fields to work as a swineherd. For a good Jew there could hardly be any greater humiliation. Pigs are unclean. To act as swineherd means incessant contact with these impure animals. The boy has effectively denied his religion. The sinner who begins with prostitutes ends by becoming a thoroughly godless apostate.

For his work the young man receives far too little food. He longs to eat some of the pods being fed to the swine. But he counts for less than the animals, and is not allowed to get down with the pigs and share their food. In his hunger and humiliation he 'comes to himself' – a wonderful, poignant expression. He has run away from so much – including himself. All alone, he must first find himself before he can find his way out of his misery and back to his family.

The prodigal son decides to go home to his father and to God. He remembers what he has lost. He will return and say to his father: 'Father, I have sinned against heaven and in your eyes.' He has only low expectations of what will follow his confession. Having already received his share of the estate, he has no further legal claim on his father. His disgusting conduct means that he no longer deserves to be treated as an honoured guest, let alone regarded as a son. For his family he is a dead outcast. At best he hopes to be taken back on the property as a hired hand, a day labourer who does not belong to the household. He remembers the kindly way his father treats even the hired hands; they have 'bread enough and to spare'. He pulls his shattered life together, and clings to the thought of his father like a life raft.

As the boy approaches home, his father sees him coming, forgets his dignity, and runs out to embrace him. Up to that point in the story, the father has said nothing – not a single word.[5] Now he begins to speak, but there are no recriminations. He cuts short his son's apologies and suggestion about being treated like a hired servant. He is not anxious to discuss matters – let alone impose conditions under which he might be willing to receive his son back into the household. The father does not even make some formal declaration of pardon.

Forgiveness is expressed by what the father does. He hugs and kisses his son. Then the boy receives the robe given to an honoured guest. He is handed a ring to wear – presumably as a sign of his right to act again as a son. He is no longer allowed to go barefoot like a common labourer, but once again he wears the sandals that the free son of a free farmer should wear. The lost son who has come home is taken into the house for a feast of joy.

THE FATHER'S LOVE

In this parable Jesus shared with his audience a vision of sin and repentance and did so through the person of the younger son. But, by shifting the focus to the father, Jesus offered an arresting answer to the question: What is God like? He invited his hearers to open themselves to the amazing love of their compassionate God. Jesus did not use either the noun or the verb 'love', but we would fail to appreciate his story unless we think in terms of love. We might single out here six qualities of human and divine love; they serve to illuminate the thrust of the parable.

Self-forgetful

Those who love reach out to others and make a gift of themselves. In doing so, they disclose themselves. Far from remaining locked up in their own private world, they forget themselves and their own immediate interests. They do not act to satisfy their own needs but to further the welfare of 'the other'. To be sure, love blesses those who love, whether they realise this or not. In that sense there is no such thing as utterly disinterested love. But those who love want to give themselves to another (or to others) in what they do and say. Their loving orientation towards the other reveals itself in their deeds and words. They love the other for himself or herself.

The father of the prodigal does not merely reach out to him, but rushes out to welcome him home. He forgets himself, his dignity, and his own interests, because he cares so much for the sinner who has returned and for his welfare. In what he does for the prodigal (by embracing him and kissing him) and in what he says to the servants, the father makes a gift of himself and discloses the love that fills his heart. He will behave, as we will see, in a similar fashion towards the elder son. This self-forgetful giving and revelation of love in deeds and words towards both sons vividly mirrors, of course, the way Jesus and his Father behave towards sinful human beings.[6]

Beyond reason

Wherever we experience it, authentic love is never the simple result of rational motivation. Unquestionably such love is not irrational and simply unmotivated. One can explain love to some extent by pointing to reasons and motives that help to explain, for instance, loving relationships with our marriage partner or with our friends. But by themselves merely rational considerations never fully account for and legitimate the choices and intensity of love. Genuine love is not against reason, but goes beyond reason. To echo Blaise Pascal (1623–62), 'the heart has its reasons of which reason knows nothing'.[7] Despite the 'passive' feel to such phrases as 'falling in love', true love is always a supreme expression of freedom. People may 'fall in love' but then they have to decide freely what they want to do. The heart of St Paul's lyric hymn to love celebrates the pure, free gift displayed in the actions of love (1 Corinthians 13:4–7). Being a supremely free decision, love is always gratuitous and never compelled. It is a mysterious act of freedom that is never forced or simply controlled by other factors – not even by the power of reason. To be sure, we run up against a real mystery here. How can a loving action be rational and yet not be fully clarified or justified by reason alone? What happens when love leads someone to do things that go beyond the merely reasonable?

Why does the father in Jesus' parable lavish such extraordinary love on the prodigal who has returned? Sheer reason fails to account for his actions. After all, the father could have imposed conditions on his runaway son. He might have required him to work for several years as a hired hand before accepting him back into the family circle. When told that his elder son was sulking outside, the father might have stayed indoors with the comment: 'He'll get over his bad mood. The smell of veal will bring him inside.' Undoubtedly, one can and should recall the parental relationship. The two brothers are his sons, and nothing can change that fact, not even the moral and religious disgrace the younger son has brought upon himself and his family. But this uniquely loving father goes well beyond what modern, western society would propose as the reasonable, mature reaction to the misbehaviour of both his sons, and certainly far beyond anything that might have been expected from a wealthy father in the patriarchal society at the time of Jesus. The father in the parable is wonderfully free in the delicate ways he shows his love towards his sons. He acts with remarkable compassion towards both of them. Reasonable motives alone cannot justify what he does, just as mere reason can never explain the intensity and mysterious freedom with which God loves human beings in their sinfulness.

In the case of divine mercy towards sinners, one might press the fact that all human beings have been made in the image and likeness of God (Genesis 1:26–27). God sees in us, one may say, divine icons. But why does God pursue us with such extravagant love, when we run away from home or sulk outside? What if the divine image and likeness have been seriously damaged and dishonoured by sin – for instance, by the immorality and apostasy of the prodigal son in the parable Jesus told? Is it reasonable for God in such cases to shower love on the sinner? Yet Jesus wants to convince us that the compassionate love of God is a 'foolish' love that goes beyond anything that we might reasonably expect.[8] Despite our horrendous sins, or even more mysteriously because of them, God reaches out in love to each one of us. God is never irrational. Yet the divine heart has its reasons that seem to go far beyond anything we might rationally justify.

The eyes of love

We have just seen how love (both human and divine), while not irrational, goes beyond the merely reasonable. We need to think a little further about the interplay between love and reason. The interplay is admittedly mysterious, but it may also help to illuminate something of the story of the prodigal son.

A modern prejudice holds that love distorts things, inevitably prevents lovers from understanding the reality of the beloved, is essentially deceptive, and necessarily produces false idealisations based on fantasy. In *A Midsummer Night's Dream* William Shakespeare (1564–1616) presents love as fostering illusions, seeing beauty that is not there, and leading us away from the real world. At the start of the final act, when Theseus equates lovers with poets *and madmen*, one is left wondering how the 'seething brains' of lovers can apprehend anything of reality. In a later play, *As You Like It*, Shakespeare has Rosalind dismiss love as being 'merely a madness' (3.2.420). In a word, love is supposed to be blind or even worse.

Undoubtedly, passionate, romantic love can lead some people astray and intoxicate them into 'seeing' what is not there. But otherwise the view of things expressed (but not necessarily held) by Shakespeare seems to be rather befuddled and runs contrary to the link that John's Gospel, St Augustine of Hippo, and many others have recognised between loving and knowing. His special love allows the beloved disciple to leap to the truth about the resurrection (John 20:8) and later to identify the mysterious stranger standing on the beach at dawn (John 21:7). 'Show me a lover and he will understand,' exclaimed Augustine when commenting on John's Gospel (26.4). Many other great voices from the Christian tradition maintain that the eyes of love lead us to the truth; we see with our hearts.

Let us apply love's insight to the case in hand. The loving father in the parable is only too painfully aware of the sinful situation of his younger son. But love makes him also aware of his real worth and potentialities for growth – a point lost on the elder son who is bitter about his sibling and can see nothing good in him. Jesus' parable not only evokes the truth seen by the merciful eyes of divine love but also rings true in common human experience. Those who love perceive the meaning and truth in people and things; love enables them to see meaning and catch sight of truth. In love with us, God knows what we can become through the grace bestowed on us, just as the father in the parable knows the basic goodness of his two sons and the greatness into which they might grow. He sees with his heart, and cherishes each of them as incomparably unique and utterly special individuals.

Loved into life

God's love is life-giving and creative; it brings into existence what has not yet existed. But even more remarkable is its 're-creative' force, which offers new life to what once existed and has now died. The story of the prodigal son presupposes the love with which his mother and father first gave him existence. The parable highlights the overflowing love with which the compassionate father gives new life to his son who has died morally and religiously – a death that is far more serious and painful than a 'mere' physical death. 'This son of mine', the father cries out, 'was dead and is alive again.' It is the father's love for his boy that makes this new life possible. He has loved him back into life.

Another father might well have become resigned to the disgraceful failure of his son. He could have let himself become indifferent to the boy's fate, even quite apathetic about what would happen to him. Or else he might have laid down conditions: 'change your life *and then* I will love you.' But not the father of the prodigal son. Deeply concerned for the real interests of his son, he gives himself in love to the young scoundrel. His love expresses itself not merely through gifts like clothing, a ring, and a family feast. It is the father's gift of himself to the returning prodigal that transforms the situation and makes all the difference.

Giving and receiving

Homecoming forms a further aspect of the divine love revealed through Jesus' story of the lost son. The loving father reaches out to welcome home his son who ran away. All true love reconciles and unites people. Of its very nature, love is a reciprocal force. It remains incomplete so long as its sentiments are not returned and there is not a full giving and receiving. Ultimately love is like a hug; you cannot give one without receiving one yourself. For me to love someone necessarily means to hope that my feelings will be reciprocated. This is not a question of selfishly trying to manipulate or even force someone into loving me. It is a matter of the very nature of love itself as reciprocal.

In Jesus' parable the father's love is perfected when his sinful son who has been away 'in a distant country' comes home again. The father's love enables a new communion of life to open up and grow. The parable contains no hint of a distorted relationship in which the repentant son will now be smothered or even psychologically swallowed up by his father. Genuine love unites without being destructive; it respects deeply the freedom of the other. The greater the loving union, the more personal identity and true freedom are safeguarded and enhanced. The father respected the wishes of the boy when he wanted to take his money and leave home. Now he welcomes him back with an exquisite respect that lets us glimpse the gracious respect with which God waits for sinners and desires to enjoy a wonderful union of love with them. Like the father of the prodigal, God puts his arms around them, kisses them, and wants to be hugged in return.

Loving always

The father of the prodigal knows only too painfully the situation into which his son has sunk, as one who is morally and religiously 'dead' and 'lost'. But he will never give him up, and cannot tolerate the thought of losing him forever. There are hints of this in the parable, not least when Jesus says that the father 'sees' his younger son 'coming'. It suggests that he has been constantly looking out for him, even anxiously waiting for him. Like all who truly love, the father cannot tolerate the idea of his son not being there; he wants to remain forever united with the boy whom he loves, and when he returns he joyfully cries out: 'he is alive again'. In this way the father reflects and reveals the constant love of God. No matter how much human beings hurt and harm themselves through sin, God's love is never withdrawn.

Clearly we should let ourselves be astonished by Jesus' parable rather than kill it with close analysis. I sense the impertinence of commenting on the love of God which comes through so powerfully. Hearing and being drawn into this story is far preferable to indulging in abstract comments. Yet we may be helped to appreciate the parable a little more by remembering how the divine love is 'self-forgetful', is seemingly beyond reason and even foolish, sees with 'the eyes of love', loves sinners into life, receives as well as gives, and is constant and never withdrawn.

THE ELDER BROTHER

Jesus' story of the merciful father gives considerable attention to the other son (Luke 15:25–32). A fairly grim sort of person, he may be the older of the two boys, but any advantage in age and family position does not stop him from behaving in a thoroughly adolescent fashion. He has been out working on what is obviously a large estate. Presumably he is coming home a little tired. When he hears the sound of music and dancing, one would expect him to brighten up and let himself feel, 'Hooray! What a nice surprise! Isn't it great to come home to a party!' Instead of rushing inside to share in the celebration, he suspiciously questions a servant to find out what is going on.

The servant speaks well of the two persons at the heart of the party: 'Your brother has come, and your father has killed the fatted calf, because he has got him back safe and sound.' The servant himself seems to share the great joy of this unexpected return. He respects the family relationships and the person with whom he is speaking by naming one of those inside as 'your brother' and the other as 'your father'. He more or less says to the elder son: 'You too should be delighted that your brother has come back safe and sound.'

But the elder son is angry. He sulks outside and refuses to join the celebration. His father loves him also, and comes out to plead with him, only to find this elder son totally self-absorbed. A little highlighting of his resentful remarks to his father brings this out: 'For all these years *I* have been working for you, and *I* have never disobeyed your command; yet you have never given *me* even a young goat so that *I* might celebrate with *my* friends.' Significantly he does not address his parent as 'Father'. He has the mind of a slave or at least of a servant who feels aggrieved that he has not received more for his loyal service. Since a young goat is of much less value than a fatted calf, it seems to him that virtue is worse rewarded than vice. He is shocked at the love shown to his sinful brother. He bitterly refers to him not as 'my brother' but as 'this son of yours'. It is a hateful phrase – one of the most unforgettable sneers in any of the Gospels. Self-pity gnaws away at the elder son. He has worked on the property for years, has always been dutiful towards his father, but he has never been given a party like this one. How terrible! He dismisses the welcome-home party as an act of soft and unfair leniency on the part of his father.

Resentment fuels the elder son's rage. One need only read the passage aloud to catch the insulting tone of his voice and words: 'this son of *yours* has devoured *your* property with prostitutes'. He almost makes it sound as if the father himself has run through his own money in some red-light district, or at least has somehow encouraged his younger son to squander everything in bad company.

If the younger son needed to give up a life of wasteful debauchery, the elder son must share his father's compassion and learn the lesson of love. A cold, unloving, self-righteous person, he is at heart no better than the fellow who took his money and went off to wallow in some high living. He is gently addressed by his father as 'child', and invited to recognise the boy who has returned as his 'brother'. To the elder son are addressed those lovely words of appeal: 'You are always with me, and all that is mine is yours.' The father's meaning is clear: 'You have never died or been lost. But you have missed the whole point. Why haven't you been happy? Why can't you love with a tender heart and join me in welcoming back your brother? Why have you turned to jealousy and bitterness?'

There the parable breaks off – in a brilliant, open-ended fashion. What happens next? Does the elder brother pull himself together, go inside, and welcome home his younger brother? What does the prodigal get up to next? Does he help with the farm work but then a few weeks later start to behave once again in a totally unacceptable fashion? We do not need to speculate about any aftermath. We should be satisfied with this story of a farmer who had two sons and loved them both. His love drives him to do what mere reason cannot justify. He sees his two sons with his heart. The younger son returns home and accepts his father's loving embrace. The father also holds out his arms to his elder son. But at this point the parable ends, leaving a challenge to Jesus' original audience and to all subsequent hearers or readers. Will the elder son and will we accept the love God offers us? Jesus' parable seems like an invitation to his hearers then and to us who read it now to reflect on ourselves.

In each of us there can be something of the younger son and

the elder brother. We may have strayed away from our Father's home – spiritually, mentally, and emotionally. We may have chosen to live our lives elsewhere – in a far country and emotionally estranged from our Father. Or we may have stayed with our Father, without really enjoying our life with him. We may have done our duty, and done it in a cold, unloving, self-righteous way. But we can always come to ourselves. No matter what our losses have been, we can always repent and return. We can always go in and enjoy our Father's home. We can always rest secure in the thought that he is always with us and that everything he has is ours. Let us explore further the two sons and their presence within each of us – which seems to be part of what Jesus wished to evoke.

A TALE OF TWO SONS

Various aspects of the story link the two sons. The verb 'to give' offers one subtle link between them. When the younger son worked as a swineherd and suffered the pangs of hunger, he wanted to take some of the pig-food. But no one *gave* him anything. Later on, the elder son complained to his father: 'you have never *given* me even a young goat so that I might celebrate with my friends.' The younger son wanted something given to him so that he might survive; the elder son wanted something given to him so that he might celebrate. The two of them had to learn that their father would give them everything – both to survive and to celebrate. There is a hint here of how all-giving the divine love is, ensuring that we can survive with strength and celebrate with joy.

Hunger links the two brothers as well. The younger son, living away from home in a distant country, dissipates his money and risks starving to death when a severe famine hits that land. 'I am dying of hunger,' he says to himself. His elder brother, however, suffers from a kind of self-inflicted starvation. He comes back from work in the fields, presumably ravenously hungry and ready for a good meal. Yet his bitter resentment keeps him outside and stops him from enjoying some choice cuts from the fatted calf waiting for him inside. But neither son should go hungry. Their father, like our heavenly Father, is lavishly generous.

In Jesus' story the father longs to satisfy the hungers of his two sons. He wants to meet their deepest needs, fill their hearts, and calm their longings with a peace that will never be taken from them. Servants slip discreetly in and out of the parable; they are there to serve the father and the family. But who is the true servant in the story? Beyond the shadow of a doubt, the father shows himself to be an exquisite servant. He runs down the road to welcome the prodigal; he organises a feast; and then he breaks away from the company to go outside and plead humbly with his elder son. Jesus pictures God as a perfectly loving father who does everything to serve, with incredible tact and delicacy, his two difficult sons.

This last thought shifts the focus away from the two sons and back to the heart of the parable: the father's love. Let me reflect on two further characteristics of that love: vulnerability and joy.

THE RISK AND JOY OF LOVE

Vulnerability

A major characteristic of love that emerges from Jesus' parable is the way in which love exposes one to suffering.[9] Real love produces vulnerability and sends lovers out over open ground under fire. Generous, self-sacrificing, and unconditional love risks being exploited, rejected, and even murderously crushed. No parable summons up more poignantly the risk of love than the story of the merciful father. He first runs down the road to greet his younger son, and later leaves the banquet to plead with his elder son. His love leads him to face and endure the insulting behaviour of the elder son, as well as some deep pain over the moral and spiritual death of his younger son. One does not have to strain to hear the sorrow in his repeated words about his son who has been 'lost' and 'dead' (Luke 15:24, 32). The father's love creates, if you like, his way of the cross or 'passion'.

In various languages a wise choice calls Jesus' own suffering and death his 'passion' – a term that combines intense love with the mortal suffering that it brought our divine Lover. The passion stories in the Gospels track the steadfastness of Jesus' loving commitment that made him vulnerable right to the end. His self-forgetful love exposed him to atrocious suffering and then death. The greatest of Jesus' parables more than hints at the 'passion' which the father risks and endures precisely because of his utterly generous love towards his two sons. Love makes God vulnerable, as we see when we gaze at the figure on the cross.

Joy

The homecoming of the younger son leads at once to a family celebration. The fatted calf must be killed; love calls for a feast of joy. Jesus reminds us how joy, even indescribable joy, is woven into the very texture of love. There is no more obvious spin-off from love than joy.

The boundless joy of God's compassionate love towards sinful human beings twice bursts through the Parable of the Prodigal Son: to round off the first part of the story (Luke 15:24), and then again at the very end when the father insists with his other son: 'We had to celebrate and rejoice, because this brother of yours was dead and he has come to life; he was lost and has been found' (Luke 15:32). The last word about divine love is that it will surprise us with joy – both in this life and in the life to come.

Jesus has much to say about the vibrant joy that our loving God holds out to us. Over and over again in his preaching, Jesus brings in the image of a feast. He pictures our future life with God that way: 'Many will come from the east and the west and will eat with Abraham, Isaac and Jacob in the kingdom' (Matthew 8:11). But such joyful feasting does not have to wait until the end, when human history finishes. Right now Jesus happily eats with sinners and outcasts; he loves them and wants to bring them forgiveness and peace of heart. He is happy and at home with them. Luke's Gospel appreciates how the joyful, forgiving love expressed by the Parable of the Father's Love serves to defend Jesus' own practice when critics grumble and complain: 'This fellow welcomes sinners and eats with them' (Luke 15:2). Jesus' happiness is unbounded when prodigal sons and daughters come home and accept the divine love.

CONCLUSION

In his preaching Jesus never offered a concept of God; at most he characterised God as 'perfect' (Matthew 5:48), 'kind', and 'merciful' (Luke 6:35–36). He let his deep experience of 'Abba' shine through such images as that of God showing love to all by sending 'rain on the righteous and the unrighteous' (Matthew 5:45) and through such parables as the Parable of the Father's Love. Jesus characterised God by telling such stories, which were also implicitly stories about himself. Occasionally Jesus characterised himself by remarking on his life as a homeless pilgrim

(Matthew 8:20), by presenting himself as a broody hen sheltering her tiny chickens (Matthew 23:37), or by quoting what critics said about his habits as a partygoer (Matthew 11:19). But, for the most part, any self-portrait of Jesus came through indirectly. His uniquely beautiful and powerful parables raise the questions: What kind of mind, imagination, and heart can we glimpse behind such stories? What must Jesus have been like if he came up with these stories and allowed us to grasp what God is like? The same questions emerge from his beatitudes, the Lord's Prayer, and the rest of his teaching. So much of what he taught was implicitly autobiographical and allows us to fill out our portrait of Jesus.

Chapter 8

♦

JESUS THE TEACHER

Amen, I tell you; no prophet is accepted in the prophet's hometown.

Luke 4:24

Amen, amen, I tell you; you will see heaven opened and the angels of God ascending and descending upon the Son of Man.

John 1:51

Some of Jesus' teaching circulates in the world's bloodstream. Several of his parables, the beatitudes, the Lord's Prayer, and other things he taught have entered languages and cultures everywhere, and become known at times even by people who remain unaware of the source of this teaching. Hence, before moving on to the story of his death and resurrection, I dedicate a further chapter to Jesus the Teacher.

THE BEATITUDES

The beatitudes summarised the essence of Jesus' programme: the best way, the only way to live. They held out the greatest good imaginable: the kingdom of heaven (Matthew) or the kingdom of God (Luke). In a concise form they pulled together Jesus' proclamation of the divine kingdom. Here, as elsewhere, Jesus never attempted to define the kingdom; he indicated the qualities of those who accepted it. As *the* teacher of wisdom *par excellence*, Jesus crafted the beatitudes, so that his hearers could memorise them, ponder them, and live by them. Like the parables, these distinctively terse pieces of teaching characterised unmistakably Jesus' style of teaching.

We find beatitudes in the Psalms (twenty-six times) and wisdom literature. On a few occasions two beatitudes occur in a row, but the Hebrew Bible contains no strings of three or more beatitudes. Occasionally such strings of beatitudes turn up in Tobit, Sirach, and the Qumran literature. Outside the Gospels, the New Testament includes hardly any beatitudes, except for Revelation, which includes seven. One of these beatitudes, at least, is clearly placed in the mouth of the risen Christ (Revelation 22:14). As regards the beatitudes recorded by Matthew and Luke, John Meier and others put a firm case for their being derived substantially from Jesus himself.[1]

Lists of beatitudes

Let me set out the two lists of beatitudes, along with the list of 'woes' that are special to Luke. I will use here the translation from the Revised Standard Version. I will set in italics the words that are special to Matthew and Luke, but without doing so for 'they' and 'you' which throughout characterise the lists of beatitudes from Matthew and Luke, respectively, except for Matthew 5:11–12, where we also find 'you'. It is most likely that Jesus expressed the beatitudes very directly by using 'you', and Matthew (or else the eyewitnesses or traditions on which he drew) made the teaching more general and formal by using 'they'.

There is much to be said for the position of John Meier, that Matthew put together in one continuous passage two separate lists of beatitudes that the tradition (or, I would say, more likely eyewitnesses) supplied and attributed to Jesus: verses 3, 4, 6, 11, and 12 made up the first list, and verses 5, 7, 8, 9, and 10 the second list. Matthew and Luke shared in common the first list (of four beatitudes). Only Matthew reproduced the second list (also of four beatitudes). Only Luke reproduced the four woes that eyewitness tradition supplied him with. (Such 'woes' belonged elsewhere in the preaching of Jesus; he also pronounced 'woes' against the towns of Chorazin and Bethsaida (Matthew 11:21).)

Matthew 5:3–12:
3 'Blessed are the poor *in spirit*; for theirs is the kingdom of *heaven*.
4 Blessed are those who mourn, for they shall be comforted.
5 *Blessed are the meek, for they shall inherit the earth.*

6 Blessed are those who hunger and *thirst for righteousness,* for they shall be satisfied.

7 Blessed are the merciful, for they shall obtain mercy.

8 Blessed are the pure of heart, for they shall see God.

9 Blessed are the peacemakers, for they shall be called sons of God.

10 Blessed are those who are persecuted for righteousness' sake, for theirs is the kingdom of heaven.

11 Blessed are you when men revile you and persecute you and utter all kinds of evil against you falsely on *my* account.

12 Rejoice and be glad, for your reward is great in heaven, for so men persecuted the prophets who were before you.'

(In vv. 4, 11, and 12 there are differences between Matthew and the corresponding beatitudes in Luke, but they seem too minor to be highlighted.)

Luke 6:20–26:

20 'Blessed are you poor, for yours is the kingdom of God.

21 Blessed are you that hunger now, for you shall be satisfied.

22 Blessed are you that weep now, for you shall laugh.

Blessed are you when men hate you, and when they exclude you and revile you, and cast out your name as evil, on account of *the Son of Man.*

23 Rejoice in that day, and leap for joy, for behold, your reward is great in heaven; for so their fathers did to the prophets.

24 But woe to you that are rich, for you have received your consolation.

25 Woe to you that are full now, for you shall hunger.

Woe to you that laugh now, for you shall mourn and weep.

26 Woe to you, when all men speak well of you, for so their fathers did to the false prophets.'

Four beatitudes in common

Let us consider the four beatitudes that Matthew and Luke have in common. The first three are simple, stark, and even laconic. Jesus declares to be blessed those who are poor, those who mourn or weep, and those who go hungry. Their situation, he promises, will be directly reversed – at the end of history and through the action of God. Those who mourn will be comforted by God; those who hunger now will be satisfied by God.

Jesus was distinctive in teaching through strings of beatitudes, but the building blocks for his beatitudes enjoyed rich precedents in the books of the Old Testament: above all the 'poor' or *'anawim'* of God. The 'poor' were, primarily, those who suffered socio-economic distress and found themselves in a situation which they had not chosen for themselves and about which they could do nothing. Their lack of money and other possessions left them vulnerable and even powerless when faced with the rapacious and ruthless masters of society. They were people who had no redress in our world. Forced to depend on the help of God, they could also be poor in their religious attitudes, as humble and needy servants of God.

The promise that Jesus made was more general in the case of the poor. For them God is inaugurating here and now the divine rule; the kingdom of heaven is already theirs and will be fully theirs in the future. In the case of the other two categories, those who mourn and those who go hungry, the promises apply simply to the future and are expressed more specifically. Those who mourn or weep will be comforted and able to 'laugh'. Those who are hungry will be satisfied or 'fed to the full' – the verb used of the prodigal son who wanted to feed himself to the full with the pods that the pigs were eating (Luke 15:16).

Jesus did not qualify his promises with any conditions. These three promises, at least explicitly, did not depend, for instance, on anyone's commitment to him. He did not say, 'blessed are the poor who follow me'; nor did he say, 'blessed are those followers of mine who weep and mourn now'; nor did he say, 'blessed are those followers of mine who are hungry now'. The promises came with no strings attached. The promises were unconditioned by any reference to Jesus himself. They also came without such qualifications as: 'Blessed are the poor who are always faithful to God. Blessed are those who weep now because they suffer for keeping the divine commandments. Blessed are those who remain hungry because they will not kill others to have more food.'

The poor, the sorrowing, and the hungry have no claim on God, or at least no strict claim. God's loving mercy will be extended to them, even though they do not deserve, or do not strictly deserve, such gracious help. Some parables carry the same message: for instance, those of the Father's Love (Luke 15:11–32), the Unforgiving Servant (Matthew 18:23–35), and the Pharisee and the Tax Collector (Luke 18:10–14). In their different ways, the prodigal son, the servant, and the tax collector are greatly in need, but they have no right to receive the help that will come their way. Thus the first three beatitudes common to Matthew and Luke focus on people who are not said to be virtuous and deserving. They are simply in need and God will help and vindicate them.[2] They are deprived and destitute, and only God will come to their aid. Jesus assures those in great distress that God intends to bring to an end the present state of things. The good news expressed in these first three beatitudes specifies wonderfully what Jesus means by saying elsewhere that 'the poor are brought the good news' (Matthew 11:5).

Some details of the four beatitudes

Any attentive reader will notice the difference between the very first beatitude that Luke and Matthew have in common. In Luke it runs 'blessed are you poor', and in Matthew 'blessed are the poor *in spirit*'. Matthew (or the eyewitnesses or the tradition on which he drew) has added 'in spirit' (or 'in the Spirit') to make the first beatitude applicable to all believers, and not merely to those who are suffering from socio-economic deprivation. The blessing goes out to the poor 'in the divine Spirit', all those who have let the Spirit open their minds and hearts to the message of Jesus. The addition brings out an aspect of this opening beatitude, without attempting to 'over-spiritualise' it and deny its primary reference to all those who are desperately disadvantaged economically and socially. It would be somewhat bizarre to think of Matthew 'watering down' this primary reference, especially if we recall the standards for the great judgement (Matthew 25:31–46). Those who have come to the aid of the hungry, the naked, the prisoner, and others in terrible distress will inherit the kingdom. One might well sum up the words of the Lord in that judgement scene as: 'I was poor and you helped me.'

The promise that those who mourn will be comforted could be a self-description; it evokes the destiny of Jesus himself. The Letter to the Hebrews recalls the agonising prayer of Jesus in Gethsemane: 'in the days of his flesh, Jesus offered up prayers and supplications, with loud cries and tears, to the One who was able to save him from death, and he was heard because of his reverent submission' (Hebrews 5:7–8). In the resurrection the suffering situation of Jesus was reversed and he was 'comforted' by God. One of Paul's central themes in his Second Letter to the

Corinthians parallels this beatitude, when he writes of 'the God of all comfort, who comforts us in all our affliction' (1:3–4). Luke's version of the same beatitude promises the gift of laughter to those who now weep. It brings to mind much in the Christian tradition. Years after their tragic separation, Peter Abelard (1079–1142/43) composed a Good Friday hymn for his beloved Heloise (c. 1110–c. 1163), by then abbess of a community of nuns. The hymn prayed to Christ: 'that you might grant us the laughter of your Easter grace (*ut risum tribuas paschalis gratiae*)'. Down to the Reformation and even later, a custom in German-speaking countries, the 'Easter laughter (*risus paschalis*)', involved the local pastor in expressing Christ's victory over death and Satan by introducing jokes into his Easter Sunday sermon. The idea was that 'he who laughs last laughs best'. In rising from the dead, the crucified Christ had, so to speak, the last laugh over suffering and all the forces of evil. The custom brilliantly embodied the beatitude: 'blessed are you that weep now, for you shall laugh.'

Where Luke has simply 'blessed are you that hunger now', Matthew represents this third beatitude as 'blessed are those who hunger and thirst for righteousness'. It could be that Jesus drew a traditional pair of words from the Old Testament Scriptures and declared 'blessed' those who endured 'hunger and thirst'. But, in the light of the first two beatitudes ('blessed are the poor, blessed are those who mourn'), which are terse and centre on a single, stark word, Jesus probably said simply, 'blessed are the hungry'. Such people will be 'fed to the full'. Here the Greek verb (*chortazo*) originally referred to the feeding of animals, like the German verb '*fressen*'. It summons up not the image of animals at the trough but that of the joyful, richly supplied banquet in the coming kingdom to which Jesus repeatedly returned.

The additional words, 'and thirst for righteousness', come from Matthew or perhaps from his sources. 'Hungering and thirsting for righteousness' make a resounding phrase that conjures up Old Testament language (e.g. Isaiah 49:10; 65:13). 'Righteousness/justice (*dikaiosune*)' turns up seven times in Matthew's Gospel, but only once in Luke and never in Mark and John. Here the evangelist intends an intense desire for the salvation that comes from God – the meaning that Matthew gives to 'justice' earlier in the Sermon on the Mount. Subsequently he will cite 'righteousness/justice' in another, related sense: as doing the will of God in the light of the teaching of Jesus (e.g. Matthew 6:33).

132

Where the first three beatitudes highlight what God will graciously do (for the poor, the sorrowing, and the hungry), the fourth beatitude (which Matthew 5:11–12 and Luke 6:22–23 share in common) spotlights the call of Jesus' followers to witness to him in the face of opposition. This beatitude is longer than the first three combined, even in the longer form that they assume in Matthew. Both evangelists cite the fourth beatitude in a second person formulation, 'you'. The beatitude envisages those who suffer persecution because they have freely committed themselves to Jesus, 'the Son of Man' (Luke 6:22). Jesus did not promise that their situation would be directly reversed, as in the case of those who mourn and then will be comforted and those who hunger and then will be fed to the full. He held out rather a general promise of a 'great reward in heaven'. Hence, even at the time of persecution when they were being reviled and excluded, they could rejoice and 'leap for joy' (Luke 6:23).

Commentators often understand this fourth beatitude to reflect persecution that would be experienced in the early Church. But it could apply also to the situation of the Twelve and other followers of Jesus at the time of his earthly ministry. When they were with Jesus, they were present on numerous occasions when he was reviled and faced with hatred; as members of his entourage they shared in this hostile rejection. When some of them were sent by him on mission for the kingdom (Mark 6:7–13; Luke 10:1–12), they were to expect not only a fruitful ministry but also unpleasant opposition. The programme Jesus summed up in the beatitudes, and not least in this fourth beatitude, was one in which he himself shared with his disciples. The programme would bring them to share with him in the fullness of life, the final kingdom 'in heaven'. But en route, like him, they too would face hostile and even murderous opposition.

Over and over again, shining examples among the followers of Jesus have embodied this fourth beatitude in their lives. To select one example from innumerable cases, Dietrich Bonhoeffer (1906–45) in the early 1930s seriously put to himself two questions: What does God demand of us? What does it mean to follow Jesus Christ? In answering these questions he resolved to take the Sermon on the Mount and, in particular, the beatitudes as the pattern for his life.[3] He began writing his *Discipleship* (originally published in 1937), which drew its inspiration from the beatitudes and the Sermon on the Mount.[4] Other decisions built on that basic commitment to Christ's programme, and eventually led to his death by hanging in April 1945, only a few days before the Second World War ended. On the morning of his execution the prison doctor saw him and had this to say: 'I saw Pastor Bonhoeffer, still in his prison clothes, kneeling in fervent prayer to the Lord his God. The devotion and evident conviction of being heard that I saw in the prayer of this intensely captivating man moved me to the depths.' Bonhoeffer's last recorded words (spoken to a fellow prisoner) expressed the spirit of the fourth beatitude and its promise of persecution being followed by a 'great reward in heaven'. He said to that prisoner: 'for me this is the end, but also the beginning'.[5]

Beatitudes special to Matthew

We saw above how the fourth beatitude marked a switch, so to speak, from the 'indicative' to the 'imperative'. The first three beatitudes put the accent on the gift of God, the fourth on the responsibility of Jesus' followers. The five beatitudes special to Matthew, beatitudes that eyewitness reports supplied him with, issue a call to action. They embody invitations to be meek, merciful, clean of heart, peacemakers, and doers of God's will in the light of Jesus' teaching. These beatitudes focus largely on 'good people doing good things', and receiving corresponding goods from God. They 'shall inherit the earth' by God's gracious gift; they 'shall be shown mercy' by God; 'they shall see God'; 'they shall be called sons [and daughters] of God'; those 'persecuted for the sake of righteousness' will receive from God the kingdom of heaven.[6] In a word, good things will happen to good people.

The first of the five beatitudes from Matthew's second list expresses Jesus' blessing on the meek – that is to say, on those who are *both* humble in their relationship with God through recognising their total dependence on God *and* behave gently in their relationship with others, not pursuing their own interests to the detriment of others. The 'meek' are non-violent people; to them 'the earth' – that is to say, 'the promised land', a way of referring to the kingdom of God – is promised. Once again, this beatitude comes across as a self-description of Jesus. In fact, he is remembered as having said: 'learn from me, for I am meek and humble of heart' (Matthew 11:29). He demonstrated this characteristic *also* through the humility of his language. He did not adopt the refined language of intellectuals, let alone the specialised terms of theological jargon, but expressed himself in the everyday speech of the 'ordinary' people of his time.

The second of the beatitudes special to Matthew, 'blessed are the merciful, for they shall obtain mercy', evokes the loving mercy constantly displayed by the actions of Jesus towards sinners and symbolised for all times in his Parable of the Father's Love. The beatitude found its expression in the Lord's Prayer: 'forgive us our trespasses as we forgive those who trespass against us'.

With his third beatitude in this list Jesus blesses the pure or clean of heart. These are people who come before God with complete honesty and sincerity. They show transparent integrity in their obedience and loyalty to God. Their reward is startling: they shall see God. According to the Old Testament, to see God is to die. Because of the greatness and awesome glory of God, human beings, even Moses who was so close to God, could not see God and live (Exodus 33:20). But Jesus promises the vision of God to those who are 'pure in heart'. Paul and then John echo memorably the reward promised by this beatitude. At the end of a lyrical hymn to love, Paul looks to the future vision of God: 'at present we see, indistinctly, as in a mirror,[7] but then we will see face to face. At present I know only partially, then I shall know fully, even as I have been fully known' (1 Corinthians 13:12). The First Letter of John probably refers to our future, heavenly vision of the glorious Christ (rather than that of God the Father) when it declares: 'we shall be like him for we shall see him as he is' (3:2). What was impossible even for Moses has become the future reward for all those who stand before God with sincerity and integrity.

Fourthly, Jesus blesses 'peacemakers', for 'they shall be called sons [and daughters] of God'. Down through the centuries, some followers of Jesus have thrown off the virus of personal and tribal interests, nationalism, and instinctive hostility towards 'the others', and proved outstanding in their efforts to bring peace on earth. St Elizabeth of Portugal (1271–1336) was one of those who took this beatitude with utter seriousness. Even in her lifetime, she came to be known as 'the peacemaker'. The daughter of Peter III, who became the King of Aragon, she suffered when a bitter quarrel between her father and her grandfather (who was still on the throne) had divided the whole kingdom. But she managed to reconcile them. She had two children by her husband, Denis the King of Portugal, who repeatedly proved unfaithful to her. Yet she cherished the children born to him out of wedlock, and cared for their education as if they were her own children. Her only son Alfonso twice rose in arms against his father, and twice

Elizabeth rode out between the opposing forces and brought about a reconciliation. She was also credited with stopping other wars. The best commentary of this beatitude comes from the life and work of such saints as Elizabeth, Francis of Assisi (1181/82–1226), St Catherine of Siena (1347–80), (Blessed) Pope John XXIII (1881–1963), and others.

The fifth beatitude in Matthew's second list declares about those 'who are persecuted for righteousness' sake' that 'theirs is the kingdom of heaven'. There is no talk here of a heavenly 'reward', but – as in the case of 'the poor (in spirit)' – the kingdom of heaven is theirs. Unlike the similar closing beatitude in the first list (that Matthew and Luke share in common), Jesus does not refer explicitly to himself or to his followers suffering persecution on his account. Nevertheless, he is implicitly present, once we agree that doing 'righteousness/justice' in this context means doing the will of God as illuminated by the teaching of Jesus.

The 'woes' in Luke

After the four beatitudes he shared in common with Matthew, Luke added four woes; one might call them a mixture of threat and lament. There are no solid reasons for doubting that Luke drew these 'woes' from the 'eyewitnesses and ministers of the word' (Luke 1:2). They belonged squarely to Jesus' style of teaching: see, for instance, Matthew 11:21; Mark 13:17; and Luke 17:1. Jesus wanted the well-fed rich to repent and not waste their lives by indulging in frivolous, empty laughter and showing themselves off, in the hope that others would speak well of them. He knew how easy it was to take for granted false values and live by them. That was the burden of such parables as the Rich Man and Lazarus and the Rich Fool. Those stories did not suggest that the rich men in question had made their money through immoral and criminal practices. The problem rather was that they did not remember God and live by the standards of neighbourly love that Jesus expected.

In the chapter where Luke places the 'woes', he immediately reports also the teaching of Jesus about 'doing good to those who hate you', being generous with others, and sharing wealth, even with one's enemies (Luke 6:27–38). The story of Jesus provides examples of well-off people practising what he preached: for instance, the women mentioned in Luke 8:1–3 and a rich tax collector, Zacchaeus (Luke 19:1–10).

Jesus addressed the 'woes' and the beatitudes to others. These concise declarations pose the question for us: What kind of mind and imagination could fashion such a programme? The remarkable quality of the beatitudes and their author emerges even more powerfully when we hear them read with dignity and even when they are read badly. To be sure, much of Jesus' teaching benefits from being read aloud, but this is especially true of the beatitudes.

Boris Pasternak's moving novel *Doctor Zhivago* covers life in Russia during the first three decades of the twentieth century. Early in the story, Lara, still only a schoolgirl, is seduced by a rich lawyer. Feeling desperate and depressed, she visits a church, feeling as if the pavement might open at her feet or the vaulted ceiling collapse on her. It would, she thinks, 'serve her right and put an end to the whole affair'. Her life has become unbearable and she would gladly die. It is her misery that makes her ready to listen.

In the echoing, half-empty church her cousin was reading at breakneck speed the beatitudes: 'Blessed are the poor in spirit . . . Blessed are they that mourn . . . Blessed are they that hunger and thirst after righteousness.' Lara shivered and stood still. These were words addressed by Christ directly and personally to her. 'He was saying: "Happy are the downtrodden. They have something to say for themselves. They have everything before them." That was what he thought. That was Christ's opinion of it.' She no longer felt meaningless and without a future. Even there, in a drab and distracting church, Lara knew Christ's gentle promise of mercy. She heard him speaking to her through the words that someone was rattling off without devotion.[8] One could add innumerable other examples from 'real' life and literature that illustrate brilliantly how the beatitudes have never stopped enjoying a powerful impact and facilitating a relationship with the mysterious and merciful person of Jesus.

The beatitudes also serve as a self-description of Jesus. If anyone was ever meek, merciful, pure of heart, and the rest, it was Jesus himself. His beatitudes, along with the 'woes', summed up the message of the kingdom. But they also provided a precise portrait of Jesus, the programme he set himself, and the way he acted. This self-portrait was further reflected in the prayer which he gave to his followers and which summarised the good news that Jesus preached.

THE LORD'S PRAYER

It is at the heart of the Sermon on the Mount, a chapter after the beatitudes, that Matthew inserts the prayer that Jesus taught his disciples: 'Our Father in the heavens, may your name be made holy. May your kingdom come, may your will be done, on earth as in heaven. Give us today our daily bread. And forgive us our debts as we also have forgiven our debtors. And do not bring us into temptation, but deliver us from the evil one' (Matthew 6:9–13). It was a prayer that Jesus prescribed for his followers ('pray then in this way', Matthew 6:9), but it was also a prayer that Jesus himself practised, at least in part. To be sure, he did not (and could not) pray, 'forgive me my sins.' But we do find him addressing God as 'Abba (Father dear)', praying 'your will be done' (Mark 14:36) and equivalently praying 'may your name be made holy' (John 12:28).

Luke provides a shorter version of the Lord's Prayer: 'Father, may your name be made holy. May your kingdom come. Give us each day our daily bread. And forgive us our sins, as we ourselves forgive everyone in debt to us. And do not bring us into temptation' (Luke 11:2–4). From the time of Origen in the second century, Christians have reflected on the existence of two, differing versions of the Lord's Prayer. Origen himself accounted for the two versions by proposing that on two separate occasions Jesus himself provided a longer and a shorter text for prayer (stage one). We cannot rule out the possibility that Jesus presented the Lord's Prayer more than once and in slightly different language. After all, it seems that there were two strings of beatitudes, originally proclaimed separately and available for Matthew to bring together. Nowadays, however, most scholars explain the two versions of the Lord's Prayer in terms of the evangelists themselves (at stage three) and/or of the different eyewitnesses and/or traditions they drew on (at stage two). Constant use of the Lord's Prayer brought some adaptations.

In appropriating fully the Lord's Prayer, the setting reported by Luke is significant. The disciples have observed Jesus at prayer. When he stops, they immediately ask him to help them also to pray (Luke 11:1–2). They want to pray like him and bond with him in prayer. The Lukan setting shows that in praying the Lord's Prayer we pray not only as Jesus taught us but also (in part) like Jesus himself. The 'Our Father' sums up in prayer much of what Jesus did and taught. The Lord's Prayer may be intriguingly simple, but it is also almost overpoweringly rich.[9]

What does this prayer tell us about Jesus himself? What does it contribute to our portrait of him? One might answer that the three 'you' petitions (only two in Luke) and then the four 'we' petitions (only three in Luke) sum up in the form of prayer seven central themes in Jesus' presence, preaching, and activity for the kingdom. Let us take the petitions in order to indicate how Jesus used them to summarise his kingdom message.

'May your name be made holy'

God proves himself holy by revealing himself as he is – that is to say, by manifesting his divine power, glory, and holiness. The presence of Jesus in the cause of the divine kingdom embodied just such a divine manifestation. In Mark's Gospel an 'unclean spirit' recognised the presence of Jesus as the revelation of the divine power and holiness: 'You are the Holy One of God' (1:24). In John's Gospel, through experiencing Jesus, Peter was moved to confess: 'We have come to believe and know that you are the Holy One of God' (John 6:69).

'May your kingdom come'

By praying for the coming of God's kingdom, the followers of Jesus aligned themselves with the very heart of his preaching, activity, and suffering: the full and final presence of the rule of God. At the Last Supper, Jesus would look forward to the consummation of this new relationship between God and human beings: 'I will never drink [again] of the fruit of the vine until that day when I drink it new in the Kingdom of God' (Mark 14:25).

'Your will be done, on earth as in heaven'

Jesus intended to found a new family, based on obedience to the divine will: 'whoever does the will of God is my brother and sister and mother' (Mark 3:35). Matthew draws the Sermon on the Mount to a close by recalling the warning of Jesus: 'Not everyone who says to me "Lord, Lord," will enter the kingdom of heaven, but only the one who does the will of my Father in heaven' (7:21).

'Give us today our daily bread'

Repeatedly Jesus had urged his audience to ask God in a simple and trusting way for their needs. He assured people that God takes a highly personal interest in everyone. God is the Father whose attentive love goes far beyond that of normal, caring parents: 'Is there anyone among you who, if your child asks for bread, will give him a stone? Or if the child asks for fish, will give him a snake? If you then, who are evil, know how to give good gifts to your children, how much more will your Father in heaven give good things to those who ask him' (Matthew 7:9–11).

'Forgive us our debts, as we also have forgiven our debtors'

The plea for forgiveness and the condition for receiving this were essential points in Jesus' programme for the kingdom. Nothing shows more clearly God's merciful love towards us than the divine forgiveness. Nothing shows more clearly our love towards others than our willingness to forgive them from our hearts. This was the one point in the Lord's Prayer where Jesus expected us to testify before God what we are doing. Our forgiveness of one another shows how far we have accepted God's forgiveness and have let it change our lives. Through the Parable of the Merciless Servant (see Chapter Six) Jesus drove this point home.

'Do not bring us into temptation'

Here Jesus asked his followers to pray, in effect, 'do not let us fall under or succumb to temptation', and not 'deliver us from temptation and suffering'. He wanted them to pray: 'protect us and help us to endure our testing faithfully' (see Mark 14:38). There is a straight line that leads from this petition to the example of Jesus himself, who was tested in the desert at the beginning of his ministry and in his passion at the end.

'But deliver us from the evil one'

This seventh and last petition of the Lord's Prayer gathers up a major element in what we see Jesus doing in his ministry for God's kingdom. Right from his baptism he struggles with the devil for the control of humanity in what is the end-time of history. Jesus is the 'stronger one' and strikingly overcomes the demonic powers through his exorcisms. Jesus enters the 'strong man's house, ties him up, and plunders his property' (Mark 3:22–27). The story of the Gerasene demoniac provides the classic example of Jesus delivering someone from the power of the evil one (Mark 5:1–20).

In this way we can read the Lord's Prayer as a masterly summary that Jesus produced of what he did and taught right through his ministry for the kingdom. The petitions from the Lord's Prayer encapsulate the message of the kingdom which Jesus preached and dramatised in his own person. But there is something even deeper to be observed here. The Lord's Prayer depended on and was shaped by Jesus' personal experience of God. As he grew up, he absorbed the rich Jewish tradition of prayer and, in particular, used the psalms. A striking instance came at the end of his final Passover meal, when he led his core group of followers in singing Psalms 115–118, the second part of the 'Hallel' psalm (Mark 14:26). What his own experience prompted Jesus to do was not to drop Jewish forms of prayer, but to move them in a new direction. The scene in Gethsemane divulged stunningly how Jesus had looked into the mystery of God and called that mystery 'Abba (Father dear)'. In the words of John Meier, 'Jesus' striking use of *Abba*' expressed 'his intimate experience of God as his own father', and 'this usage made a lasting impression on his disciples'.[10]

According to the Old Testament Scriptures, God was known by many names, above all by the intensified plural 'Elohim' (divine God) and by the personal name of YHWH (e.g. Exodus 3:14; 6:6–8), the holiest of names that occurs about 6,800 times in the biblical text, both by itself or in compounds. Since devout Israelites judged it too sacred to be pronounced, they read in its place 'Adonai' (Lord) or 'Elohim'. In the light of this practice many English translations render YHWH as LORD or in some cases GOD, both in capital letters. As regards metaphors for God, 'God is king' was the predominant one in the Old Testament, appearing much more frequently than other such metaphors as 'God is a lover/husband' or 'God is a father'. What do we find about the last metaphor, the one that particularly interests us in connection with the opening of the Lord's Prayer, when we examine the proto-canonical books of the Old Testament (those thirty-nine books accepted by all Christians as inspired and canonical) and the deutero-canonical books (the six books and further portions of the proto-canonical books found in the Greek but not in the Hebrew canon of Scriptures)?

Hardly twenty times in the entire Old Testament 'Father' was used in speaking of God (or addressing God). Naming God 'Father' expressed the divine involvement in the history of Israel, its kingly leaders, and its righteous people. The 'Father' metaphor centred, above all, on the free, divine choice of a people whom God had delivered from Egypt and steadfastly cherished. Despite their sinful failures, the people could always experience God as their 'Father'. Nevertheless, while occurring in the Pentateuch (e.g. Deuteronomy 32:6), and in some historical (e.g. 2 Samuel 7:12–14), prophetic (e.g. Jeremiah 3:4–5, 19), and sapiential (e.g. Wisdom 2:16) texts, this divine name was not frequent in the Old Testament. It hardly ever occurred in prayers addressed to God (e.g. Psalm 89:26–29; Isaiah 63:16). Jesus changed that, influenced more by his experience in prayer than by his Jewish heritage.

The Gospel of Mark several times calls God 'Father', most strikingly in Jesus' prayer in Gethsemane: 'Abba, Father, all things are possible to you; take this cup from me. Yet not my will but thine be done' (Mark 14:36). In Aramaic, the mother tongue of Jesus, 'Abba' was the way children and grown-ups addressed their male parent as 'my own dear father'. It was rather like the situation in modern Italian, where adults continue to speak to their male parent as they did when they were children: 'babbo (daddy)'. Jesus evidently spoke of and with God as his 'Abba', in a direct or highly familial manner that seems to have been unknown, or at least extremely unusual, in the earlier Jewish tradition in Palestine. 'Abba' was remembered as a characteristic and distinctive feature of Jesus' prayer life. It reproduced the unaffected attitude of children who totally trust their loving father. It introduced the Lord's Prayer, in which short and direct petitions mirror a childlike dependence on an all-powerful and loving father in whom one can have unconditional confidence.

In several passages in Matthew (e.g. 6:9; 11:25–26; 16:17), in at least one passage in Luke (11:2), and probably in further passages in these two Gospels, 'Father' (patêr in Greek) stands for the original 'Abba'. The example of Jesus encouraged his followers, at least in the early days of Christianity, to address God with the familiar 'Abba' (Romans 8:15; Galatians 4:6). St Paul regarded the 'Abba' prayer as a distinctive mark of those who had been baptised into Christ and had received the Holy Spirit (Galatians 3:27; 4:6).

As we concluded in Chapter Two above, Jesus spoke at least fairly frequently of God as 'Abba (Father dear)' and, as the Son, claimed a unique mutual knowledge and relationship to the Father, a unique mutual relationship out of which Jesus revealed, not a previously unknown God, but the God whom he alone knew fully and really. He invited his hearers to accept a new relationship with God as Father; yet it was a relationship that depended on his relationship with God (Luke 22:29–30) and differed from their relationship.

Recalling how Jesus gave himself totally to proclaiming the kingdom of God, many have called the Lord's Prayer the prayer of the kingdom, the prayer which summarised the entire message of the kingdom. Its very first word, 'Abba (Father dear)', set the tone and was the heart of the matter. In proclaiming the kingdom, Jesus announced the God of his deepest experience: the loving, merciful Father, the God with whom we can enjoy a truly intimate and privileged relationship. This was the Father whom Jesus experienced as utterly good to all, the God whose goodness knows no bounds (Matthew 5:48).

THE LOVE COMMAND

As well as instruction on prayer that reached its high point in the Lord's Prayer, Jesus had much to say about human behaviour. That teaching found its climax in the Golden Rule. Where others had formulated things 'negatively' ('do not do to others …'), Jesus positively required that we actively contribute to the welfare and happiness of others: 'in everything do to others as you would have them do to you' (Matthew 7:12). Along with the Golden Rule, we should recall also Jesus' reformulation of the love command.[11]

When questioned about 'the first commandment', Jesus responded from within the Jewish tradition by first quoting the *Shema* ('Hear, O Israel') on the love of God (Deuteronomy 6:4–5) and then adding another scriptural text on the love of neighbour (Leviticus 19:18): 'Hear, O Israel, the Lord our God, the Lord is one; you shall love the Lord your God with all your heart, and with all your soul, and with all your mind, and with all your strength. The second is this, You shall love your neighbour as yourself' (Mark 12:28–34). In the context of the *Shema*, faith in YHWH as 'the one and only God' provides the motive for loving this God with total love and an undivided dedication that holds nothing back – i.e. with all one's being ('heart', 'soul', 'mind', and 'strength'). Deuteronomy repeatedly introduces the wider background and basis for this commitment: the story of God's saving acts in delivering the chosen people from Egypt and bringing them to the promised land (e.g. Deuteronomy 6:20–25; 26:5–10).

Jesus innovated in two ways: first, by combining the two classic Old Testament texts about love of God and love of neighbour, respectively. He distinguished but would not separate the vertical relationship to God and the horizontal relationship to neighbour. Together they form one commitment of love that transcends all the other commandments in importance, summarises the key values of the Jewish Torah, and furnishes a basic framework for understanding and applying the law of God.

The second innovation introduced by Jesus was to go beyond defining 'neighbour' narrowly as one's kin and one's people. In Leviticus 19:18 'neighbour' meant one's fellow Israelite; a few verses later 'neighbour' was slightly extended to include 'resident aliens' (Leviticus 19:33–34). Jesus, however, defined 'neighbour' in a way that went beyond family and ethnic relationships and contacts with resident aliens. He spoke out on the need to love even one's enemies, whoever they were (Luke 6:27–35).

When Luke records the teaching of Jesus on love for God and neighbour, he at once has Jesus tell the story of the Good Samaritan in answer to the question, 'and who is my neighbour?' (Luke 10:29). Even if this parable may not have belonged originally in that setting, it goes back to Jesus and lets us glimpse his universal application of neighbourly love. In this story the hero is neither the Jewish priest nor the Levite but a despised and even hated outsider, a Samaritan. Jesus holds up this compassionate person as an example for everyone, a practical model for human conduct when faced with someone who is distressed and afflicted and to whom we should 'show pity and kindness, even beyond the bounds of one's own ethnic and religious group'.[12]

This chapter has limited itself to three major items in the teaching of Jesus: the beatitudes, the Lord's Prayer, and the love command. All three raise the question: What kind of mind, imagination, and heart could produce such teaching? What kind of person can we glimpse behind these fresh religious ideas and commanding intuitions about God and the human situation? All of this teaching draws its force from a unique experience of God that we can only grope after in a bewildered fashion.

The teaching of Jesus is like a stream of life and not a watertight, sharply articulated system. But to say that is to take nothing away from its authoritative character. Repeatedly the Gospels testify to the striking authority with which Jesus taught. The Synoptic Gospels express this in various ways, and not least through an expression which at times introduces some teaching from Jesus: 'Amen, I tell you'. John's Gospel maintains this practice and makes it even more solemnly authoritative. Twenty-five times the Fourth Gospel represents Jesus as saying, 'Amen, amen, I tell you'. As a unique witness Jesus gives authoritative testimony to the things of God with which he enjoys firsthand contact.

Jesus' life and, even more, his death authenticated his teaching. Take, for instance, the beatitudes, the Lord's Prayer, and the love command. It is not difficult to recognise how they were played out in Jesus' suffering, death, and resurrection. For instance, the sixth petition in the Lord's Prayer, 'do not bring us into temptation', received its dramatic embodiment through the crucifixion. The noun 'temptation (*peirasmos*)' and the corresponding verb 'tempt/test (*peirazo*)' turn up here and there in the New Testament and, not least, in connection with Jesus himself. After telling how Jesus was led by the Spirit into the wilderness and tempted by the devil, Luke ends his account with the ominous hint: 'When the devil had finished every test, he departed from him until an opportune time' (Luke 4:1–13). That time would come when Jesus faced his arrest and said to those who came to seize him: 'This is your hour and the power of darkness' (Luke 22:53). At the Last Supper he had already acknowledged his disciples to be those 'who have stood by me in my trials (*peirasmois*)'. In the Garden of Gethsemane Jesus warns Peter, James, and John about the time of trial they will now face: 'watch and pray that you may not come into [succumb to] temptation/ trial' (Luke 22:46). They will be very shortly faced with a terrifying test at the arrest, passion, and death of Jesus.

Some film directors have developed these hints to bring Satan quite blatantly into the story of Jesus' suffering and death. In a 1999 American/Italian film, *Jesus*, the devil appears in the desert as a plausible, contemporary crook – a bit overweight, with greasy hair and wearing an Armani suit. He returns in the same garb during the agony Jesus undergoes in Gethsemane. Mel Gibson's *The Passion of the Christ* opens with Jesus' agony in the garden and introduces Satan into the scene. He appears both as a loathsome, androgynous figure and a menacing snake. He will turn up again as the androgynous figure in scenes that follow.

This penultimate petition in the Lord's Prayer, 'do not bring us into temptation', can appropriately make us think of Jesus and how he was tested by forces actively hostile to God, especially at the beginning of his ministry and at the end of his earthly life.

Chapter 9

♦

FACING DEATH

Jesus was not crucified on a marble altar between two
golden candlesticks, but on a city garbage dump, outside
the walls, between two thieves.

George Macleod

THE SINGLE-MINDED DEVOTION with which Jesus proclaimed the kingdom quickly led him into conflict with
groups of Pharisees, Sadducees, and others. As Mark tells the
story, that opposition showed itself from the start (2:1–3:6). At
the end, some highly placed Sadducees joined forces with one of
Jesus' disciples (Judas) and Pontius Pilate, the Roman governor
of Judea, Samaria, and Idumea (AD 26–36) to bring about the
crucifixion. How did Jesus face and understand death when it
closed in on him? Did he interpret his death in advance as the
climax of his mission? Or did he experience panic and even
succumb to the fear that 'all might come to nothing'? We can
glean some answers by taking matters in stages.[1]

WHAT JESUS SAID OF HIMSELF

At some point in his ministry, and not simply at the very end,
Jesus began to anticipate his own violent death. He referred to
himself as 'the bridegroom' whose presence gave joy to the
wedding guests or to the groom's close attendants. But, as he
ominously added, the bridegroom would be 'taken away' from
them. This portrayal of himself as a tragic bridegroom alluded to
his violent end (Mark 2:18–20).[2]

Jesus saw his ministry as standing, at least partially, in

continuity with the prophets, right down to John, his prophetic precursor from whom he received baptism.[3] In his own prophetic role Jesus seemingly had a premonition that he would inevitably die a martyr's death and apparently expected that to happen in Jerusalem, the city that 'murders prophets and stones those sent' to it (Luke 13:33–34; see 11:47, 49–51).[4] There was a tragic tradition about various messengers of God being persecuted and killed in Jerusalem.[5] Apparently Jesus sensed that he would share the fate of those already done away with in that city. Not only past history but also contemporary events had their lesson to teach. The execution of John, someone whose prophetic activity directly prepared the way for the ministry of Jesus, showed how perilous such radical religious activity was in the Palestine of that time. Jesus would have been remarkably naive not to have recognised the danger.

In this connection we should cite the Parable of the Vineyard and the Tenants (Mark 12:1–12), which came from a discourse of Jesus in controversy with some religious leaders.[6] It is the only parable in which Jesus spoke clearly about his own mission. The owner (who evidently symbolises God) leases to some tenant farmers a vineyard (which, in the light of Isaiah 5:1–7, inevitably evokes Israel), and eventually sends a series of servants to collect his share in the produce. But the tenants refuse to honour the claims of the owner, they mistreat his agents, and even kill some of them. Finally, the owner despatches his son, a fully accredited representative. The tenants murder him, throw the corpse out of the vineyard, and plan to seize the property for themselves. Jesus probably ended the parable with a question and a response: 'What then will the owner of the vineyard do? He will come and destroy the tenants and give the vineyard to others.' Many scholars argue that the quotation from Psalm 118 (in the next two verses) about the 'rejected stone' becoming the 'cornerstone' was added in stage two of the tradition. Many also hold that the qualification of the 'son' as 'beloved' was likewise added at stage two. Some commentators maintain that Jesus originally ended his parable with the question: 'What then will the owner of the vineyard do?' Yet it has been argued convincingly that the language about the transfer of the vineyard to others came from Jesus himself (at stage one).

What then may we draw from the parable for our portrait of Jesus? The 'servants' stood for the prophets who, on God's behalf, had over the centuries confronted the religious and political leaders of Israel. Jesus may have intended to include

John the Baptist among these biblical figures. He thought of himself as the 'son' through whom 'the owner of the vineyard' made a final bid to the 'tenant farmers', the leaders of Israel. But a violent death overtook the 'son' – a clear pointer to the fate that Jesus anticipated for himself. Who were the 'others' to whom the property was to be given (and not merely leased)? Seemingly they were the Jewish disciples of Jesus and the Gentiles, who together would form the reconstituted Israel. Yet the identity of these beneficiaries was not clarified, nor did any resurrection from the dead appear as the aftermath of the violent death endured by the 'son'.

The major conclusions we draw should be limited to four. First, Jesus understood himself to be in person the climax of God's dealings with the chosen people. Second, he found himself in dangerous controversy with some of the religious leaders of Israel. Third, the outcome of that unflinching conflict would be Jesus' violent death, the nature of which was not specified. Fourth, there would be a dramatic change in God's relationship with his 'vineyard', Israel.

Even before reporting the Parable of the Vineyard and the Tenants, Mark has inserted three predictions of the passion in which Jesus announced the suffering and death of 'the Son of Man' and his vindication through resurrection (Mark 8:31; 9:31; 10:33–34). Frequently these predictions have been dismissed as 'prophecies after the event', created by early Christians who wanted to show that the death of Jesus was a necessary part of the divine plan. To be sure, the precise details of Jesus' passion, especially those in the third prediction (e.g. about being 'mocked', 'spat upon', and 'scourged') look like episodes that occurred in the course of the passion and were later added by early Christians. Nevertheless, we should distinguish between the essential content of the predictions and their formulation. Even if they were to some extent embellished during stage two (the post-Easter tradition), they need not be later statements retrospectively attributed to what Jesus said during his ministry. Some of the content could well derive from the earthly Jesus (stage one).[7] In particular, the second passion prediction, the shortest and the vaguest of the three, seems likely to be an authentic saying: 'The Son of Man will be delivered into the hands of men, and they will kill him, and when he is killed, after three days he will rise again' (Mark 9:31).[8]

Let us pull matters together. We can conclude that (at least to the core group of his disciples) Jesus announced his coming death and affirmed that his Father would quickly or 'in a short time' (in that less precise, biblical sense of 'after three days'[9]) vindicate him through resurrection. We may be cautious about tracing any precise wording back to Jesus (stage one). But we have good reasons for concluding that he anticipated his violent death and hoped for his speedy, subsequent vindication. Such a conclusion says something about Jesus' view of what that death entailed for himself: a contrast between a human verdict on him and a divine verdict on him. A rejection on the human side would be reversed by a resurrection on the divine side. But what did he make of his impending death *for others*? What did Jesus expect that his fate would bring to others, even to the whole human race? We return to those questions below.

That Jesus predicted his violent death is hardly surprising. Menacing opposition had built up against him long before he went to Jerusalem for his final Passover. The exact order in which most events in his ministry took place is lost forever, the details of various episodes remain unclear, and not all the sayings attributed to him derive from him – at least not in the precise form in which they are set down by the evangelists. Nevertheless, there is undoubtedly an historical core to certain charges (of violating the Sabbath, working wonders through diabolic power, rejecting the purity regulations, acting as a false prophet, and making blasphemous pretensions about such matters as the forgiveness of sins) that are reported as being provoked by his radical mission for the kingdom. Then his protest in cleansing the Temple, if it did happen at the end of the ministry (Mark 11:1–19) and not at the beginning (John 2:13–25), was a final, unflinching challenge to the religious authorities in the city and to the power they exercised through the Temple. Let us examine that climactic challenge which Jesus made with righteous anger but also with tears (Luke 19:41).

ENTRY INTO JERUSALEM AND CLEANSING THE TEMPLE

John Donahue and Daniel Harrington observe that the prophetic actions of Jesus in entering Jerusalem (Mark 11:1–11) and cleansing the Temple (Mark 11:15–19) 'go a long way toward explaining why the Jewish and Roman leaders acted so quickly to arrest and execute Jesus'.[10] Jesus was not ingenuous; he must have been aware of that danger. Let us see some of the details.

According to John's Gospel, Jesus went up to Jerusalem at least four times during his ministry (2:13; 5:1; 7:10; 12:12). On the first occasion he cleansed the Temple and spoke of the Temple being destroyed and restored (John 2:13–22). Since the cleansing is separately attested by the Synoptic tradition (Mark, followed by Matthew and Luke) and the Johannine tradition, its historical status seems to be established satisfactorily. The dating is another question, and I am inclined to follow Mark by locating the cleansing at the end of Jesus' ministry.[11]

The Synoptic tradition records only one journey that Jesus made to keep the Passover in Jerusalem. As Mark, followed by Matthew and Luke, tells the story of *the entry into Jerusalem*, it was a royal gesture, a prelude to the passion of Jesus, a symbolic action oriented towards what was coming in his death and resurrection. We can reasonably accept this episode as historical and as understood by friends and foes in a messianic sense. They interpreted Jesus' action of riding into Jerusalem on a colt as claiming royal authority. Yet it remains difficult to establish precisely what Jesus himself intended. Did he consciously associate himself with Zechariah 9:9: 'your king comes to you, triumphant and riding on a donkey' (Matthew 21:5; John 12:15)? Or did early Christians adopt this and other scriptural verses to present what had happened at Jesus' entry into Jerusalem? It is hard to decide. It seems easier to take a position on what Jesus intended *when he cleansed the Temple* – the incident which became a major reason for the authorities moving to do away with him.[12]

Merchants had turned the Temple precincts into a place of business. Such commercialism, perhaps allied with dishonest practices in the sale of animals (for sacrifice) and in the exchange of money, worked against the purpose of the Temple, which was meant to be a place of worship and instruction for the Jews and for the world (e.g. Isaiah 2:2–4; 66:22–23). *The* place of prayer had become a place where business transactions were distracting people from the real purpose of the Temple. What then did Jesus intend by driving out the money-changers and those who were buying and selling in the Temple? As Mark (followed by Matthew and Luke) describes matters, Jesus did not aim at symbolising any coming destruction of the Temple and the building of a new and perfect temple; his action in cleansing the Temple was not as such a portent of its destruction. Jesus seems to have been inspired by a 'vision of a purified and renewed Temple' that would also 'welcome non-Jews'.[13]

To sum up. In cleansing the Temple Jesus did something that

he knew to be dangerously provocative and could precipitate his death. He may well have hoped that his action might benefit Jews and non-Jews alike, by making the Temple once again 'a house of prayer' for everyone.

Jesus also said something about the *'replacement' of the Temple,* a saying closely connected with the destruction of the Temple. Joseph Fitzmyer surveys the evidence and concludes that Jesus did say something about the fate of Jerusalem and the fate of the Temple. Let us see the details.[14]

John's Gospel links the episode of the cleansing of the Temple with some words of Jesus about the coming destruction of the Temple and its rebuilding. To those who demanded a 'sign' to legitimate what he had done in cleansing the Temple, Jesus replied: 'Destroy this temple and in three days I will raise it up.' The evangelist comments: 'he was speaking of the temple of his body' (John 2:13–22).

In Mark's Gospel (followed by Matthew and Luke) the Temple action comes not at the beginning but at the end of Jesus' ministry. Moreover, in the versions of the cleansing provided by these three evangelists nothing is said about the destruction and replacement of the Temple. It is a little later in Mark's narrative that Jesus, when predicting the destruction of Jerusalem, begins by announcing the destruction of the magnificent Temple (Mark 13:2). But nothing is said there about rebuilding or replacing it. At the trial of Jesus some report that they had heard Jesus say: 'I will destroy this temple [or perhaps 'this sanctuary', the holiest part of the Temple rather than the whole complex] that is made with [human] hands and in three days I will build another, not made with hands' (Mark 14:58). Where Mark speaks here of 'false' witnesses, Matthew avoids calling them 'false' and also has the witnesses testify that Jesus said: 'I am able to destroy the temple of God and to build it in three days' (Matthew 26:60–61). Apparently Matthew regards their witness as true and does not want 'to deny that Jesus had said what is reported by the witnesses'.[15] Matthew also differs from Mark by alleging a power or possibility ('I am able to destroy') and by not including the contrast between human agency ('made with hands') and divine agency ('not made with hands'). In Mark's passion narrative, the charge recurs when some of those present at the crucifixion taunt Jesus by saying: 'You who would destroy the temple and build it in three days, save yourself, and come down from the cross' (Mark 15:29). In his Gospel, Luke does not include any such saying about the Temple. But in his second work he represents

Stephen being charged with prophesying against the Temple by claiming that 'Jesus of Nazareth will destroy it', as if the prophecy were still unfulfilled some years after the crucifixion and resurrection (Acts 6:13–14).

The convergent evidence from the Johannine and Synoptic traditions suggests that the Temple saying in some form went back to Jesus. Yet the differences remain: in John the destruction of the Temple is seemingly attributed to the critics of Jesus, whereas in Mark and Matthew Jesus himself will be the agent of that destruction.[16] The saying points to some radical break with the past. Jesus announces that the coming divine kingdom will involve refashioning God's people at the heart of their religious existence, the Temple. In life and in death, Jesus understands his mission as that of replacing the Temple and its cult with some new, better, and final temple ('not made with hands'). The expression used for a short period of time ('in three days') seemingly alludes to Christ's death, followed by resurrection after three days. By associating the Temple saying with the risen body of Christ, John (the only eyewitness among the four evangelists) may well have unpacked something of Jesus' intended meaning (John 2:19–22).

THE COMING KINGDOM

The theme of God's kingdom can help us appreciate how Jesus understood his death. It would take a sceptic with nerves of steel to deny the centrality of the kingdom in the preaching of Jesus.[17] From the outset he announced the divine rule to be at hand. It would be false to separate this proclamation of the kingdom from his acceptance of his own victimhood. Jesus saw suffering and persecution as characterising the coming of that kingdom (see e.g. the beatitudes and the Lord's Prayer). The message of the kingdom entailed and culminated in suffering the ordeal to come: a time of crisis and distress which was to move towards 'the day of the Son of Man' (Mark 13), the restoration of Israel (Matthew 19:28), the banquet of the saved, and the salvation of the nations (Matthew 8:11). Thus the arrest, trial, and crucifixion of Jesus dramatised the very thing that totally engaged Jesus, the rule of God that was to come through a time of ordeal.

At the Last Supper Jesus linked his imminent death with the divine kingdom: 'Amen, I say to you, I shall not drink again of the fruit of the vine until that day when I drink it new in the kingdom of God' (Mark 14:25).[18] It is widely agreed that this text derives from something Jesus himself said during his last meal with his friends. Death is approaching; he will have no occasion again to have a festive meal of any kind. But after his death, God will vindicate the cause of Jesus by fully establishing the divine kingdom. Jesus will be seated at the final banquet – obviously with others at his side – when he 'drinks wine new'. He looks forward with hope to this final time of eschatological 'feasting'.

In this saying the death of Jesus remains implicit, since what we call 'the Last Supper' will be the final festive meal of his life. The resurrection as such is not mentioned, but it is implied that God will rescue Jesus out of death and let him enjoy the final banquet. The saying, simply as such, does not attribute to Jesus any redemptive function in the ultimate triumph of the kingdom. It is not stated, or at least not stated implicitly, that he will restore the fellowship with his disciples which will be broken by death – let alone that he will mediate to others their access to the final banquet.

In these and further ways the saying from Mark 14:25, taken by itself, leaves much unsaid. Yet it turns up in Mark's Gospel as *the final kingdom saying* from Jesus, a saying about the kingdom which is connected with his approaching death. The saying should be interpreted in the light of what Jesus has already said. He has constantly preached the future reign of God, which will be *the* saving event for all human beings. By linking his imminent death with the coming kingdom, Jesus implicitly interprets his death as somehow salvific for all. Through his preaching he has promised salvation for human beings at large.[19] Now he associates his death with that future salvation and communion at the final banquet in the coming kingdom of God. The kingdom saying at the Last Supper may be laconic. But Jesus charges it with meaning through what he has already said about the coming kingdom.

It is hardly surprising that Jesus made such a positive integration between the coming kingdom and his death. The message about the divine reign was inseparable from the person of Jesus (see Chapter Two above). This essential connection between the message of Jesus and his person meant that the vindication of his person in and beyond death entailed the vindication of God's kingdom and vice versa.

ROYAL ANOINTING AND LAST ARRANGEMENTS

Undoubtedly the religious authorities in Jerusalem took Jesus' entry into Jerusalem (with its perceived messianic significance) and cleansing of the Temple to be two major challenges to the way they understood faith and conducted affairs at the heart of Jewish life. Add too the dramatic 'sign' of Lazarus' resurrection from the dead (John 11), which had a profound impact on the Jerusalem public and prompted the Sanhedrin, the official Jewish council, presided over by the high priest Caiaphas, to proceed with the arrest of Jesus and his execution (John 11:45–57).

Following Richard Bauckham's judicious explanation of anonymous persons in Mark's passion narrative,[20] we can add a fourth episode which fuelled official hostility to Jesus in the days leading up to his death. Mark tells of an anonymous woman who anointed Jesus during a meal at the home of 'Simon the leper'. Jesus accepted her act, defended her, and underscored the significance of what she had done: 'wherever the good news is proclaimed in the whole world, what she has done will be told in remembrance of her' (Mark 14:3–9). Why then does Mark decline to name her? Bauckham suggests convincingly that 'at the time [AD 40–50] when this tradition took shape in this form in the Jerusalem church, this woman would have been in danger were she identified as having been complicit in Jesus' politically subversive claim to messianic kingship'.[21] Her action carried messianic impact, and was to be interpreted against the background of the anointing of kings in the Hebrew Scriptures. She was understood to have anointed the Messiah. Jesus himself (or perhaps Mark), instead of reading the episode in terms of a coming messianic triumph, connected it with the cross: 'she has anointed my body beforehand for its burial.'

Judas reported the episode of the anointing to the chief priests (Mark 14:10–11) who had already decided to arrest Jesus and have him killed (Mark 14:1–2). The messianic anointing must have seemed the last straw to the religious authorities, who may well have feared that Jesus and his disciples were dangerously intent on a messianic uprising. The anointing at Bethany also led Judas, whatever shape the motives took for his final defection, to make his definitive break with Jesus. The anointing provided 'both added cause for the chief priests to take swift action against Jesus and also the means to do so in the shape of Judas's offer'.[22]

They had clinching motivation for their decision and further 'evidence' of Jesus' seditious behaviour. It helped the 'case' they could present to Pilate about Jesus' challenge to Roman rule: Jesus was claiming to be 'the king of the Jews' and planning an uprising.

By the time John wrote his Gospel, the 'protective anonymity' of the woman who anointed Jesus was no longer an issue. She was named as Mary, the sister of Martha and Lazarus (John 12:1–8). The sequence of events reported by John may well have been correct: first the messianic anointing in Bethany and then, the very next day, Jesus' messianic entry into Jerusalem (John 12:12–15). In the politically charged atmosphere of Jerusalem, the sequence of those two episodes strengthened the resolve of the chief priests to do away with Jesus.

Jesus knew that Jerusalem was a danger zone and had become aware of Judas' defection. That accounts for the cautious, clandestine way in which he personally made arrangements to secure the colt on which to ride into Jerusalem (Mark 11:1–7) and to make preparations for his last Passover meal (Mark 14:12–16).[23] In particular, he did not want to reveal in advance the whereabouts of the house where he would eat that meal. If he was going to keep it secret from Judas, he had to keep it secret from the Twelve. Jesus expected to be arrested, but he did not want that to happen before he could celebrate a final meal with his disciples. He had made prior arrangements with an anonymous person (a disciple or merely an acquaintance?), and approached the Last Supper like someone in charge of a covert operation. This prudent self-control will make his 'breakdown' in Gethsemane even more startling.

THE LAST SUPPER

Convergent evidence from St Paul and the Gospels clearly establishes as historically certain that Jesus celebrated a farewell meal with his core group of disciples.[24] Biblical scholars widely agree that the 'bread saying' derives from the historical Jesus. Many argue as well that the 'cup saying' is also traceable to him. The 'words of institution', if taken at face value, show Jesus defining his death as a sacrifice which will not only representatively atone for sins but also initiate a new and enduring covenant between God and human beings. Yet here we must reckon with the question: How far have the sources of Paul, Mark, and the other evangelists been shaped by liturgical usages in the early Christian communities? In 1 Corinthians 11:23–25 we read: 'The Lord Jesus on the night when he was betrayed took bread and when he had given thanks, he broke it, and said: "This is my body which [is given] for you. Do this in remembrance of me." In the same way [he took] also the cup, after supper, saying: "This cup is the new covenant in my blood. Do this, as often as you drink it, in remembrance of me." ' In Mark's account of the Last Supper, however, the instructions calling for a future repetition of the Eucharist ('do this in remembrance of me', and 'do this, as often as you drink it, in remembrance of me') are missing. The qualification of 'my body' as being 'for you' is also missing. Yet, unlike the Pauline tradition, Mark describes the blood as being 'poured out for many'. His version runs as follows: 'He took bread, blessed and broke it, and gave it to them, and said: "Take, this is my body." And he took the cup, and when he had given thanks, he gave it to them, and they all drank of it. And he said to them, "This is my blood of the covenant, which is poured out for many" ' (Mark 14:22–24).

Obviously there are differences between the Pauline tradition (to which, apart from adding, apropos of 'my blood', 'which is poured out for you', and not including, apropos of the cup, 'do this in remembrance of me', Luke 22:19–20 approximates) and the Markan tradition (which is more or less followed by Matthew 26:26–28, apart from the latter adding that the blood is shed 'for the forgiveness of sins'). Confronted with these differences, some writers back away from relying too much on the words of institution as accurate sources for settling the way Jesus understood his death and its impact. In some form the words of institution go back to Jesus. But in what precise form? Admittedly the breaking of the bread, identified as his body, and the pouring out of his blood imaged forth the sacrificial surrender of his life, the action of total self-giving that was about to take place in his violent death. Clearly those followers present at the Last Supper shared in his body that was being given up to death and in his blood that would be shed. They were invited to participate in Jesus' destiny and enjoy a new, permanent communion or covenant with him. Whether Jesus spoke of a 'new covenant' (Paul and Luke) or only of a 'covenant' (Mark and Matthew) that was being instituted through his 'blood', he inevitably evoked key biblical passages (e.g. Exodus 24:3–8; Jeremiah 31:31–33) which illuminated his words and gestures. He was making a new covenant, sealed and ratified by the shedding of his blood.

But, beyond the group present at the Last Supper, whom did Jesus intend to be the beneficiaries of his death and the new covenant? The 'for you' of the Pauline and Lukan tradition pointed immediately to his disciples who shared the common cup at the Last Supper. But he clearly intended the group who participated in his final meal to represent others, even many others. If Jesus explicitly called for a *future* repetition of the bread ritual ('do this in remembrance of me' – Paul and Luke) and of the cup ritual ('do this in remembrance of me' – Paul only), he evidently wanted to confer on an indefinite number of others the saving benefits of his life and impending death. Even if Jesus did not literally express the directive 'do this in remembrance of me', one can reasonably argue that this addition from the Pauline and Lukan churches rendered explicit his intentions. He wanted to establish for countless others his continuing place and presence in the meal fellowship that he was establishing with a small, core group of disciples.

Mark (followed by Matthew) has Jesus speaking of his blood poured out 'for many', an inclusive Semitic expression for a great multitude or countless number (= 'for all'). But, granted that 'for you' and 'for many' point to an indefinitely large group, we are still left with the question: Did Jesus intend the benefits of his violent death and new covenant to be conferred only on all those who were sharing and would share in the ritual and the fellowship he was creating? Would the benefits of his sacrificial death 'for many' be passed on only to the new covenant community, the fellowship of those who would share in the saving power of Jesus' death through eating his 'broken body' and drinking from the common cup?

A short answer to those tempted to imagine Jesus limiting the saving impact of the new covenant comes from a feature of his ministry we recalled in Chapter Two: the meals he shared with all manner of people, not least with the disreputable. That table fellowship conveyed forgiveness to sinners and celebrated in advance the happiness of the heavenly banquet to come, a banquet to which all were invited. Jesus' practice throws light on his intentions at the Last Supper. It was intended to be 'the last supper' or climax of a whole series of meals that revealed his saving outreach to everyone.[25] Ultimately the pressure on us to establish precisely what Jesus said and intended at the Last Supper can be eased by recalling his characteristic attitudes. They illuminate the scope of his saving intentions.

CHARACTERISTIC ATTITUDES

In general, characteristic ways in which people act and speak can fill their death with meaning, even when they have no chance at the end to express their motivation and make an explicit declaration of intent. Archbishop Oscar Romero (1917–80), for instance, was abruptly shot dead when celebrating the Eucharist. He had no last-minute opportunity to blurt out some statement interpreting the death which confronted him. Nevertheless, all that he had been saying and doing during his three years as archbishop of San Salvador served to indicate his basic intentions and fill his martyrdom with significance.

Jesus himself consistently behaved as one utterly devoted to his Father's will and completely available for the service of all those who needed mercy and healing. His words and actions brought divine pardon to those who, in various ways, felt a great need of redemption. He never drove away the lepers, taxation agents, sinful women, children, and all those anonymous crowds of people who clamoured for his love and attention. He valued every individual as unique and irreplaceable.

Now it would be strange to imagine that the threat of the passion abruptly destroyed Jesus' resolution to show himself the servant of others. Rather, a straight line ran from his serving ministry to his suffering death. He who had shown himself the servant of all was ready to die for all – to release them from various forms of oppressive servitude. As many scholars have insisted, the service of Jesus had been offered especially to the outcasts and religious pariahs. Part of the reason why his ministry led to this crucifixion stemmed from the fact that he faithfully and scandalously served the lost, the godless, and the alienated of his society. The physician who came to call and cure the unrighteous eventually died in their company. His serving ministry to the reprobates closed when he obediently accepted a shameful death between two reprobates. His association with society's outcasts and failures ended with his solidarity with them in death. In these terms the passion of Jesus became integrated into his mission as a final act of service. In death, as in life, he served and sacrificed himself for others. Luke 22:27 ('I am among you as one who serves') was an authentic pointer to this basic pattern in Jesus' behaviour.

Israel was the context for the ministry of Jesus; yet that ministry had a universal dimension. His message of the kingdom reached beyond the frontiers of religious and racial separations. God's reign here and hereafter was for all human beings. The parables of Jesus show this universal horizon. Even in the Parable of the Tax Collector and the Pharisee (Luke 18:10–14), the only parable set in the most Jewish of settings, the Temple in Jerusalem, this universality showed through. Jesus asserted that the full extent of God's generosity had hitherto been ignored: the divine pardon was offered to all.

By rejecting or at least relativising dietary laws and merely external purity regulations (Mark 7:14–23), which preserved the boundaries between Jews and Gentiles, Jesus implied that these distinctions had no ultimate significance before God. What mattered was the internal state of the 'heart' – its purity or its corruption.[26] Hence Jesus' vision of Israel's future entailed 'many coming from the east and the west to sit at table with Abraham, Isaac and Jacob in the kingdom of heaven' (Matthew 8:11). The ministry of Jesus envisaged salvation for the nations. Having lived and preached such a universal vision, at the end Jesus, one can reasonably suppose, accepted in some sense that he would die for all people.

CONTEMPORARY IDEAS

Some contemporary ideas can also point to the intentions of Jesus in the face of death. Various Old Testament books endorse the notion that the righteous will suffer (e.g. Psalms 34:19) and do so at the hands of the unrighteous (e.g. Wisdom 2:10–20). Prophets could expect to be persecuted because of their faithfulness to God. Such notions, as we saw in the last chapter, surface in the beatitudes taught by Jesus (e.g. Matthew 5:10–12).

The experiences of the Maccabean martyrs in the second century BC helped to give rise to a further development that was in the air at the time of Jesus. The suffering and violent death of righteous persons brought healing and forgiveness to others and expiated their sins. The martyrdom of even one individual could representatively atone for the sins of a group (e.g. 2 Maccabees 7:37–38). Martin Hengel has marshalled evidence to show how earlier Greek and Roman literature, history, and customs supported the notion that someone could die 'for' his/her city or people and so atone for their sins. The Jewish conviction to this effect may have been taken over from Greek sources.[27]

But my aim here is not to discuss questions of provenance but rather to recall a relevant belief found at the time of Jesus. Once the threat of violent death loomed up, it would have been somewhat strange if Jesus had never applied to himself that religious conviction shared by his contemporaries and had not done so through the universal horizon that characterised his ministry. Through his martyrdom he could vicariously set right for all people a moral order disturbed by sin.

Here I should add a parenthesis on the poem from Second Isaiah (52:13–53:12) about the Servant of the Lord, who – whether understood primarily as an individual or in a collective sense – suffers for the sins of 'the many'.[28] Although this poem dates from the sixth century BC and could obviously support reflections on vicarious atonement, the text is never *quoted* either by later books of the Old Testament or by non-canonical books of the intertestamental period. Even where *allusions* to the poem about the Suffering Servant can be detected in subsequent texts (e.g. Zechariah 12:10), we do not find the notion of a death which representatively atones for others. Nevertheless, this fourth poem about the Servant helped to shape early Christian thinking and preaching. There are hints in Paul's letters (e.g. Romans 4:25), and the First Letter of Peter was to develop the theme of Christ as the servant whose vicarious suffering brings healing and forgiveness. Eventually, the New Testament was to include eleven quotations from this poem and at least thirty-two allusions to it. Early Christians were to see Isaiah 53 as an elaborate prefiguration of Christ in his atoning suffering. In the late first century St Clement of Rome simply quoted the whole of this text when expounding the meaning of Jesus' death (*1 Clement*, 16). In his *Dialogue with Trypho* St Justin Martyr would quote Isaiah 53 in full (no. 13).

What conclusions does this parenthesis point to? We should be cautious about invoking the fourth poem on the Lord's Servant to establish contemporary ideas about vicarious atonement which Jesus could easily have applied to himself. As we have seen above, Palestinian Judaism of the first century AD included the belief that the death of a martyr could representatively atone for the sins of others. But, curiously, it is not clear that this belief drew on the song of the Suffering Servant. We have no unambiguous text from pre-Christian Judaism which speaks of the anointed Messiah's vicarious suffering in connection with Isaiah 53. That fact *by itself* does not, of course, rule out the possibility of Jesus' sense of mission in the face of death being shaped by Suffering Servant imagery. Yet it was one thing for him to

161

envisage his vicarious suffering as Messiah and quite another thing for him to have done so in terms of the Suffering Servant of Isaiah 53. We have no strong evidence that Jesus clearly made this association.

CONCLUSION

This chapter has aimed at establishing that Jesus not only anticipated a violent death but also interpreted it in advance as atoning for the sins of Jews and Gentiles alike. Faced with death, Jesus understood it as a representative and redemptive service that would bring a new relationship between God and all human beings. In reaching these conclusions I have largely drawn on the Synoptic Gospels. But what might we glean from the Fourth Gospel?

In the Preface to this book I proposed that, through decades of prayerful experience of the exalted Lord, the 'beloved disciple' gained richer insights into the events in which he had participated. He reflectively remembered the events of the Last Supper, the passion, and the crucifixion that had shaped the rest of his life. When he came to write the Fourth Gospel, he could express the deep truth of those events. Precisely because he had participated so closely in what had happened (from his privileged position at the Last Supper to his standing with Jesus' mother under the cross and visiting the tomb with Simon Peter), he could allow himself a higher degree of interpretative appropriation of what he had personally witnessed. In particular, he fashioned the long discourse and prayer with which Jesus interpreted his imminent suffering, death, and resurrection and giving of the Holy Spirit (John 13:1–17:26).

Those chapters are far from being a brilliant piece of fictional writing. Let me mention three examples. First, those chapters contain, for instance, the poignant climax in the history of Judas' betrayal of his Master. Jesus washed the feet of Judas, seated the traitor next to himself, and handed him a piece of bread – gestures of honour through which he hoped to dissuade him from pressing ahead with his treachery. Jesus concealed what he knew about Judas' treachery from everyone except his intimate friend, the beloved disciple (John 13:21–30). Second, the Fourth Gospel does not include the institution of the Eucharist. But it has already dedicated a long section to the Bread of Life (6:25–59), and in the last discourse (chapters 13–17) it brings out the true and rich significance of the Eucharist: a fruitful life in Christ (15:1–11); a loving relationship with other disciples (13:34–35); and a willing service of others that imitates the humble act of Christ who washed the feet of his companions (13:3–17). John's Gospel goes well beyond the Synoptic Gospels in expressing what the Eucharist, historically instituted by Jesus at the Last Supper, means and should mean in the life of Christians. The beloved disciple had participated intimately in the institution of the Eucharist, and was concerned to plumb for others its unique significance. Third, the other Gospels portray Jesus as singing some psalms (Mark 14:26) and then praying, both in the Garden of Gethsemane and at the crucifixion. John's Gospel omits the prayer in Gethsemane but, before doing so, introduces a long, high priestly prayer that expressed the sentiments with which, as the beloved disciple knew, his Lord had faced death. Jesus prayed for himself that he might 'finish the work' by securing 'eternal life' for all people (John 17:1–5). He then prayed for his disciples that they might be united, experience joy, and fulfil their mission (17:6–19). Finally, he prayed for the whole Church that all might share in a loving communion with the Father and the Son (17:20–26).

How did the beloved disciple sum up in chapters 13–17 the meaning of what Jesus went through on Holy Thursday, Good Friday, Holy Saturday, and Easter Sunday? Firstly, he saw those events as inspired by love and releasing a new power of *transforming love* into the world. The chapters begin by declaring that Jesus, 'having loved his own who were in the world, loved them to the end' (or 'to the uttermost') (13:1). Both explicitly (e.g. 13:34–35) and implicitly (e.g. 14:3) love threads its way through what follows. The chapters end by announcing that the redeeming death and resurrection of Jesus aimed at nothing less than bringing human beings into a communion of love with Jesus and his Father (17:26). Secondly, looking back at the climax of Jesus' earthly story, the beloved disciple understood it all as the supreme highpoint of the effective self-disclosure of the Father, Son, and Holy Spirit. Through the death and resurrection of Jesus, the tripersonal God was fully revealed and the mission of the Holy Spirit inaugurated. Chapters 13–17 of John's Gospel put Jesus himself at centre stage, since he is the one who washes the disciples' feet, speaks, and prays. These chapters refer explicitly to the 'Father' sixty times (named as 'God' in ten of these occurrences), and to the Holy Spirit (named as 'Advocate' or 'Helper') seven times. Thus the beloved disciple recalled in a deeply *trinitarian* way Jesus' passing from this world to his Father.

Chapter 10

◆

JESUS THE SUFFERING SERVANT

> God defined himself as love on the cross of Jesus.
>
> *Eberhard Jüngel*, God as the Mystery of the World

> Any version of the gospel that substitutes the message of
> personal success for the cross is a manipulative
> counterfeit.
>
> *A. C. Thiselton*, The First Epistle to the Corinthians

THE ARREST, SUFFERING, DEATH, and burial of Jesus unfolded with breathless speed. Unlike John the Baptist, Paul the Apostle, and Joan of Arc, he did not face an extended period of imprisonment before being executed. In less than twenty-four hours everything ended on a cross, *the* sign of weakness, folly, and failure. Had his life been successful? A disgraceful and humiliating death challenged the 'normal' assumptions and values for assessing what makes for true and lasting success. Paul had endorsed the contemporary view that crucifixion signalled being 'cursed' by God (Galatians 3:13),[1] but came to realise that the crucified Jesus was and is 'the power of God and the wisdom of God' (1 Corinthians 1:24).

In portraying the passion and death of Jesus, we are blessed by the lengthy accounts of all four evangelists.[2] We cannot dream of doing better than them. To remain within manageable limits, this chapter will draw on two Gospels: one produced by an eyewitness (John) and the other (Mark) coming from the testimony of Peter the Apostle.

The beloved disciple frames the entire story of Jesus within the context of his pre-existence (or 'pre-history') and his post-existence (or 'post-history'). The prologue of the Fourth Gospel opens with words that take us back to the eternal life of God: 'in the beginning was the Word, and the Word was with God, and the Word was God' (1:1). The epilogue takes us forward to the second coming of Christ (21:22–23). The majestic, divine frame for this Gospel will have its counterpart in the way the beloved disciple sets out the passion, death, and burial of Jesus.

As we saw in the Preface, there are good reasons for retrieving the view that Simon Peter was the major eyewitness source behind the Gospel of Mark. Peter is present in much of the narrative from 1:16 to 16:7. He is named twenty-six times in the Gospel – nineteen times as 'Peter' and seven times as 'Simon'.[3] Throughout the Gospel and, in particular, through the passion narrative, readers can share the eyewitness perspective that the testimony of Peter embodied.

Before they read what follows, I ask readers to refresh their memory of those two passion narratives by quietly going through Mark 14:26–15:47 and John 18:1–19:42. If they can envisage the first passion narrative coming from Peter and the second from the beloved disciple, they will be in an even better position to appreciate what I have to say.

PETER ON THE PASSION

The agony in the Garden

Nothing brings alive more vividly the attitudes and feelings of Jesus when confronted with death than what he said and did at the Last Supper and in the Garden of Gethsemane. He took stock of his perilous situation, but refused to let imminent danger interfere with his unwavering commitment to his mission. As we saw in the last chapter, his words and gestures at the Last Supper incorporated his suffering and death into the great project of universal salvation, God's coming kingdom.

In Gethsemane Jesus 'began to be distressed and agitated' and admitted to Peter and the sons of Zebedee that he was 'deeply grieved'. He 'threw himself on the ground' and uttered a prayer that came up from the depths of his being: 'Abba, Father, for you all things are possible; remove this cup from me; yet, not what I want, but what you want' (Mark 14:33–36). Jesus addressed his Father in his usual, affectionate way as 'Abba'. But his intimate experience of God was now being played out, not during a period of early morning prayer alone in a deserted place (Mark

1:35), but in the darkness of night as a traitor was leading a bunch of paramilitary police (apparently from the Temple) to arrest him. Jesus made the hard decision. He would not slip away through the olive grove and take refuge with his friends in Bethany, Mary, Martha, and Lazarus.

Arrest and death

There is a chilling loneliness in the unfolding story of Jesus' arrest, of what he faced in the proceedings before Caiaphas and Pilate, and of his suffering and death. As Simon Peter told the story to Mark, Jesus remained isolated and undefended through it all. No one spoke up for him, let alone did anything for him. From the time of leaving the supper until the moment of his death on a cross, Jesus received no visible, human support from anyone. A whole series of people proceeded to take action against Jesus and 'hand him over' (*'paradidômi'*). At the start of his ministry Jesus had announced that he had come to call sinners (Mark 2:17). At the end he was 'handed over' into the power of sinners (Mark 14:41). At the beginning Jesus stretched out his hands to heal and forgive sinners; at the end the hands of others stretched out to seize him and carry him off to death. In his ministry Jesus had taken action against the invisible powers of evil. He was often in conflict with the invisible, demonic powers and took a strong initiative against them (Chapter Five above). At the end, in a very visible way, the powers of evil took the initiative against Jesus. There was a whole visible chain of those who took action against Jesus and handed him over.

Even before the Last Supper, Judas had already decided to 'betray' or 'hand over' Jesus to the chief priests (14:10–11, 21, 42, 44). Then the Sanhedrin, led by Caiaphas and other priests, acted against Jesus, had him bound, and 'handed him over to Pilate' (15:1, 10). Finally, Pilate acted against Jesus by having him scourged, and then 'handed him over to be crucified' (15:15). It is easy to identify the motives of expediency (and worse) that prompted the actions of Caiaphas and Pilate. The first, who was appointed high priest around AD 18 and deposed in AD 37, had a shadowed record.[4] We also know something from both the Gospels and non-Christian sources (e.g. Josephus and Philo) about Pontius Pilate, the governor of Judaea from AD 26 to 36; the evidence presents him as unprincipled and harsh.[5] But, apart from the claim in John 12:6 about Judas being a thief, the motivation of Judas for betraying Jesus remains obscure, even if the literature about him is vast and continues to grow – both academic publications and works of fiction.[6]

At the time of Jesus' arrest all of his disciples 'deserted him and fled'. A mysterious 'young man' (Lazarus?) followed him for a few minutes. When the Temple police tried to seize him as well, he fled naked into the night (Mark 14:50–52).[7] Whatever one concludes about his identity, this young man who fled naked into the night symbolised powerfully the failure of Jesus' male disciples. Peter had spoken up for these disciples when he declared: 'we have left all things to follow you' (Mark 10:28). Now an anonymous young man, presumably a disciple, left all his clothing as fear drove him to run away from Jesus. It was only after the death of Jesus that anyone took a stand for him. Seeing the way he died, the officer in charge of the execution squad declared: 'Indeed this man was the Son of God.' At that point Mark, drawing on Peter, refers to a number of female followers of Jesus who had witnessed the crucifixion and names three of them, Mary Magdalene, Mary the mother of James the younger and of Joses, and Salome (Mark 15:39–41). Thanks to them, the loneliness of Jesus in his passion and death had not been complete.

After the death of Jesus, an outsider appeared to take charge of his burial: Joseph of Arimathea, 'a respected member' of the Sanhedrin, the official Jewish court presided over by the high priest. He 'went boldly to Pilate and asked for the body of Jesus'. The request was granted and Joseph, in the presence of Mary Magdalene and Mary the mother of Joses, wrapped the body of Jesus in 'a linen cloth' and buried him in 'a tomb that had been hewn out of the rock' (Mark 15:42–47). Luke adds that Joseph was 'a good and righteous man' who, though a member of the Sanhedrin, 'had not agreed to their plan and action' in condemning Jesus (Luke 23:50–56). In Matthew's Gospel, Joseph is called a disciple of Jesus and is said to have used 'his own new tomb' for the burial of Jesus (Matthew 27:57–61; Luke also says that the tomb had not previously been used). John's Gospel also calls Joseph a disciple of Jesus, and pictures him as being helped by Nicodemus in the burial (John 19:38–42). Even if at the time of the crucifixion Joseph was apparently not yet a disciple of Jesus (Mark and Luke), it could well be that he joined the followers of Jesus subsequently. Matthew and John simply anticipate what Joseph did later. He was clearly remembered with gratitude by the followers of Jesus for his courageous help in seeing that Jesus was buried honourably. Sooner or later Joseph learned the awesome news that Jesus had been raised from the tomb that he had provided, and hence that there was no need to open the tomb nine months or more later and pack the bones of Jesus in an ossuary for their final resting place. The amazing news about what had happened in the tomb that he had provided must have shaped the life of Joseph forever.[8]

The way Mark (guided by Peter) tells the story, the male disciples, unlike the women and Joseph of Arimathea, failed dismally – a failure that is also expressed linguistically. The last time they are named as 'disciples' occurs when Jesus led them to Gethsemane. 'He said to his *disciples*, "Sit here while I pray"' (Mark 14:32). After that they are referred to several times as 'they' or (more often) 'them', until at the arrest of Jesus 'all of *them* deserted him and fled'. They will not again be called 'disciples' until the angel instructs the three women in the empty tomb: 'Tell his *disciples* and Peter that he is going ahead of you to Galilee; there you will see him' (Mark 16:7). The male disciples re-emerge at that point, and it is implied that Peter and the others will now be rehabilitated through their encounters with the risen Jesus.

Among the male disciples Peter stood out poignantly for his failure, a moral and religious breakdown that he described to Mark. Peter had shone by recognising and confessing the messianic identity of Jesus (Mark 8:29) and by exuberantly protesting loyalty: 'we have left everything and followed you' (Mark 10:28). After the Last Supper, Jesus led his disciples to Gethsemane and warned: 'you will all become deserters'. But Peter vehemently insisted that he would never become a deserter, even if he had to face death with Jesus. Peter's bravado encouraged all the other male disciples to protest that they too would be faithful (Mark 14:27–31). Yet he was not strong enough to stay on the watch with Jesus in Gethsemane. He fell asleep and was reproached by Jesus: 'Simon, are you asleep? Could you not keep awake one hour?' (Mark 14:37). When the Temple police arrested Jesus, it was Peter – as we know from John's Gospel (18:10–11) – who drew his sword and struck out in defence of Jesus. Since Peter injured the slave of Caiaphas the high priest, neither Mark nor the other two Synoptic Gospels identified Peter as the one who cut off the ear of Malchus. When the beloved disciple wrote his Gospel late in the first century, there was no longer need to maintain any 'protective anonymity'.[9]

After standing out for his insight into the identity of Jesus and loyalty towards him, Peter went on to fail blatantly and miserably. After running away in Gethesemane, he turned back and made his way to the courtyard of the high priest – evidently to be near Jesus, now on trial before the Sanhedrin (Mark 14:53–65). But then Peter's courage failed him. He not only three times denied knowing Jesus, but ended by utterly repudiating his Master. When pressed the third time for being a follower of Jesus, Peter 'began to curse, and he swore an oath, "I do not know this man you are talking about"' (Mark 14:66–72).

From the time of his arrest until his death on the cross, Jesus said very little: a few words in Gethsemane when he was arrested (Mark 14:48–49); a brief reply that combined Daniel 7:13 and Psalm 110:1 when answering the high priest's question 'are you the Messiah, the Son of the Blessed One?' (Mark 14:61–62); a cryptic answer to Pilate's question 'are you the King of the Jews' ('you say so' – Mark 15:2); and at the end on the cross a cry of abandonment which followed the opening words of Psalm 22 (Mark 15:34). Thus Jesus spoke only four times: three times in the presence of those who had joined forces to bring about his death (Judas, Caiaphas, and Pilate) and then once to God in a final prayer. That prayer ('my God, my God, why have you forsaken me?') has triggered endless speculation and writing.[10] Some Christians, especially since the sixteenth century, have interpreted the words to mean that Jesus felt himself to be the object of divine anger, a substitute for sinful human beings, and even punished with the pains endured by those condemned to the eternal sufferings of hell. But what can we make of this final cry of Jesus as a guide to the feelings with which he died?

The cry of abandonment

The high probability that Jesus, when dying on the cross, quoted the first words of Psalm 22 and did so in Aramaic, his mother tongue (Mark 15:34), makes this verse and the whole psalm uniquely important for understanding what he went through in his last moments. What should be said about Psalm 22 first in its Old Testament setting and then on the lips of the dying Jesus? We need to recall the whole psalm, since Jesus and devout Jews of his time found in the full texts of the psalms familiar and constant nourishment for their life of prayer.

The protagonists of the psalm are the psalmist, God, and the others (evildoers, brothers, the people, and all the nations). The psalm divides into two major sections: the personal lament which is almost an accusation of God (vv. 1–21), and then thanksgiving and praise which respond to the dramatic change in the situation (vv. 22–31). The psalm opens with God not offering help (v. 1) and ends by proclaiming the 'deliverance' which God has effected (v. 31). The psalmist suffers atrociously, even to the point of feeling abandoned by God; yet God vindicates and saves him. Let us look more closely at the two sections and the movement from complaint to praise.

The sufferer feels God to be 'far off' or distant in space (vv. 1, 11, 19), absent by 'day' and 'night' or in time (v. 2), and failing to 'answer' or remaining silent (v. 2). The intensity of the psalmist's prayer is indicated by the doubled 'My God, my God' of verse 1 – something 'unique in the Bible'.[11] Everything is concentrated in a cry: 'Why am I suffering? Why is God silent and seemingly inactive?' Unlike other psalms, the one who suffers does not protest his innocence (e.g. Psalm 17:1, 3–5), does not confess any personal guilt (e.g. Psalm 38:18), and does not call for vengeance on his enemies (e.g. Psalms 2–3; 5–7; 9–10). Psalm 22 does not offer any explanation for the suffering being undergone, still less any hint about the expiatory value either for the sufferer or for others.

The repeated 'my God' (vv. 1, 2, 10) rather than 'our God' supports a very personal note in the first section of the psalm. What is happening in the psalmist's personal experience seems radically different from what God has done in the story of his people. Their 'trust' (repeated three times) called for deliverance and salvation from God: 'In you our ancestors trusted; they trusted and you delivered them. To you they cried, and were saved; in you they trusted, and were not put to shame' (vv. 4–5). The psalmist feels as low as possible, 'a worm' (v. 6) who is utterly inferior to the throne of the holy God (v. 3). Nevertheless, in praying to God, he recalls the tender, divine care shown from the very beginning of his life and closely associated with his own mother's love: 'It was you who took me from the womb; you kept me safe on my mother's breast. On you I was cast from my birth, and since my mother bore me you have been my God' (vv. 9–10).[12]

Views differ about the nature of the suffering that the psalmist undergoes. Often it has been understood to be a serious illness. He suffers even more when others mock him because they believe sickness to be a sign of God's displeasure (vv. 6–8). Those who favour this view interpret some verses as vividly describing the psalmist's fever: 'I am poured out like water, and all my bones are out of joint; my heart is like wax; it is melted within my breast; my mouth is dried up like a potsherd, and my tongue sticks to my jaws' (vv. 14–15). His feverish state has left him emaciated and debilitated: 'My hands and my feet are shrivelled. I can count all my bones' (vv. 16–17). An alternative explanation proposes that the sufferer has been put on trial, within a cultural system which, in the case of conviction, involves his clothing being given to the prosecutor or to the one who arrested him: 'they divide my clothes among them, and for my clothing they cast lots' (v. 18). The powerful men or 'bulls' who persecute him are led by a 'lion'; the sufferer is about to be executed by the 'sword' (vv. 12–13, 20–21).[13]

Whether we follow the first or the second explanation, the enemies of the sufferer are presented as savage beasts: bulls, wild oxen, dogs, and a lion (vv. 12–21). Yet they too (as we shall shortly see) undergo a remarkable change, when God acts to transform radically the situation. Dramatically delivered from danger and persecution, the psalmist vows to make a formal thanksgiving to the Lord: 'I will tell of your name to my brothers and sisters; in the midst of the congregation I will praise you' (v. 22). Then follows a hymn (vv. 23–31), sung 'in the great congregation' (v. 25) – apparently in the context of worship in the Temple. God has once again proved to be the defender of the 'afflicted' (v. 24) or 'the poor' (v. 26). Powerful human beings have threatened to kill the sufferer or at least mocked him in his serious illness, but his prayer has been heard by God. He has not died from his sickness or been sentenced and put to death. God has rescued him and heard a prayer that is similar to one that concludes (rather than opens) another psalm: 'Do not forsake me, O Lord; O my God, do not be far from me; make haste to help me, O Lord, my salvation' (Psalm 38:21–22).

Seemingly the persecutors themselves undergo a change. At all events, the psalmist abruptly begins to speak of 'my brothers and sisters' (v. 22), the 'offspring of Jacob/Israel' (v. 23), and those who make up 'the great congregation' and can join in praising God (v. 25). The psalmist then looks beyond the Israelites to 'all the families of the nations', who will turn to the Lord and worship before him (v. 27). 'Future generations' will be told about the Lord and serve him (vv. 30–31). The divine rule will also extend to the dead (v. 29). Thus the psalm which begins with the cry of an individual who suffers ends with a vision of God's final, universal rule.

We have seen above how some of the language from the opening verse of Psalm 22 recurs in the final verse of Psalm 38: 'Do not forsake me … O God, do not be far from me.' Other psalms pray to God for deliverance from enemies or from illness (e.g. Psalm 17), and with few exceptions (e.g. Psalm 88:10–18) such deliverance is confidently expected. In general, the psalms of lament are also psalms of praise and thanksgiving. While falling into this category, Psalm 22 has its own particular 'shape': in the movement from personal lament to praise in the context of Temple worship, and on to a vision of God's future rule over the nations.

The dying Jesus was remembered (by the women disciples present at the crucifixion and Simon of Cyrene)[14] as having invoked the opening verse of Psalm 22. With these 'last words' the crucified Jesus, according to Mark 15:34, spoke for the first and last time during the crucifixion. This use by Jesus of Psalm 22 encouraged the eyewitnesses, Mark, and the other evangelists to find in that psalm a key source for the language in which they told the story of the last hours of Jesus.[15] Thus what was originally a psalm of lament and thanksgiving became *the* passion psalm or, more accurately 'the crucifixion psalm'.

In particular, there was a dramatic shift from the familial confidence with which Jesus, even in great distress, prayed on the eve of the crucifixion to God in a distinctive way as 'Abba, Father' (Mark 14:35–36). On the cross he spoke to God in words that all suffering human beings can share, 'My God'. The difference between the prayer in Gethsemane and that on the cross became even more poignant, since in both cases Jesus prayed in his mother tongue, Aramaic.

To sum up: first, the cry of dereliction did not represent Jesus on the cross as bearing the sins of the world, nor did it support the idea that he felt himself to be the object of God's anger. Such ideas are imported from elsewhere, and do not emerge from a careful example of the text itself. As Raymond Brown observes, 'the issue of Jesus' prayer on the cross is God's failure to act, without any suggestion as to why. Nothing in the Gospels would suggest God's wrath against Jesus as the explanation.'[16] Second, the cry of abandonment expressed both the frightful suffering that Jesus was undergoing and (through what followed in the same psalm) his confidence that God would deliver him. One can assume that Jesus aligned himself with further features of Psalm 22. From the way he had lived and from what he had taught, one can properly hold that Jesus, like the psalmist, did not pray that the evildoers would be punished and expected that a divine reversal of his own dreadful situation would change them and bring all nations to worship the God of Israel (now identified as 'Abba' or the loving Father) and to receive final salvation.

THE BELOVED DISCIPLE ON THE PASSION

I have followed Richard Bauckham in accepting the Fourth Gospel as written by an eyewitness, who participated personally in the ministry, death, and resurrection of Jesus and is to be identified with the beloved disciple. He set the whole story of Jesus in a magnificent, divine frame, and that remained true for his passion narrative. Many human, historical details, however, match those in the passion story of Mark: for instance, the betrayal by Judas (who does not, however, kiss Jesus), the triple denial by Peter, the hearing before Caiaphas, the scourging of Jesus, the crucifixion of two other men alongside Jesus, the presence of holy women at the death of Jesus, and his burial by Joseph of Arimathea. Some further details (not found in Mark or the other Gospels) are recalled by the beloved disciple: for example, the hearing before Annas, a former high priest and the father-in-law of Caiaphas, the presence of Jesus' mother at his crucifixion, and the role of Nicodemus in the burial of Jesus. Some of the features of Mark's narrative do not appear: for instance, the prayer in Gethsemane, the flight of the naked young man into the night, the help that Simon of Cyrene gave Jesus in carrying the cross to Calvary, and the cry of abandonment. Finally, a few 'vague' details in Mark's story are clarified: for instance, the name of the man (Peter) who used a sword on the servant of the high priest and the name of that servant (Malchus). When the Fourth Gospel was written, Peter was dead and no longer needed the protection of anonymity.[17] We might press ahead and closely compare and contrast the passion narratives of Mark and John. Standing back from many particular details, we can see, however, that the two narratives divulge a greater stress on Jesus' human loneliness and divine majesty, respectively. It is not difficult to discern the majestic tone of John's version, or what we might call the 'divine composure' of Jesus.

The arrest of Jesus

In the way he tells the story of Jesus' arrest, the beloved disciple introduces a striking contrast between light and darkness or warmth and cold. Through the Gospel Jesus has been pictured as the Light of the world (1:4–9; 3:19; 8:12; 9:5), the true source of warmth and vitality. When Judas led a detachment of Roman soldiers and Temple police into the garden, they came with 'lanterns, torches and weapons'. They arrived with their puny lights and weapons to arrest the One who was and is Light of the world (18:1–3). These forces of darkness and death needed 'illumination', otherwise they could not have seen the Light of the world. This irony was to surface a little later in the story, when Peter warmed himself at a charcoal fire (18:18). He was cold, and wanted warmth and light. But he went to the wrong source. He relied on a charcoal fire, instead of relying on the Light of the world.

Later in this book we will examine the remarkable questions that Jesus poses in the Fourth Gospel. One example appears when Jesus asks the arresting party: 'Whom are you seeking/looking for?' (18:4). Right through this Gospel people look for Jesus. Some seek him because – whether or not they realise it at the time – he gifts them with light and life (e.g. 1:38; 20:15). Others seek Jesus because they want to put him to death (e.g. 5:18; 7:1, 19, 25). Those who are bent on his destruction are finally successful when they look for Jesus in the garden, find him, and arrest him. Remembering the whole story of Jesus' life, death, and resurrection in which he closely participated, the beloved disciple recalls numerous 'Jesus-seekers' and divides them into two groups: those who sought him in order to receive life from him, and those who sought him in order to do away with him, the One whom the beloved disciple knows to be divine Life in person.

When the soldiers and Temple police declared whom they were looking for, 'Jesus of Nazareth', he replied: 'I am [he] ($\epsilon\gamma\omega\ \epsilon\iota\mu\iota$)' – a clear evocation of the divine name revealed to Moses at the burning bush (Exodus 3:14). Faced with the divine name and its awesome power, all those who had come to arrest Jesus, including Judas, stepped back and fell to the ground (18:5–6). In the beloved disciple's picture of what happened in the garden, Jesus did not kneel or lie on the ground, not even in prayer. It was those who had come to arrest him who fell to the ground. The worldly might of the Roman and Temple authorities, exercised through their soldiers and police, proved pathetically feeble when confronted with the power of the incarnate Son of God. The scene anticipated an exchange between Jesus and Pontius Pilate. When Pilate asked: 'Do you not know that I have power to release you, and power to crucify you?', Jesus replied: 'You would have no power over me unless it had been given you from above' (19:10–11). God permits evil, but remains sovereignly powerful over all human might.

Another detail in the narrative of Jesus' arrest can catch our attention. He repeats what he has already said and adds something significant for the whole thrust of the story: 'I told you that I am he [Jesus of Nazareth]. So if you are looking for me, let these others go' (18:8). This added detail hints at the whole meaning of Christ's passion; it took place – to echo the Creed – 'for us and for our salvation'. The others go free, but Jesus will allow himself to be arrested and put to death for all others and for their everlasting benefit. At the moment of his betrayal and arrest, Jesus does not try to slip away or to shield himself behind the others. He is prepared to be seized and led away to death. The soldiers and the police, along with those who sent them, have no right to touch Jesus, let alone to punish him. As he has said and will say, repeatedly and to different authorities, he is innocent (e.g. 8:46; 18:23). But, to echo the 'bread of life' discourse, he is the bread given and broken 'for the life of the world' (6:51).

The arrest of Jesus enacted the truth: 'I have not lost a single one of those whom you [my Father] have entrusted to me' (18:9; see 10:28; 17:12). Looking back at the passion and death of Jesus, the beloved disciple knew that those entrusted to Jesus were not merely the few persons with whom he had just shared a last meal but all men and women of all times and places.

The death of Jesus

When the beloved disciple recalled what followed the arrest of Jesus, he recognised the divine glory and majesty that shone through it all: the hearing before Annas (18:19–24), the proceedings before Pilate (18:33–19:16), and the way to Calvary on which Jesus himself carried the cross (19:17).

In death itself Jesus remains, as it were, divinely in charge of what happens. His last words ('it is finished' – 19:30) express the conviction that he has completed all that the Father has sent him to do for the salvation of the world (see 17:4). He can die now, since his work is finished. The beloved disciple who witnessed the death of Jesus says that 'he handed over his spirit' (19:30). It conveys a sense not only of Jesus actively 'departing from this world' (13:1) but also of his already sharing with others the Holy Spirit. At the moment of death he imparts the Spirit to the little group gathered around the cross. The evangelist describes Jesus in his very death as being divinely active.

The majesty of the Son of God that enfolds the whole story should not, however, allow us to slip over some human details that also shape the narrative of the passion and death of Jesus. The beloved disciple recalls those who stood with him on Calvary: the mother of Jesus, her sister (also called Mary), and Mary Magdalene. Jesus would not die before making some arrangements for his mother (who had obviously lost her husband Joseph years before). He asked his intimate friend, the beloved disciple, to take care of her (19:25–27).

When Jesus died (or even before?), the Jewish authorities asked Pilate to have the legs of the three crucified men broken and their bodies removed. With heavy mallets the soldiers broke the legs of the two others and so hastened their death. But when they came to Jesus, they found that he was already dead and so did not need to break his legs in order to hasten death. Instead, one of them was seen by the beloved disciple to pierce the side of Jesus with a spear. The eyewitness recalled: 'at once water and blood came out' (19:34). This detail showed the reality of the genuine death that Jesus had undergone, as well as symbolising the gift of the Holy Spirit imparted by Jesus in his return to the Father (7:37–39; see 1 John 5:6–8).[18]

A sense of Jesus' divine identity permeated the passion narrative provided by the beloved disciple, but this did not lead him to neglect the human face of his Master's suffering and death. One might say that the opposite was true of the passion narrative presented by Mark on the basis of the eyewitness testimony of Peter and others. Mark highlighted the human loneliness and suffering of Jesus, but he did not ignore his divine identity. The evangelist had begun his work by presenting Jesus as the Son of God (Mark 1:1, 11); the first human being to acknowledge this truth appeared at the end, the Roman officer in charge of the crucifixion. Seeing the way Jesus breathed his last, the centurion said: 'Truly this man was the Son of God' (Mark 15:39). The passion narratives of John and Mark, for all their obvious differences, match each other at a deeper level by acknowledging divine and human elements in the story.

LOOKING BACK AND LOOKING FORWARD

No one can narrate the suffering and death of Jesus without introducing some of the meaning which is to be found in that story. In telling the story of Jesus, it is above all when addressing the passion that it is impossible to detach oneself from making any judgements about value and significance. At the start of this chapter I quoted two modern examples: the first from a theologian and the second from a biblical scholar. Eberhard Jüngel understood the crucifixion to be the supreme point in the revelation of divine love: 'God defined himself as love on the cross of Jesus'.[19] Anthony Thiselton pointed to the judgement which Calvary passed on the real point and purpose of human life: 'any version of the gospel that substitutes the message of personal success for the cross is a manipulative counterfeit'.[20] For two thousand years innumerable scholars, saints, and other Christians have wrestled with the meaning of Jesus' passion and death. They will continue to do so until the end of human history. Let me complete this chapter by suggesting two directions in which one might look when mulling over the significance of the crucifixion.

Looking back

In a medieval church where I once helped during Lent and Holy Week, the Good Friday services ended with a ceremony re-enacting what Joseph of Arimathea and Nicodemus did when they took the body of Jesus down from the cross. There was a procession from a scene of the crucifixion to a statue of the Virgin Mary with the dead Jesus lying limply across her lap. That familiar composition, called the *Pietà*, has provided countless Christians with much food for thought and prayer. Many visitors to Rome carry away at least one vivid picture from the Basilica of St Peter's: the *Pietà* by Michelangelo. The lifeless body of Jesus allows us to look back at his whole story, recalling what he did for human beings and what they did to him. One can focus in turn on his eyes, his mouth, his ears and face, his hands, and his feet.

One can think, first, of his *eyes*. At home in Nazareth they looked with love on Mary and Joseph. When he was growing up, those eyes noticed so much: farmers sowing seed, women leavening batches of dough with yeast, and pushy guests claiming the best places at table. His eyes took in so much – in fact, the whole scene around him in ancient Galilee. Then in his ministry the eyes of Jesus looked across crowds of people who were like sheep that were lost and anxious to find a true shepherd. His eyes gazed with compassion on the sick, looked with love at little children, and blazed with anger at those who put their version of the law above the real needs of those who were suffering. Tears came into those eyes over the death of a friend. At the end, in his passion, what did the eyes of Jesus see? Judas coming to betray him with a kiss, the other disciples running away through the olive trees in Gethsemane, and Peter breaking down in grief at denying his Master. What did the eyes of Jesus see when he stood before Caiaphas and Pilate? Or when he made his way to Calvary and hung on the cross? And then those eyes finally closed, not in sleep but in death.

From the eyes of Jesus our gaze might take us to his *mouth*, that mouth that delivered so much truth and so many blessings. With his mouth he preached the good news of God's kingdom, told unforgettable parables, declared sins forgiven, and invited people: 'Come, follow me.' It was that mouth which declared the merciful, the sorrowful, and the pure of heart truly blessed. From that mouth came prayers and his own self-dedication at the Last Supper: 'This is my body, given for you; this is my blood, poured out for you.' From that mouth came his last words: in the Garden of Gethsemane, at the moment of his arrest, during the hearings before the religious authorities and Pontius Pilate, and then his final prayers on the cross. At the end, that mouth, which had said so many golden, truthful, and loving words, was finally closed in death.

We might think too of his *ears* and of all that they heard during his lifetime: from what those ears heard out of the mouths of Mary and Joseph right through to what those ears heard on the cross. Jesus heard and listened to so much: from the centurion's cry for help ('Say only the word and my boy will be cured'), to the cry of the blind beggar ('Jesus, Son of David, have mercy on me'); from the prayer that burst from the father of the epileptic boy ('I do believe; help thou my unbelief') to the accolade when Jesus rode into Jerusalem on a donkey ('Blessed is he who comes in the name of the Lord'). Think too of what Jesus' ears had to hear at the end: from Peter's boast ('Even if others fall away, I will not') to the cry for his death ('Crucify him, crucify him') and the mockery on the cross ('Save yourself and come down from the cross'). And then in death his ears could listen no more to any of the words or sounds of our world.

179

From his eyes, his mouth, and his ears, we might turn to Jesus' *face* which rested in death in the arms of Joseph of Arimathea and, one can presume, on his mother's breast. At the end his face had been kissed by the betrayer, Judas. It has been slapped, beaten, and spat upon. From his wounded head, blood had trickled down onto that face. And then life went out of that face.

When Michelangelo and other great artists portrayed Jesus dead in his mother's arms, they made much of his hands and feet. His *hands* had touched a disfigured leper, healed blind eyes, and multiplied loaves and fish for the hungry. They had lifted up Peter's mother-in-law and given her health. Those hands had also gripped a whip, lashed out at traders, and flung down the tables of money-changers in the Temple. His hands had taken his disciples' feet and washed them. With his hands he broke bread at the Last Supper and passed around the cup. Those hands were finally stretched out on a cross, and in death hung down torn and lifeless in the arms of Joseph of Arimathea and Mary.

What of the *feet* of Jesus? They had walked the roads of Galilee to bring the good news to thousands of sinners and sufferers. They had taken him up mountains to pray or down to a lakeside to call fishermen to a new vocation. Those feet had finally brought him to Jerusalem for his last days and hours. They were then pinned helplessly to a cross. In death they hung motionless in the arms of Joseph of Arimathea and across the lap of Mary.

The lifeless body of Jesus, when taken down from the cross and about to be buried, suggests so much about what he intended, what he did, and what he experienced. All praise to Michelangelo, Caravaggio, and other artists who showed us the way to read the whole story of Jesus by reflecting on his body lying dead in the arms of his mother and others. All praise to Jesus whose love for humankind is written there in his lifeless body.

Looking forward

In one of his most haunting lines, Blaise Pascal (1623–62) declared: 'He [Christ] is in agony until the end of the world, and we must not sleep during all that time.'[21] This was to look forward from the crucifixion and see the passion of Christ being re-enacted day after day in our world of suffering human beings.

Under the impact of Psalm 22 and other classic scriptural passages, some notable Christian writers understood the passion to have been *anticipated* by Old Testament figures. Thus St Melito of Sardis (d. c. 190) wrote of Christ: 'He was present in many so as to endure many things. In Abel he was slain; in Isaac bound; in Jacob a stranger; in Joseph sold; in Moses exposed; in David persecuted; in the prophets dishonoured' (*On the Pasch*, 69). This was not, however, to exclude recognising how the suffering of Christ continued not only in his ministers but also in human beings at large. St Paul and Jesus himself had pointed in this direction.

St Paul interpreted the dangers and sufferings that he faced in his missionary work as means for sharing in the death of Jesus and his risen, victorious life: 'we carry in our body the death of Jesus, so that the life of Jesus may also be made visible in our bodies' (2 Corinthians 4:10). A letter by the Apostle or one of his associates classically expressed the conviction that afflictions endured by Christians for the sake of the Church and her mission can also be called the sufferings of Christ: 'I rejoice in my suffering for your sake, and in my flesh I am completing what is lacking in Christ's afflictions for the sake of his body, that is, the church' (Colossians 1:24). In other words, we can see the passion of Christ continuing in the work of his ministers.

Jesus himself universalises that picture through the great judgement scene in which 'all the nations' and, seemingly, every individual will appear before 'the Son of Man' (Matthew 25:31–46). He will bring the final blessings of the kingdom in all its fullness for the righteous and pronounce condemnation for the wicked. The two groups will be, respectively, approved for their deeds of mercy towards Jesus himself ('I was hungry and you gave me to eat') and faulted for their lack of loving deeds towards him ('I was hungry and you gave me no food'). Jesus lists six needs (being hungry, thirsty, a stranger, naked, sick, and in prison) which he repeats four times in the text, with a corresponding list of remedies (e.g. 'I was a stranger and you welcomed me'). The list is open-ended, representing needs of all kinds and open to be expanded ('I was ignorant and you taught me'; 'I was dying and you gave me blood'). Jesus mentions various situations when, in a hidden way, he was in need and when, without recognising him, the righteous met that need.

In the perspective of Jesus, all human beings in desperate need belonged to him; he identified himself with them; they were members of his family. The scene of final judgement elaborated and universalised what Jesus said elsewhere about identifying himself with his disciples, with little children, and with others

(Matthew 10:40–42; 18:5–6). The teaching from that scene could be summed up as 'wherever there is suffering, there is Christ (*ubi dolor, ibi Christus*)'.

This axiom corresponds to Pascal's vision of Christ 'in agony till the world's end', a vision shared by many painters, composers, and writers of the past and the present. Painters such as Georges Rouault (1871–1958) and Marc Chagall (1889–1985) portrayed the passion of Christ within a wide context of human suffering. In his *War Requiem* written for the consecration of Coventry Cathedral in 1961, Benjamin Britten (1913–76) evoked the horror of modern warfare and the awful suffering of combatants and civilians alike.[22] In his powerful poem from the Second World War, 'Ecce Homo' (see John 19:5), David Gascoyne (1916–2002) pictured the crucifixion of Christ as being re-enacted through perpetrators and victims of our times; he ended by praying that our 'long journey through the night may not have been in vain'.

Down through the centuries, such painters, composers, and writers have intuitively and sometimes very consciously acknowledged a central truth that has often been ignored by biblical scholars and theologians: the cross of Christ permeates the whole of history. The story of all human suffering vividly and constantly reveals the passion of Christ: '*ubi dolor, ibi Christus*'. We should distinguish but never separate the passion of Christ from the passion of all suffering human beings.

Recent years have seen a revival of a popular devotion, 'the Stations of the Cross', a devotion in which the participants prayerfully move around (normally) fourteen scenes from the suffering and death of Christ – from his trial before Pontius Pilate to his burial. Occasionally artists fashion stations of the cross in which Jesus himself nowhere appears. His sufferings are expressed by various human beings whose pain and sorrow represent and re-enact what Jesus went through.

Chapter 11

♦

JESUS THE LORD OF GLORY

And all alone, alone, alone
He rose again behind the stone.

Alice Meynell, 'Easter Night'

B EFORE MOVING INTO THE Easter section of this portrait of
Jesus, I should make two preliminary statements. First, I
understand the resurrection of Jesus to mean that, through a
unique divine action which set the ultimate seal of approval on
his life and work, Jesus was personally delivered from the
situation of death. With his earthly body transformed and taken
up into his new, glorified existence, he thus initiated the end of
all things for human beings and their world (Romans 8:18–25).
Second, historical evidence for the appearances of the risen Jesus
and for the discovery of his empty tomb, converges with personal experience, the power of the Holy Spirit, and the testimony
of others in making faith in the risen Jesus a reasonable and
viable option for one's life. In many earlier publications I have
expounded the meaning of the resurrection and the case for
Easter faith.[1] On the basis of that previous work, I want now to
use the Gospels and elaborate a possible Easter portrait of Jesus.

THE EASTER CHAPTERS

Those who set themselves to portray Jesus during his public
ministry can draw on some rich testimony. All four Gospels have
much to report about his words, which include parables, beatitudes, and a range of other kinds of teaching about the present
and future kingdom of God. The Synoptic Gospels often report

those words in more or less the same way, even though they do not normally provide a verbatim agreement. Likewise the Synoptic Gospels recount a conspicuous variety of actions: joining sinners for meals, delivering people from diabolic possession, calling and training the Twelve, associating with women and children, healing the sick, and performing a range of further miraculous deeds. None of the Gospels, as we saw in Chapter One, ever describes the face of Jesus or his appearance, but they do say something about his 'face in action' – mentioning how on occasions he looked at people with love, compassion, grief, and even anger. They do not set themselves to document his interior life. But at times they let us glimpse his intentions and catch sight of his emotions: in particular, his deep grief over the failure of Jerusalem to respond to his preaching, his tears at the death of Lazarus, and the profound distress which he experienced in the Garden of Gethsemane. Right through his ministry Jesus let his feelings show through. What is the situation when we move to the Easter chapters of the Gospels?

When we move to their Easter chapters, the Gospels recount *only a few words from Jesus*. In his brief final chapter, Mark simply indicates that Jesus will appear to Peter and the other disciples in Galilee but includes no such encounters (Mark 16:1–8). The words of the risen Jesus in Matthew are primarily concerned with commissioning the disciples to begin their work for the whole world (Matthew 28:16–20). The Easter chapter of Luke is likewise oriented towards the mission of Jesus' followers, for which they will be empowered by the outpouring of the Holy Spirit (Luke 24:49). John's Gospel ends with two Easter chapters, which are directed towards the disciples' mission: Jesus prepares them by actually imparting the Holy Spirit (John 20:21–23) and by commissioning Simon Peter to 'feed his lambs and sheep' (John 21:15–19). John includes one beatitude when, after a profession of faith from Thomas, Jesus declares all those 'blessed' who will come to believe, without having seen him as Thomas has (John 20:29). The Easter chapters of the Gospels include no further teaching – never, for instance, any such words from Jesus that might evoke his own experience 'the resurrection is like ...'

If we set side by side the words attributed to the risen Jesus in Matthew, Luke, and John, they do not parallel each other to any great extent but seem rather stamped with the characteristics of each particular evangelist. Matthew, for instance, concludes with what looks like his own construction: 'All authority in heaven and on earth has been given to me. Go therefore and make disciples of all nations, baptising them in the name of the Father and of the Son and of the Holy Spirit, teaching them to observe all that I have commanded you; and behold, I am with you always, to the close of the age' (Matthew 28:16–20). These words take up language and summarise themes of Matthew's Gospel in a way that makes the section 'a climax and conclusion to Matthew's particular presentation of the gospel material and of the figure of Christ, and which would make it as out of place at the end of any other gospel as it is completely in place here'.[2] We might, however, suggest that their meetings with the risen Lord conveyed to the disciples a profound sense of their being sent definitively on mission – a conviction that three of the evangelists eventually articulated in their own language and with their own emphases.[3]

The Easter chapters of Matthew, Luke, and John include 'the breaking of the bread' at Emmaus with two minor disciples who have left the community of Jesus' followers (Luke 24:30–31), a hint of a meal back in Jerusalem (Luke 24:41–43), and a breakfast on the shore of Lake Tiberias at which the penitent Peter makes loving amends for his triple denial of the Lord during the passion (John 21:9–14). In a sense, *Jesus' table fellowship with sinners* continues beyond the resurrection.

One major feature of his ministry is notably absent in the Easter chapters: *miracles and exorcisms*. At best one might point to the remarkable catch of fish (John 21:4–11) and perhaps to the new powers exhibited by Jesus. He suddenly appears behind closed doors (John 20:19, 26) and abruptly disappears at will (Luke 24:31, 51). Any post-resurrection healing affects the spiritual state of the disciples rather than their bodily infirmities. The miraculous activity of Jesus will continue, according to Luke, through the marvellous deeds performed in his name by his followers (e.g. Acts 3:1–8).

The training of the Twelve (now minus Judas) and, more generally, of the disciples continues after the resurrection. The promise of a rendezvous with the risen Jesus in Galilee hints at the rehabilitation of the male 'disciples and Peter' after their disastrous failure during the passion (Mark 16:7). Matthew depicts the final schooling and commissioning of 'the eleven disciples' by Jesus (Matthew 28:16–20). Luke narrates what the risen Jesus does for 'the eleven and those who were with them' (Luke 24:33) – a wider group that obviously includes various named and unnamed women, as well as Cleopas and his companion. Through his closing two chapters, John repeatedly calls

185

Jesus' followers 'the disciples', naming 'the Twelve' only once and that in connection with Thomas 'one of the Twelve' and his refusal to accept the resurrection without palpable proof (John 20:24–25). Terminology apart, the disciples undergo the final stage of preparation through their encounters with the risen Jesus.

The Easter chapters of the four Gospels never introduce any children. But *women lead the way*, especially through the figure of Mary Magdalene. She is mentioned in four out of five resurrection narratives (Mark 16:1–8; Matthew 28:1–20; Luke 24:1–53; and John 20:1–29) but not in John 21:1–23. However, she appears in the (later) appendix to Mark (Mark 16:9–20). Along with other women she has been recalled by Mark, Matthew, and John as present at the death of Jesus and by Mark and Matthew as present at his burial. Long before that, Luke has introduced her among the followers of Jesus, together with Joanna (Luke 8:1–3), who will also be named as an Easter witness (Luke 24:10). Female disciples fashion a firm bridge between the public ministry of Jesus, his passion, and then his risen life beyond the resurrection.

Such continuity between the pre-Easter and post-Easter Jesus is, however, missing in the case of two final items: his *emotions* and his *appearance*. First, what do we read of emotions in the final chapters of the four Gospels? Deep feelings of sorrow and then joy characterise the disciples. Mary Magdalene and her two female companions are profoundly alarmed, shaken, and even terrified by the news of the resurrection (Mark 16:5, 6, 8). Matthew also speaks of their feelings but modifies them by writing of 'fear and great joy' (Matthew 28:8). Luke depicts the women as being 'perplexed' and even 'terrified' by their confrontation with the event of the resurrection (Luke 24:4–5). Cleopas and his companion are characterised as 'sad' before their hearts begin to 'burn' within them when Jesus explains to them the Scriptures (Luke 24:17, 32). Back in Jerusalem, 'the eleven and their companions' are 'startled and terrified' when Jesus suddenly appears to them (Luke 24:33, 37–38). That mood gives way to 'joy' at the resurrection and even 'great joy' after Jesus is 'carried up into heaven' (Luke 24:41). John's Easter chapters run through a memorable range of emotions: the tears of Mary Magdalene that end when she rapturously holds onto the risen Jesus (John 20:11, 13, 15, 17); the 'joy' of the male disciples when they see the Lord (John 20:20); and the 'hurt' that Peter feels when Jesus continues to question him about his love (John 21:17). To be sure, feelings are ascribed to the disciples during the public ministry of Jesus: for example, amazement and fear when they learn of the suffering destiny faced by Jesus (Mark 9:32; 10:32), anger when James and John put themselves forward for special places in the coming kingdom (Mark 10:41), and the tears shed by Peter after he denied his Master three times (Mark 14:72). But the four Gospels excel in recalling the deep emotions felt by the disciples in the post-resurrection situation.

But the witnesses never recall, or at least explicitly recall, the risen Jesus as betraying any emotions. He never expresses any satisfaction at what he has achieved, no radiant joy at his intimate experience of resurrection, no deep happiness at being reunited with Mary Magdalene, the male disciples, and his other friends. No feelings show through the testimony provided by the Gospels. Luke's use of Psalm 16:8–11 (in Acts 2:25–28) encouraged later Christians to ascribe its sentiments to Jesus and depict him in his death as praying with joyful trust to the Father: 'you will not leave my soul among the dead, nor let your beloved know decay. You will show me the path of life, the fullness of joy in your presence, at your right hand happiness forever' (Psalm 16:10–11). It became a commonplace to understand this and various other psalms as expressing the feelings of Jesus when praying to his Father not only in his life but also in his death and resurrection.[4] In their prayer, preaching, and art, Christians sometimes spelled out the feelings that they thought appropriate to attribute to the risen Christ. But the Easter chapters in the four Gospels remain silent, at least explicitly, about any emotions felt by Jesus in his risen state.

They are likewise *silent about any bodily transformation* of Jesus and the way he looked. There is a remarkable, albeit mysterious, 'ordinariness' about him. The resurrection stories lack the traits of apocalyptic glory found in the narratives of the transfiguration (Mark 9:2–8). According to Luke's account of the walk to Emmaus, for several hours two disciples entertain Jesus unawares. As C. F. Evans comments 'the story is the furthest possible remove from the category of heavenly vision of the Lord in glory'.[5] Bewitched by the luminous phenomenon Luke associates with Paul's Damascus road encounter, by the conviction that the transfiguration is a misplaced Easter appearance, by the apocalyptic language of Revelation 1:12–20 and, at times, by alleged Gnostic parallels to the resurrection stories, some have attempted to smuggle glorious features into the Easter appearances.[6] But the only glorious figure in the Gospel accounts of the appearances is the 'angel of the Lord' whose appearance terrifies the guard at Jesus' tomb and causes the two holy women some fear (Matthew 28:2–5). None of the Gospels ever describes the risen Jesus himself like that angel. St Paul writes about 'the glory of God in the face of [the risen] Christ' (2 Corinthians 4:6). But in their Easter chapters the Gospels maintain a sober silence about the glorious transformation that Jesus' resurrection from the dead entailed.

The evangelists maintain a reverently discreet respect when they reach the mysterious truth of Jesus' new life. In later centuries the challenge of depicting his resurrection was taken up by Christian artists such as Piero della Francesca (1416–92) and Titian (c. 1488–1576), and by wonderful Eastern icons of the 'Anastasis', such as the one in the monastery of Chora (Istanbul). Settings of the Creed for the Latin Masses by Bach, Beethoven, Bruckner, Mozart, and other classical composers evoke the joyful mystery of Christ's resurrection (*'et resurrexit tertia die'*), as do Mahler's Second (*Resurrection*) Symphony and the works on the resurrection, risen bodies, and the resurrected environment by Olivier Messiaen (1908–92). Music, like literature and the visual arts, can lend credible insight into the glorified, bodily existence of the risen Jesus and risen humanity.

Since this book draws above all on the four Gospels, we move now to ask: How did the evangelists take in the awesome mystery of Christ's resurrection, (implicitly) portray themselves in doing so, and suggest lines of theological interpretation of that mystery? The response that the risen Jesus evoked in them belongs essentially to his story. Following the pattern of the last chapter, let me confine myself to the first evangelist (Mark) and the last evangelist (John).

MARK 16:1–8 ON THE RESURRECTION

Mark points to the divine *self-revelation* connected with the discovery of the empty tomb. At first glance, the spare eight verses which conclude Mark's Gospel do not look that promising for any theological reflection on divine revelation, but these laconic lines prove rich for such a theology. The verses report a pair of elements which persistently shape God's self-revelation: *events* (here the divine action which has already reshaped the whole situation before the arrival of the three women) and *words* (here the angelic proclamation). As the Second Vatican Council taught, revelation occurs 'sacramentally' – through the interplay of words and deeds.[7] Moreover, three *contrasts* are built into the story: darkness/light, absence/presence, and silence/speech. They enhance the telling of the episode and play their role in communicating the revelation of God.

Firstly, Mark's text contrasts not only the darkness of the night (between the Saturday and the Sunday of the resurrection) but also the darkness that enveloped the earth at the crucifixion (Mark 15:34) with the light of the sun that has just risen when the women visit the tomb (Mark 16:2). The three women go to the tomb with light streaming into the sky and with something they never imagined about to be revealed: God has definitively overcome darkness and death.

A preliminary hint of what is to be revealed comes when the women 'raise their eyes and see' that the enormous stone, which blocked the entrance to the tomb and their access to the body of Jesus that they intend to anoint, 'has been rolled away' (Mark 16:4). From the 'theological', passive form of the verb, the attentive reader knows that God, while not explicitly named, has been at work in bringing about what is humanly impossible – by opening the tomb and raising the dead Jesus to life. The women catch the first hint of what God has already done in unexpectedly reversing the situation of death and vindicating the victimised Jesus. Without yet being properly aware of it, the women find themselves confronted with the first disclosure of God's action in the resurrection.

A second contrast emerges once the women enter the tomb itself. The absence of Jesus' body is set over against his personal presence, mediated through an interpreting angel in the form of a well-dressed 'young man'.

A third contrast pits the confident *words* of the heavenly figure ('He has been raised. He is not here. See the place where they laid him') against the *silence* of the three women when they flee from the tomb. Its triple shape adds force to the announcement. The angel proclaims, first, the great truth that concerns everyone and will change the universe for ever: 'He has been raised.' Then he turns to the particular place in which he is addressing the women: 'He is not here.' Finally, he points to the specific spot in the tomb where the body of Jesus had been buried: 'See the place where they laid him.' Both these words of the angel and then the silent flight of the women highlight the dramatic and numinous moment of revelation. Let us see the details.

When the three women enter the tomb, they do not find the

body of Jesus but a 'young man, dressed in a white robe, and sitting on the right' (Mark 16:5). His shining apparel is the traditional dress for heavenly messengers. Like the Old Testament figures who remain seated to deliver a judgement, the angel does not rise to greet the women but speaks with authority to deliver a most unexpected message. At the sight of the angel, the women respond by being 'greatly amazed' (v. 5) – a reaction which matches the normal biblical response to God's presence in a theophany. After countering their startled reaction with a word of comfort ('do not be amazed') and revealing the resurrection ('he has been raised' – v. 6), the angel commissions them: 'Tell his disciples and Peter that he is going before you into Galilee. There you will see him' (v. 7). But the women 'fled from the tomb. For trembling and astonishment had seized them, and they said nothing to anyone, for they were afraid' (v. 8).

Some commentators, like Norman Perrin and Francis Moloney, explain the silent flight of the women as their disobedient failure. First of all, the male disciples of Jesus have failed, and now three women prove to be disobedient failures. They break down and disobey the commission they have received from the angel. So Mark's Gospel is alleged to close with total human collapse. But other commentators, like R. H. Lightfoot and Rudolf Pesch, do not agree with such exegesis of Mark's narrative, and find that it misses something very important about divine revelation.[8] It also glosses over the difference between the 'track record' of the male disciples from chapters 6 to 15, and the women's 'track record' in chapters 14, 15, and 16.

Beyond question, the male disciples of Jesus start going downhill from Mark 6:52, where the evangelist states that they do not understand what the feeding of the five thousand signifies and their hearts 'are hardened'. Their lack of faith leads Jesus to reproach them with their failure to understand and believe (Mark 8:14–21). A little later he rebukes Peter sharply for perpetuating Satan's temptations by refusing to accept the suffering destiny that awaits his Master: 'Get behind me, Satan' (Mark 8:31–33). Then James, John, and the other male disciples prove just as thick-headed (Mark 9:32; 10:35–40). Judas betrays Jesus into the hands of his enemies. When their Master is arrested in the Garden of Gethsemane, all the male disciples desert him (Mark 14:50). Peter creeps back and goes into the courtyard of the high priest while Jesus is being interrogated. But under pressure Peter twice denies being a follower of Jesus and then swears that he does not even know him (Mark 14:66–72).

None of the male disciples show up at the crucifixion, and it is left to a devout outsider, Joseph of Arimathea, to give Jesus a dignified burial (Mark 15:42–47). The progressive failure of Jesus' male disciples – and, in particular, of the core group of the Twelve – begins at Mark 6:52 and reaches its lowest point in the passion story. Meanwhile, women have entered Mark's narrative (Mark 14:3–9; 15:40–41, 47). They function faithfully as the men should have done but have failed to do. The women remain true to Jesus right through to the end, and are prepared to play their role in completing the burial rites. They have 'followed' Jesus and 'ministered' to him in life and in death (Mark 15:41). Does, then, the frightened silence with which they react to the angel's message represent a sudden, unexpected collapse on their part? Those who endorse such a dismal explanation should reread Mark's Gospel and notice how from the very start (Mark 1:22, 27) people over and over again respond to what Jesus does and reveals with amazement, silence, fear, and even terror (e.g. Mark 4:40–41; 6:50–51). His teaching and miracles manifest the awesome mystery of God come personally among us.

In a detailed study Timothy Dwyer has shown how 'wonder' is a characteristic motif in Mark's Gospel and occurs at least thirty-two times.[9] Comprising 'all of the narrative elements which express astonishment, fear, terror and amazement', it is the appropriate human response to the awesome presence and power of God revealed in the teaching, miracles, death, and resurrection of Jesus. Apropos of the three key terms in Mark 16:8 (flight, fear, and silence), Dwyer appeals to earlier passages in Mark and other relevant texts to show that the terms do *not* always bear negative connotations. Far from being always defective and the antithesis of faith, 'flight is a common response to confrontation with the supernatural'. The reactions of trembling, astonishment, *and fear* in Mark 16:8, as Dwyer demonstrates, 'are consistent with reactions to divine interventions early in the gospel', reactions which 'co-exist with faith'.[10] As for 'silence', he illustrates how in biblical stories silence for a time can 'result from a divine encounter'.[11] The silence of the three women is properly understood as provisional: in due time they spoke to the disciples.[12] They remained silent until they could pass on their message to the appropriate persons, the disciples.

To sum up: it is with flight, trembling, astonishment, silence, and fear that the women initially receive the angel's message about God's action in raising Jesus (Mark 16:6) and about Jesus' appearance(s) to take place in Galilee. But these, as Lightfoot, Pesch, Dwyer, and others have argued in various ways, are proper reactions to the climax of divine revelation which has occurred in the resurrection of the crucified Jesus. God's action has transformed the whole situation. The women have experienced the death of Jesus and his burial (Mark 15:40–41, 47); they expect to find a crucified corpse when they arrive at the tomb. Their intense response to the angel's words matches the awesome power of God, now disclosed in that 'which is greater and indeed sums up all the other acts in the gospel' of Mark.[13] God has triumphed over evil, the divine kingdom is breaking into the world, and the victimised Jesus is known to have been finally vindicated as the Son of God (Mark 1:1, 11; 9:7; 15:39).

In Mark's Gospel the crucifixion and resurrection stand over against each other. But they interpret and 'reveal' each other and may never be separated. Mark exemplifies this mutual 'illumination' through two juxtaposed statements, which the interpreting angel makes to the three women: 'You are looking for Jesus of Nazareth who was crucified' and 'He has been raised' (Mark 16:6). To that message of the resurrection of the crucified One the women react appropriately.

Read this way, Mark's concluding eight verses provide a rich commentary on the divine self-revelation conveyed by the numinous wonder of the resurrection. The later Gospels of Luke and John were to fill out the picture of the divine revelation at the resurrection by highlighting the outpouring of the Holy Spirit. Matthew, albeit discreetly, also does so by associating the formula of baptism 'in the name of the Father, and of the Son, and of *the Holy Spirit* with the post-resurrection rendezvous of Jesus with 'the eleven disciples' (Matthew 28:16–20). Thus Matthew, Luke, and John press beyond the Easter revelation of the Father and the Son (found in Mark 16) to acknowledge the 'trinitarian' disclosure of Father, Son, and Holy Spirit.

What God reveals changes any situation. As the Old Testament prophets insist, the revealing word of God is effective and transforming (e.g. Isaiah 55:10–11). Revelation and *redemption* can be distinguished but never separated. Mark's empty tomb narrative also exemplifies this truth, by presenting or at least hinting at some major aspects not only of revelation but also of God's redeeming activity. At least three points merit retrieval.

1. God, while never formally named in the eight verses of Mark's concluding chapter, has triumphed over the evil and

injustice that struck Jesus down. Glorious new life and not death have the final word. Two verbs in the passive voice indicate the divine activity which utterly transforms the situation established by the crucifixion and burial of Jesus. The link between the crucified Jesus and the risen Jesus is the victorious power of God. The great stone blocking the entrance to the tomb 'has been rolled away', and one understands 'by God'; Jesus himself 'has been raised' and one understands 'by God'. Even before the women arrive, the divine power has dramatically reversed the situation of death and injustice.

2. Many commentators find a firm hint of redemptive rehabilitation in the angel's words to the women: 'Tell his disciples and Peter that he [Jesus] is going before you into Galilee. There you will see him' (Mark 16:7). The male disciples sinfully failed when Jesus was arrested. They fled into the night and never showed their faces at the crucifixion and burial of Jesus. Peter denied that he even knew Jesus. But now their failure is forgiven. Once again they are named 'disciples', and their discipleship is to be restored when they meet their risen Lord in Galilee. Using the promise to be conveyed to the male disciples, Mark hints at the way in which redemption involves the reconciliation of sinners.

3. Then the angelic figure in the tomb offers a subtle hint of the redemptive power of love. Almost inevitably attentive readers of Mark's Gospel, when they come to the young man 'dressed in a white robe' ('stole' in Greek, Mark 16:5), recall another 'young man' who left his 'linen cloth' ('sindon' in Greek) in the hands of those who had come to arrest Jesus, and fled into the night (Mark 14:51–52). In chapter 14 the nakedness of the young man, the linen shroud, and the darkness of the night readily evoke the sense of Jesus now being led away defenceless and facing imminent death and burial. Three days later a 'young man' clothed at dawn in the white robe of resurrection also symbolises what has happened to Jesus, who has been executed, buried in a 'linen cloth' ('sindon'; Mark 15:46), and raised gloriously from the dead. The shroud of death has given way to the shining robe of resurrection.

In reflecting thus on the last chapter of Mark's Gospel, I have hoped to bring out its rich treasure of thought for those who want to catch something of how the evangelist (and Simon Peter on whose eyewitness testimony he drew) responded to the awesome mystery of Christ's resurrection. In portraying that mystery, they were also implicitly portraying themselves and something of how they too belonged to the encompassing story of the crucified and resurrected Christ.

REDEEMING LOVE (JOHN 20–21)

The Synoptic Gospels yield material for those who appreciate the resurrection of the crucified Jesus, with its aftermath in the outpouring of the Holy Spirit, as the climax of loving salvation. For instance, in Luke's story of the meeting with Jesus on the road to Emmaus, Cleopas and his companion (his wife?) experience how the presence and teaching of the risen Jesus set their 'hearts burning within them'– a hint of the way in which the gloriously risen Christ has his impact.

But it is John who sets out more clearly the redemptive power of divine love at work through the death and resurrection of Jesus. The evangelist has already repeatedly signalled the theme of saving love in the farewell discourse of Jesus and, not least, through an 'inclusion' which links the start of chapter 13 with the close of chapter 17. At the end of his long prayer, Jesus asks the Father that his suffering, dying, and rising will bring his followers into the communion of love which is the life of God (John 17:26). At the beginning of the farewell discourse, John has told us about Jesus: 'Having loved his own who were in the world, he loved them to the end [or to the uttermost]' (John 13:1).

John portrays Jesus in his dying and rising as bent on sharing with his followers and all people his transforming love. Here the evangelist reaches the climax of his portrait of Jesus. It is also the section of this Gospel where its author, the beloved disciple who was so intimately bound in friendship to Jesus, emerges clearly and depicts himself. His own self-portrait merges with his portrait of the risen Jesus.

When we move to the two Easter chapters of John, so many verses can speak to us of the redeeming love deployed by the risen Jesus. We find beautifully exemplified here the observation of Vincent Bruemmer: 'Our identity as persons is bestowed on us in the love which others have for us ... Our identity is equally determined by the love we have for others. In both senses we owe our identity as persons to others.'[14] In the encounter, for instance, between Jesus and Mary Magdalene we see her lasting identity being bestowed on her through the love which Jesus has for her and through her love for him (John 20:11–18). But let me dwell rather on the closing chapter of John's Gospel and the case of Simon Peter.

Many readers of John notice how the theme of Peter's sin and forgiveness is resolved and settled in chapter 21. Three times in the courtyard of the high priest he denies being a disciple of Jesus (John 18:15–27). That sombre episode ends when the cock crows, but without any repentant tears shed by Peter. Alerted by Mary Magdalene after the resurrection he visits the open and empty tomb, but that sign does not bring him to Easter faith as it does in the case of the beloved disciple (John 20:8). Peter is there with the other disciples when, behind locked doors, Jesus suddenly appears, breathes the Holy Spirit into them, and gives them the power to forgive sins (John 20:19–23). Peter's threefold declaration of love matches his denial of a few days earlier and brings the commission to feed the Lord's lambs and sheep (John 21:15–17).

Beyond question, John's final chapter shows Peter being lovingly forgiven for a recent act of cowardice. But the text says much more about love than that. It shows us the risen Jesus bringing up a buried past, and with loving delicacy healing old memories for Peter *and for the reader*. As so often in John's Gospel, the text invites us to identify with the men and women who meet and experience Jesus and are transformed by him.[15] In this case our identification with the disciples in John 21 entails remembering situations into which we have been drawn right from the first chapter of the Gospel. This is an exercise that can recall and heal our own buried past. Let us see how the final chapter of John can lovingly bring about a healing redemption.

After chapter 20 the situation we meet in the final chapter is astonishing. Summoned by Mary Magdalene's unexpected discovery, Peter has visited the empty tomb of Jesus. On Easter Sunday evening, along with the other disciples, he 'rejoices' to see the risen Lord, receives the Holy Spirit, and is sent on mission by Jesus. Thomas, 'called the Twin', is absent on Easter Sunday evening, and expresses his crass doubts about the resurrection. A week later, along with Peter and the other disciples, Thomas sees the risen Christ and blurts out his confession: 'My Lord and my God' (John 20:24–29). Then we suddenly find Peter, Thomas, and five other disciples out fishing, almost as if Jesus had never existed and had never turned their lives around.

Peter's announcement, 'I am going fishing' (John 21:3) seems as if he is ignoring or even denying the association with Jesus which has so shaped his recent past. At the least it suggests deep uncertainty about the future and the way Peter and his fellow disciples should begin their ministry to the world. The text evokes what we already know, not from John but from the other Gospels. Peter and 'the sons of Zebedee' (John 21:2) were fishermen when Jesus first called them. Something of their past is showing through.

John's final chapter opens by stating that it will describe how the risen Jesus manifests himself again to the disciples (John 21:1), his third self-manifestation after the resurrection (John 21:14) – actually his fourth if we include the appearance to Mary Magdalene alone (John 20:11–18). Three times in John 21:1 and 14 we find the verb 'manifest', the same word used to close the story of the changing of water into wine: 'This, the first of his signs, Jesus did in Cana in Galilee, and *manifested* his glory; and his disciples believed in him' (John 2:11). The narrative in chapter 21 encourages the reader to remember that episode by noting that one of the seven fishermen, Nathanael, comes from 'Cana in Galilee' (John 21:2). Once again the past is being recalled. Just as Galilee saw Jesus working his first sign to manifest his glory, so now in the same Galilee the risen Jesus manifests himself as 'the Lord' (John 21:7, 12).

He does so 'just as day is breaking' (John 21:4). He is there on the beach when the dawn comes and darkness slips away. The scene evokes the cure of the blind man (John 9:1–41) and the claim of Jesus: 'I am the light of the world' (John 9:5). The spring dawn at the end of the Gospel can also take the reader back even to the very beginning of the Gospel and the 'Light' which shines in the darkness to give light and life to every man and woman (John 1:4–9). In the closing chapter of John the seven disciples have fished all night without catching anything.[16] Now the stranger on the lakeside tells them to cast their net on the right side of the boat. They do so and make an enormous catch of 153 fish (John 21:6, 8, 11) – a symbol of fullness[17] and an echo of the 'life in abundance' (John 10:10), which the Gospel, right from its prologue, has promised that the Light of the world will bring (John 1:4).

The extraordinary catch of fish, the only such miraculous or semi-miraculous event of its kind in the Easter stories of all four Gospels, recalls the multiplication of the loaves *and fishes* (John 6:1–15). In the discourse which follows that sign, Jesus speaks of people being 'hauled' or drawn to him (John 6:44), a verb which turns up later in the promise: 'When I am lifted up from the earth, I will draw [literally, 'haul'] all people to myself' (John 12:32). Now in the closing chapter of the Fourth Gospel the same verb recurs when Peter 'hauls' ashore the unbroken net containing 153 fish. Symbolically Peter the fisherman is now engaged in the work of 'hauling' others to the Lord (see Mark 1:17) or gathering around Jesus 'the scattered children of God' (John 11:52).

The remarkable way in which the net remains unbroken, despite its enclosing so many large fish, can bring to mind the unity of believers promised by Jesus through the image of gathering all into 'one sheepfold' (John 10:16). The images of fish and sheep differ, but the basic meaning is the same.

When the disciples reach land, they see that Jesus has already prepared for them some fish and bread (John 21:9). In preparing a meal Jesus has done something which none of the Gospels ever report him doing during his lifetime. (That might prompt us in giving him a new title, Jesus the Cook.) But then, with words and gestures that evoke what he has done when multiplying the loaves and fishes (John 6:8–11), Jesus asks the disciples to bring some of the fish which they have just caught (John 21:10). He then 'takes' and 'gives' them bread and fish (John 21:13), just as he had done earlier (John 6:11). The reader is being lovingly challenged to recall an earlier story. Once more the text works to summon up a past grace by which we can be touched again.

Many readers link 'the disciple whom Jesus loved' (John 21:7, 20) with the figure repeatedly characterised in this way from the Last Supper to his visit to the empty tomb (John 13:23; 20:2). But the beloved disciple has made his appearance much earlier in the Gospel, as the anonymous companion of Andrew when they stayed (literally, 'remained') with Jesus for the better part of a day (John 1:35–40). Richard Bauckham has drawn attention to the way in which the language of that first meeting with Jesus is echoed in chapter 21 – not least in the final words of Jesus (addressed to Peter and concerned with the beloved disciple): 'if it is my will that he *remain* until I come, what is that to you?' (John 21:23). At the beginning that disciple 'remained' with Jesus and bore witness to him even before Peter became a disciple. The beloved disciple's 'ministry of bearing witness will continue into the future even after Peter has completed his discipleship'. In a sense that witness stretches from the first 'coming' of Jesus (John 1:29, 30) to his second 'coming' in the future (John 21:22, 23).[18]

Readers often rightly link the 'charcoal fire' (John 21:9) around which the disciples take their breakfast with the charcoal fire in the high priest's courtyard, the scene of Peter's denial (John 18:18, 25). On both occasions a charcoal fire forms the background to what happens. The morning scene on the beach prompts a new evaluation of Peter and ourselves. A broken past can resurface and be lovingly redeemed.

However, despite the explicit recall of the Last Supper in John 21:20, what may pass unnoticed is the way the lakeside breakfast works to heal the memory of earlier meals in John's narratives. Those earlier meals proved occasions of deadly threats against Jesus (John 12:1–11), disputes about 'wasting' precious nard to anoint the feet of Jesus (John 12:4–8), the betrayal of Jesus (John 13:21–30), and a 'misunderstanding' when the wine ran out during a marriage feast (John 2:3–4). The miraculous feeding of the five thousand (John 6:1–15) is also significant here. It led to a discourse about the bread of life, which ended with many disciples leaving Jesus and the first warning about Judas' treacherous conduct (John 6:25–71). In a loving and healing way, the Easter breakfast at dawn evokes those earlier meals and the crises associated with them, and promises Jesus' saving presence through the eucharistic meals to come.

Most readers have a sense of what the Gospel is saying through Peter's threefold profession of love (John 21:15–17). Peter must acknowledge and come to terms with his sinful failure. Renouncing his threefold denial (John 18:15–17), he is lovingly forgiven and rehabilitated. Undoubtedly the professions match the denials. But the author of the Gospel wants to convey a richer sense of healing than just that.

Right from the outset of the Gospel, Jesus has put questions to various individuals and groups: 'What are you looking for?' (John 1:38), 'Will you also go away?' (John 6:67), and so on. The end of the Gospel features the only question that Jesus ever repeats, and he puts it three times to Peter: 'Do you love me?' In this closing chapter an old habit returns and is intensified. Peter faces Jesus the loving questioner, from whom he receives forgiveness and a lasting commission.

At their very first meeting, before giving him a new name ('Cephas' or 'Peter'), Jesus had spoken to Peter as 'Simon, son of John' (John 1:42). Jesus now goes back to that original name when he addresses him that way three times at their last, post-resurrection encounter (John 21:15–17). In the imagery of the Good Shepherd and his sheep, the Good Shepherd calls his sheep by their names (John 10:1–8). Peter is now named and commissioned to feed the Lord's lambs and sheep. The great catch of fish with which chapter 21 opens might have shaped the missionary charge as 'cast my net, catch my fish'. Yet in John's imagery it is not fishing but shepherding the flock that entails danger and even death (John 10:11–15, 17–18). Peter's commission will bring him to martyrdom (John 21:18–19), in the service of the flock. No longer is it a matter of his deciding whether or where to go and stay (John 6:67–68). He will be carried where he does not wish to go (John 21:18–19). Like Philip at the beginning of the Gospel (John 1:43), Peter at the end hears the simple but radical call to faithful discipleship: 'follow me' (John 21:19, 22).[19]

John's narrative shows us Peter recovering his past before he begins the pastoral ministry which will eventually lead to his martyrdom. As we have seen, the last chapter of John recalls much of Jesus' ministry and story, right back to the prologue. Peter is taken through all this, down to his shameful failure during the passion. The past is not denied, but recalled, forgiven, and lovingly redeemed. A healing through love becomes the basis for Peter's new future.

John 21 begins with Peter going out fishing. He is, as it were, taking time off while he seeks for a pattern of meaning in his life and, particularly, in his recent experiences. It is almost as if, for the moment at least, the grand design has eluded him. But the Lord appears at dawn to heal Peter's past and enrol him in an heroic mission that will lead to a martyr's death (John 21:18–19).

By the way he has crafted his final chapter, the author of the Gospel lets something of that redemptive process also come true for the readers.[20] To the extent that they have allowed themselves to become involved with Jesus in the whole of John's story, the closing chapter will have its saving effect on them. It will bring up memories of Jesus and past encounters with him, so as to heal and redeem that past. For the readers, no less than for Peter, the 'follow me' of the last chapter can evoke and heal their memories as the basis for a new future.

This way of looking at John 21 accounts for the deeply haunting quality which many find in it. Somehow we have heard and experienced it all before. There is an affinity and continuity between our lives and what we read at the end of John. The closing chapter works to bring back to the surface painful and sinful memories. But they can become the start of a fresh future – through the loving presence of the risen Lord, who is our goal (because we have accepted the 'follow me') and our necessary support.

Some observations from John Rist converge with the redemptive love embodied in John 21. 'Only love', Rist writes, 'could induce us to take responsibility for our past; yet without taking that responsibility, we cannot complete a *single* "narrative" of our own life.'[21] I have suggested that by the power of his love the risen Christ encourages Peter to take responsibility for his past. Thus the Apostle can move beyond his divided self and eventually – through martyrdom – complete the single narrative of his life. The love of the risen Christ, I would add, can also have a similar impact on the readers of John's Gospel; they too are called to complete the single narrative of their lives.

The author of this Gospel, whether or not he was the beloved disciple (which following Richard Bauckham I think more likely) or someone else, held together through further 'inclusions' his total portrait of Jesus. First, the Fourth Gospel opens its majestic prologue with the eternal pre-existence of the Word (John 1:1); it closes by looking ahead to the end of all history when the risen, 'post-existent' Christ will 'come' at the end (John 21:22–23). The evangelist puts his portrait of Jesus in an immense framework, which runs from the divine pre-existence to the final coming. Second, on their side human beings are summoned to faith. The prologue states that John the Baptist 'came for a witness to testify to the light, so that all may *believe* through him' (John 1:7). At the end the Gospel states its purpose for the readers, 'so that you may *believe* that Jesus is the Messiah, the Son of God' (John 20:31). John's portrait of Jesus illustrates the shape of such believing, the theme of our final chapter.

Chapter 12

♦

JESUS THE ABIDING PRESENCE

If we let Christ into our lives, we lose nothing, nothing,
absolutely nothing of what makes life free, beautiful and
great.

Pope Benedict XVI, St Peter's Square, 24 April 2005

We thrive on love, and bereft of it we languish.

Peter Steele, Georgetown University, 2 August 2006

J ESUS REMEMBERED WAS ONE of three truly major works on
Jesus published in 2003.[1] By expanding its title, I could sum up
the scope of my present book: a portrait that remembers and
experiences Jesus. One could also express the thrust of the
Fourth Gospel in those terms. Written by a witness who had
enjoyed firsthand contact with the events of Jesus' history, that
Gospel merged two horizons: those of memory and experience.
Through decades of prayerful contemplation, the author recalled
a past which had ended with the resurrection of Jesus and the
gift of the Holy Spirit. A lifelong process of understanding and
interpretation, along with the abiding presence of the risen Jesus
himself, allowed the beloved disciple to gain ever deeper
insights into the meaning of the events in which he had participated. He wrote his Gospel to share with others that intimate,
personal knowledge of Jesus which embraced both memory
from the past and ongoing experience in the present. At the end
he frankly addressed his readers and explained his purpose in
writing: 'so that you may come to believe that Jesus is the
Messiah, the Son of God, and that through believing you might
have life in his name' (John 20:31). Let us see something of the

exquisite strategy that shaped the evangelist's presentation and took the form of questions, encounters and the dynamism of faith.

JESUS THE QUESTIONER

It has often been said that a wise person is one who pauses to ask the right questions rather than rushing at once to give the 'correct' answers. John's Gospel, along with the Bible, implies, however, that the wise person would be one who pauses to hear and ponder the right questions that God poses.

In the Book of Genesis God soon confronts Adam with a question: 'Where are you?' (Genesis 3:9). Right through the Old Testament, God continues to challenge people with utterly basic questions: 'What have you been doing?' 'Where are you going?' 'Why have you abandoned me?' In the face of Job's complaints about his unmerited sufferings, the divine Questioner does not offer explanations, but speaks out of a whirlwind: 'I will question you' (Job 38:3). The climax of that book (38–41) shows God searching Job with a battery of questions about the power, beauty, and mystery of the created universe. Here one might adapt the opening line of 'The Wreck of the Deutschland' by Gerard Manley Hopkins (1844–89): 'Thou questioning me God!'

To be sure, the Old Testament records various truths, commands, invitations, and warnings which God communicated to individuals and through them to the chosen people. But the Scriptures also indicate that at times the word of God took the form of a question. Isaiah, for example, recalls the vision in the Temple that brought his prophetic vocation. His mouth was purified, and then he heard 'the voice of the Lord' asking: 'Whom shall I send, and who will go for us?' (Isaiah 6:8). God could prove a questioning God.

It comes then as no surprise that in John's Gospel, with its clear statement of the divinity of Jesus, his very first words are a question: 'What are you looking for?' (John 1:38). The divine Questioner has become flesh to dwell among us. His opening words take the shape of a terribly simple but profound question: 'What are you looking for?' The God who says to Adam, 'Where are you?', and to Job, 'I will question you', has come among us and slips at once into the divine habit of asking questions. Before he presents his message, Jesus first calls human beings into question. He wants them to examine what their hearts are set on

– what they finally hope to discover in life. His opening question ties in with the spiritual search of Andrew and his anonymous companion (arguably the beloved disciple). Such a question does not erect a barrier in the way that answers can sometimes do. Rather than pressing ahead at once to provide them with the true answers, Jesus wants to help them move forward by hearing and weighing the right questions.

John's Gospel invites its readers to let themselves be drawn into the beloved disciple's experience by noting and mulling over such questions of Jesus as: 'What are you looking for?' (1:38), 'Will you also go away?' (6:67), 'Do you believe this?' (11:26), 'Do you know what I have done to you?' (13:12), 'Have I been with you so long, and yet you do not know me, Philip?' (14:9), 'Woman, why are you weeping? Whom are you looking for?' (20:15), and through to the awesomely direct question 'Do you love me?' (21:15–17). Let me take up these seven questions in turn.

'What are you looking for?'

At one level the question Jesus puts to Andrew and his companion ('*What are you looking for?*') is straightforward.[2] Jesus turns around and sees two men trailing along behind him, and asks them what they are after. What is their motive in following him? But his question plays on a possible, deeper meaning: 'What are you seeking in life?' Without forcing himself on them, Jesus confronts and gently challenges their most fundamental aspirations and intentions. As the story unfolds in the Gospel, the question takes on deeper significance. The verb 'seek (*zeteo*)' will 'be employed to speak of people's attitude to Jesus and their deepest commitments'[3]: when people 'seek' him (e.g. 6:24, 26; 13:33; 20:15). Sadly, the same verb will also be used of those who 'seek' to arrest Jesus (e.g. 18:4, 7, 8) and to kill him (e.g. 5:18; 11:8).

Some deeper meaning likewise shines through what the evangelist twice says that the two men are doing: they are 'following Jesus' (1:37–38). The verb can easily move beyond mere physical movement to express faithful discipleship. Andrew and his friend respond to Jesus' question by calling him 'Rabbi' and asking: 'Where are you staying?' (1:38). This counter-question seems mundane, but hints at deeper dimensions. C. K. Barrett catches the profound sense of what is at stake in their question:

'Nothing is more important than to know where Jesus abides and where he may be found.'[4] Then the two verbs that make up Jesus' seemingly matter-of-fact reply, 'Come and see' (1:39), likewise convey a deeper meaning. 'Coming' in John's Gospel may express the state of someone 'believing' in Jesus (e.g. 6:35, 37, 44, 45, 65); 'seeing' can be equivalent to personally 'knowing' in faith (e.g. 9:37–38; 12:45; 14:6–7, 9). To complete the picture, 'staying/remaining/abiding (*menein*)' conveys more than a superficial meaning of stopping or hanging around somewhere. Andrew and his companion want to know where Jesus is 'staying'; after 'coming' and 'seeing' where he is 'staying', they 'stay' with him that day (1:38–39). The two men initiate a relationship of 'staying/abiding' with and, in fact, 'in' Jesus, who will be disclosed to them as the 'true vine' in whom they will allow themselves to be incorporated (15:1–11, a passage which uses the verb '*menein*' ten times).

Along with the verb enshrined in the question of Jesus, 'What are you looking for?', the further four verbs ('follow', 'stay/abide', 'come', and 'see') that shape these three verses (1:37–39) all enjoy a more profound, spiritual meaning. The question, as well as what follows immediately in this passage, reaches out beyond the situation of Andrew and his companion to confront the readers of the Fourth Gospel: What are they/you really looking for in life? The question and its setting blend the commonplace with the marvellous. Do the readers also wish to 'come' and 'see' Jesus, and 'remain' with him for ever?

'Will you also go away?'

At the end of the long discourse on Jesus as the bread of life, numerous disciples find it all too much, a teaching that is difficult to accept. Many of them break off their relationship with Jesus (6:60–66). This prompts him into challenging the Twelve with the question: '*Will you also go away?*' (6:67).[5] Once again the question bears a profound sense. Much more than mere physical separation is at stake, as the immediate context suggests. Jesus refers to the coming betrayal by Judas Iscariot (6:70–71). Outwardly the traitor remains in the company of Jesus, but at that point in the narrative he has already abandoned his loyalty and interiorly 'gone away'. His apostasy marks out one extreme answer to the question. The response of Peter, as representative of the Twelve, marks out the other extreme: 'Lord, to whom shall we go? You have the words of eternal life. We have come to believe and know that you are the Holy One of God' (6:68–69), the One who shares in the holiness of the Father (17:11).

In his words Jesus deals with nothing less than eternal life, and his words impart that life to those who respond to him in faith. In Peter's reply, 'know' overlaps with 'believe', as can happen elsewhere in John's Gospel (e.g. 4:42). He and those for whom Peter speaks have acknowledged the truth about Jesus and hold it fast in faith. Only Jesus is worthy of their total allegiance. The mysterious God has been revealed to them through the person, works, and words of Jesus, the divine Revealer. As the One 'close to the Father's heart' (1:18) who has been 'sanctified' by the Father and sent into the world (10:36), Jesus can make known the truth of God and human destiny. The searching question of Jesus ('Will you also go away?') prompts an appropriately profound answer.

When presenting the question of Jesus, the evangelist knew that, between the response of Peter and that of Judas, all kinds of other responses were possible. Disciples could stay with Jesus in a half-hearted way that was not truly sharing his life. They may not have gone away from him, yet they did not truly belong to him. They remained near him rather than fully with him. If there was more than one way of leaving Jesus, there were also many ways of not staying fully with him. Nothing in the New Testament expressed more vividly the situation of those who remained only half-heartedly with Jesus than the rebuke delivered to the Christians of Laodicea for their lukewarm discipleship (Revelation 3:14–22).

'Do you believe this?'

After his friend Lazarus has died and been buried, Jesus arrives in Bethany and is met by Martha, the sister of the dead man. She expresses the hope that her brother will rise one day: 'I know [= believe] that he will rise again in the resurrection at the last day' (11:24). Jesus accepts her profession of hope in the final resurrection of the dead, but puts it in a fuller, personal context by identifying himself: 'I am the resurrection and the life. Those who believe in me, even though they die, will live; and everyone who lives and believes in me will never die. *Do you believe this?*' (11:25–26).[6] The question challenges Martha to acknowledge the power of Jesus to give life here and now, as well as at the end of history. Those who believe in him 'will live' and 'never die', precisely because he is in his own person 'the resurrection and the life'. Not only in the future but right now in the present he shares in the divine power to give life and, in particular, to give new life to those who have died. Wherever Jesus is, there is resurrection and life; as we might say, 'where there is Christ, there is resurrection and life (*ubi Christus, ibi resurrectio et vita*).' 'Do you believe this?' is a demanding question, addressed not only to Martha but also to the readers of the Gospel.

But Martha answers it superbly: 'Yes, Lord, I believe that you are the Messiah, the Son of God, the One coming into the world' (11:27). This magnificent confession, which anticipates the full-blown, closing confession of 20:31 (that promises life to those who believe that Jesus is the Messiah and Son of God), acknowledges Jesus as the One who has come into the human world from the divine world. There the conversation between Jesus and Martha breaks off; 'if Jesus is what Martha believes him to be there is no more to say'.[7]

The raising of Lazarus is the crowning 'sign' that reveals Jesus to be *the* Life-giver (11:1–57). The question at the heart of this story ('Do you believe this?') also confronts the readers of the Gospel. Such questions belong to the way in which the evangelist reaches out to engage them and encourage them to give their allegiance in faith to Jesus, who is 'the resurrection and the life'.

'Do you know what I have done to you?'

A question that Jesus puts to his disciples after he has washed their feet, '*Do you know what I have done to you?*' (13:12), concerns the example of humble service that he has just given them. Jesus himself at once answers his own question: 'You call me Teacher and Lord, and you are right, for that is what I am. So if I, your Lord and Teacher, have washed your feet, you ought also to wash one another's feet. For I have given you an example, that you should do as I have done to you' (13:13–15). Jesus appeals to the enormous difference between his identity as Teacher and Lord and the servant role he has just adopted by washing their feet. If and when the disciples follow his example by serving one another, 'the status reversal' could never be anywhere 'near as massive as in the case of Jesus'.[8]

The question goes, however, beyond the immediate context. It occurs after the disciples have shared the company of Jesus for several years and now face the separation that his death will bring. Do they really know what he has done to them – in both the consoling happiness and painful struggles he has brought to them over many months and now in the suffering that threatens him and them? Can they truly know what their relationship to Jesus has done to them and is doing to them? For the disciples and, I would suggest, for the readers of John's Gospel, the question ('Do you know what I have done to you?') has an even wider significance than the touching example of service Jesus offers. It summons up the whole story of one's experience of Jesus and must be wrestled with for a lifetime.

'Have I been with you so long, and yet you do not know me?'

A little later in John's narrative of the Last Supper, Philip lets his longing to see/know God lead him into making a somewhat foolish request to Jesus: 'Lord, show us the Father, and we will be satisfied.' This draws from Jesus a response which is both a question and a rebuke: *'Have I been with you so long, Philip, and yet you do not know me?'* At once Jesus adds: 'Whoever has seen me has seen the Father' (14:8–9). Philip's request has in fact already been granted, but he has failed to grasp that in his person and activity Jesus is totally taken up with revealing the Father (1:18). The disciples and others have 'never seen the form' of the Father, but the One whom the Father has sent has completely represented and disclosed him (5:37–38). From the beginning, Jesus has been mediating his vision and knowledge of the Father (e.g. 6:46; 8:19, 38). Philip is rebuked for not recognising that Jesus is *the* revelation of the Father.

The attentive reader will remember that, at the very start of his ministry, it was Jesus himself who had 'found' Philip and invited him: 'Follow me.' Philip accepted at once this call and showed his new faith in Jesus by 'finding' Nathanael and bringing him to Jesus (1:43–51). Before miraculously multiplying the loaves and fishes, Jesus had singled out Philip and 'tested' him by asking him: 'Where are we to buy bread for these people to eat?' (John 6:5). At the conclusion of Jesus' ministry, Philip joined Andrew in telling Jesus that 'some Greeks' wanted to 'see' him (12:20–22). Philip has been with Jesus a long time, and yet has not appreciated what Jesus' presence has been mediating to him.

Thoughtful readers of the Gospel could well transfer to themselves Philip's predicament. They too may have 'been with

Jesus' for a long time, but missed the full meaning of their experience. They may become painfully aware that, after being with Jesus for many years, they hardly 'know' him. The question Jesus asks remains poignantly relevant for all of his followers: 'Have I been with you so long, and yet you do not know me?'

'Why are you weeping? Whom are you looking for?'

My sixth example of Jesus playing the role of questioner shows him putting two questions to Mary Magdalene: '*Woman, why are you weeping? Whom are you looking for?*' (20:15).[9] Overcome with grief and absorbed with the desire to locate the corpse of Jesus, she fails to recognise at once the risen Lord and supposes him to be a local gardener. She responds to his two questions by saying: 'Sir, if you have carried him away, tell me where you have laid him, and I will take him away.' Her initial reaction embodies a remarkable, 'ironic' misunderstanding: 'not only does she think Jesus is the gardener but she also asks him about the location of his own body'.[10] When Jesus addresses her by name ('Mary'), she recognises him, calls him 'Rabbouni (Teacher)' as Andrew and his companion did when they first met Jesus (see above), and clings to him (20:14–17). Some commentators picture her as trying through physical contact to recapture a past relationship; she has to learn that the risen Jesus is not the 'old Jesus' all over again. There is clearly some truth in such comments. But in the Gospel narrative what other reaction might one expect from someone who courageously and lovingly attended Jesus' crucifixion (19:25), came to his tomb 'early on the first day of the week', found his body missing (20:1–2), and was in deep anguish at the thought that grave-robbers had been at work? The evangelist has made much of Mary's grief at the disappearance of Jesus' body by noting three times that she was weeping. But now he declines to capture in a net of words her joy that Jesus is gloriously alive. The evangelist lets that joy come through her gesture as she clings impulsively to Jesus.[11]

The pain of Mary Magdalene can readily touch thoughtful readers of this Easter story; they too have their sufferings and grief. Like her, they may have their immediate answers to give anyone who asks them about the cause of their tears: 'Why are you weeping?' But in their sorrow they may also be open to the second question: 'Whom are you looking for?' They can then hear the Good Shepherd calling them by name (10:14) and know the immense consolation of his presence, as happened in the case of Mary Magdalene. The evangelist, as commentators regularly observe, wants his readers to recall the earlier passage about Jesus 'shepherding' and knowing personally all his 'flock'. That link will encourage perceptive readers to appreciate the force of the two questions in their own lives.

'Do you love me?'

My final example of Jesus the Questioner involves not two distinct questions (as in the case of Mary Magdalene) but one and the same question repeated three times: 'Simon, son of John, do you love me?'[12] The first time the question is phrased by Jesus more fully: 'Simon, son of John, do you love me more than these [other disciples]?' (21:15–17). The three questions correspond to the three times Peter denied Jesus (18:15–18, 25–27) and to the threefold commission Peter receives from Jesus to care for the flock ('feed my lambs, feed my sheep'). The relationship between Jesus and Peter is being formally re-established but not without pain.

Jesus recalls something painful by the longer form of the first question: 'Do you love me more than these other disciples do?' The addition evokes the boast of Peter that he would 'lay down his life' for Jesus (13:37–38), a boast that was followed within hours by Peter denying his Master and so failing more completely than the others. Now Peter does not pick up the comparison suggested by the question of Jesus, 'but assures Jesus of his love and appeals to Jesus' knowledge of that love'.[13] Twice he says, 'Yes, Lord, you know that I love you,' and, finally, 'Lord, you know everything; you know that I love you.' He makes a poignant appeal to 'Jesus' sovereign knowledge' – something that Peter had traumatically experienced for himself when Jesus, who 'knows all things', had predicted Peter's threefold denial (13:38). Now Peter 'will demonstrate the genuineness of his love by caring for those who belong to Jesus', the Good Shepherd (10:3),[14] by shepherding the Lord's flock, and by dying a martyr's death.[15] Love will sustain Peter's fidelity, right through to his martyrdom by crucifixion.

Any reader of John's Gospel will be struck by the power and depth of the repeated question 'Do you love me?' – coming as it does soon after Peter's threefold denial. But for him, as for all followers of Jesus, failure should not have the last word. Love will always make possible a new union with Jesus, a union that may well entail ministry on his behalf and a life of witness that could even lead to martyrdom. Peter's obedient love implies sharing fully in the meaning Jesus proposes for life and in the great project that Jesus has set in train for the world.

It is worth noting that Jesus does not ask Peter: 'Have you a good plan for organising the missionary campaign? Will you prove a successful leader of my disciples?' Very simply Jesus questions him: 'Do you love me?' Loving friendship is all that Jesus wants from Peter or any other follower. Finally, Jesus will question us only about our love.

We have examined seven passages that picture Jesus the Questioner. To be sure, such questions enter essentially into the vivid, dramatic dialogues that characterise John's Gospel. But these questions also express the strategy of the evangelist in drawing his readers to share his own faith and lifelong experience of the risen Lord. Taken together, these questions make up a list of the truly great questions of life – not only for followers of Jesus but also for others.

ENCOUNTERS WITH JESUS

Encounters with Jesus form another, distinctive perspective that shapes the narrative of the Fourth Gospel. Through such encounters the evangelist brings on stage a range of people who feel various needs or face diverse challenges. Through this further 'tactic' used by the evangelist, his readers will gain insight into what the risen, exalted Christ might bring them and how they might negotiate for themselves a relationship with him. From the first to the last chapter we can read this Gospel in that key – as a series of one-to-one encounters with Jesus. Unquestionably, he also meets groups or even crowds of people. But much of the story concerns meetings with individuals and Jesus' impact on them: from Andrew in chapter 1 to Simon Peter in chapter 21. This is part of the portrait of Jesus that readers will carry away from John's Gospel.

Sometimes those individuals are given names, like Nicodemus, Martha, and Mary Magdalene. Sometimes they are simply called a Samaritan woman, a royal official, a man sick for thirty-eight years, a woman taken in adultery, or a man born blind. In all these people we can spot representative problems and recurrent human needs. It is not difficult for readers to transfer what they read to their own human and Christian experience.

I want to reflect on some of these encounters with Jesus, taking these stories in their own terms as John presents them. Patterns will begin to emerge when we put some questions to our texts. How do the individuals come to meet Jesus? What might they expect from him? What does encountering Jesus do to them? How are they changed and even spiritually transformed? How does the outcome go beyond their expectations?

Andrew

Andrew and his companion meet Jesus because they have been in John the Baptist's company (1:35–42). Then the Baptist 'looks at' Jesus as he walks by and says, 'Behold, the Lamb of God!' That significant glance and remark are enough to send Andrew and his friend trailing off after Jesus. They have taken the initiative. But what precisely do they expect? At this point we are not told. John has directed them towards this stranger as the One who can relieve the terrible burden of sin. Prompted and encouraged by Jesus, they signal some 'intention of attaching themselves' to him as their rabbi or teacher.[16] They exit to 'remain' the rest of the day with Jesus; the perceptive reader will soon become aware that the evangelist uses here this distinctive verb for the ongoing relationship between Jesus and his followers.

The Gospel includes no account of what Jesus talks about with the two men. Once they have accepted the invitation to 'come and see' where he is 'staying', the dialogue takes place offstage. Their question, 'Where are you staying?', may have moved alert readers beyond the purely superficial matter of Jesus' current address to ponder the deeper meaning of his permanent home as Son of God in his Father's 'house' (8:35; 14:2, 10; 15:10). As for the two disciples themselves, when Andrew returns from these first hours with Jesus, we see at once how much he has been changed. He goes looking for his brother Simon and, in the remarkable first words from an individual disciple of Jesus, he tells Simon: 'We have found the Messiah.' Andrew and his friend have been looking for nothing less and no one less than their Deliverer who has been appointed and sent by God.

Every believing person can echo Andrew's cry of joy at

finding the One who will set us free or rather at being found by him. The search is over and the burden is lifted. No writer has expressed this quest more poignantly than Dostoevsky in *The Brothers Karamazov*: 'I've been waiting all my life for someone like you. I knew that someone like you would come and forgive me' (see above, Chapter Five).

Finally, the 'missionary' impulse in Andrew is unmistakable. He immediately wants to share with others what he has found and bring them to the One he has experienced. The missionary desire to share Jesus with others runs through the stories of encounters in John's Gospel: from the Samaritan woman's invitation, 'Come and see a man who told me all that I ever did' (4:29) to Mary Magdalene's joyful announcement, 'I have seen the Lord' (20:18).

Nicodemus

Nicodemus meets Jesus because he has gone looking for him (3:1–21).[17] Admittedly he comes 'by night'. As a Pharisee, a ruler of the Jews, and a teacher in Israel, Nicodemus is someone who has arrived and who is sensitive to his own reputation and importance. He is afraid of compromising himself, and so he decides to visit Jesus under cover of darkness.

What expectations does Nicodemus have? He has already reached certain conclusions about Jesus: 'Rabbi, we know that you are a teacher come from God; for no one can do these signs that you do, unless God is with him.' Apparently Nicodemus simply wants reassurance and confirmation about Jesus being a divinely endorsed teacher.

But what happens in the dialogue suddenly goes far beyond the limited agenda that Nicodemus has proposed. Jesus abruptly assures him: 'Amen, amen, I say to you, unless one is born again, he cannot see the kingdom of God.' Jesus spells out this unexpected invitation to enter the kingdom as involving new birth through water and the Holy Spirit. Is Nicodemus ready to submit to God's Spirit that, like the unpredictable and invisible wind, 'blows where it wills'? Must he become a born-again Pharisee?

Nicodemus knows what can happen and what cannot happen. The words 'how' and 'can' recur in his three questions to suggest a limited view of God's power: '*How can* a man be born when he is old? *Can* he enter a second time into his mother's womb and be born? ... *How* can this be?' It is disturbing to be called when one is 'old' to start once again from the beginning. Is it possible to do so? Nicodemus is a professionally religious man, a rigid individual who has life under control but who also feels an ill-defined sense of some personal need. He does come to Jesus of his own accord, and seems to betray a feeling that something needs to be changed in his life. But for the time being he has only limited trust in the power of the Holy Spirit.

The story of Nicodemus' encounter with Jesus trails off. There is no clearly indicated ending in the text of the Gospel. A change does come over Nicodemus but it will come slowly. It comes precisely in terms of public courage, the very quality Nicodemus has seemingly lacked. First, he disagrees with 'the chief priests and the Pharisees' and defends Jesus' right to a proper hearing (7:50–51). Then after the crucifixion he throws in his lot with the faithful disciples of Jesus and turns up with an enormous quantity of myrrh and aloes (19:39). He sees to it that Jesus is buried like a king. Although he first visited Jesus under cover of darkness, by acting truly he has finally come to the light (3:21). He has grown slowly but dramatically in his relationship with Jesus.

The Samaritan woman

It looks like an accident that the Samaritan woman meets Jesus (4:4–42).[18] If he had not been so tired, he might have gone with his disciples into Sychar to buy food. She could have gone to draw water earlier or later in the day. The midday encounter at Jacob's well might seem a perfectly chance meeting. But what begins like a random exchange ends very differently.

Unlike the encounter with Nicodemus, it is Jesus this time who takes the initiative and opens the dialogue: 'Give me a drink.' To begin with, their interchange centres on something which is not only simple and basic but also an elemental necessity for human beings and their world: water. The first part of the dialogue ends with Jesus' promise: 'Those who drink of the water that I will give them will never thirst; the water that I will give them will become in them a spring of water welling up to eternal life.'

When I read that promise, I always think of the fountains in the Villa d'Este outside Rome. The spouts of crystal-fresh water leap into the air and become charged with sunlight. Like those fountains Jesus gives himself away with joy. The Samaritan woman and the rest of us are not asked to search or dig for water, let alone store it up in some reservoir. We simply have to cup our hands and drink.

The encounter at high noon abruptly moves on when Jesus says to the woman: 'Go, call your husband.' Jesus has touched on her irregular home situation. She has had five husbands, and is now living with a man who is not her husband. But she does not break off her conversation with Jesus in embarrassment. The magic of his presence speaks for itself. Little by little she lets him lead her on, right to the point when he no longer speaks merely of living water but reveals himself as the living Messiah.

Once more we see the missionary impulse in a person who has experienced Jesus at such depth. She does not hoard the good news but brings it at once to the people of Sychar. Many are so impressed by the woman's testimony that they come to believe in Jesus. Later, others tell her that she is now redundant: 'It is no longer because of your words that we believe, for we have heard him for ourselves and we know that this is indeed the Saviour of the world.' They no longer need the woman's witness to her own experience. They have experienced Jesus for themselves, and they call him by a remarkable title that we find nowhere else in the New Testament, 'the Saviour of the world'.

If Nicodemus is a slow learner, the sinful Samaritan woman is quite the opposite. This might seem all the more surprising in someone who is no impressionable teenager but a grown woman with a steady habit of getting married. In the encounter with Jesus, she lets herself be touched, changed, and loved by him. Within a few hours she has become a missionary for him. This is a story of someone who gets up in the morning suspecting and expecting nothing. The day ends with her a totally changed person. She has let Jesus challenge her and reveal himself to her.

The officer

John's Gospel moves at once to the story of an *officer in the royal service*, who leaves Capernaum and hurriedly seeks out Jesus in Cana (4:46–53).[19] He meets Jesus because he wants one particular thing – a cure for his sick son, 'my little boy' as he calls him poignantly. The royal official moves from trusting that Jesus can work a miracle provided he comes in person to visit the dying boy to accepting that Jesus' all-powerful word can heal at a distance.

The official receives not only what he wants but also much more as well. He and his entire household become believers. Meeting Jesus leads him to found a community of faith. What happens to the man goes far beyond his hopes and expectations.

Let us note some further precious details in the story of the encounter with the man from Capernaum. As we saw above, Jesus speaks to Nicodemus of *rebirth to new life* and to the Samaritan woman of *living water* that springs up to *eternal life*. In the cure of the official's son *life is restored*. This theme of life will continue in what Jesus will *say* later about the bread of life (6:25–59) and in what he will *do* in bringing Lazarus back to life (11:1–44). Jesus is in the business of giving life and giving it in rich abundance.

A lovely detail, which one could easily miss, concerns the person whose son is cured. The Gospel gives him various names, calling him first a 'royal official' (4:46, 49), then 'the man' or rather 'that human being' (4:50) and, finally, 'the father' (4:53). He enters the story as what he is in public life – an official who carries out a state function. Then he becomes 'the man' who believes the word Jesus addresses to him. In meeting Jesus he loses, as it were, his public mask. He is simply a human being, face to face with the Lord. He is offered and accepts the only gift that ultimately matters: 'the man believed the word that Jesus spoke to him.'

Then he becomes 'the father'. His new faith has not reduced but reinforced his humanity. He is no longer merely an 'official' but 'the father' who returns to his family and finds his son restored to health. Then 'all his household' also come to believe. So, far from being a private, isolating force, faith speaks out, spreads itself, and builds communities of believers. What has been just a household now becomes a household of faith.

The lame man

The setting now switches in the Gospel to the pool of Bethesda in Jerusalem and to a man who has been lame for thirty-eight years (5:1–18).[20] He fell into that condition before Jesus was born. The man lies there – incurable and incredibly helpless. During the early years of his crippled state he could hope for healing, but now his friends have abandoned him and he has given up on himself. The poor man is the impotent slave of his own condition. He has become utterly used to the way he is.

He cannot move himself and go looking for Jesus, as Nicodemus and the official from Capernaum do. Jesus simply turns up and stands there looking at the crippled man. In that great crowd of invalids (5:4) Jesus picks out the one who seems most in need. The others can to some extent help themselves, but this man has been lame for so long that he cannot do anything for himself and has lost all heart.

What does the crippled man expect when he notices Jesus gazing at him? Some food or some alms perhaps? Instead, Jesus tries to rouse a little hope by asking, 'Do you want to be healed?' The man reacts by making excuses for himself: 'Sir, I have no one to put me in the pool when the water is troubled. While I am going another steps down before me.' The lame man's situation has been tragically paradoxical. He has lived so close to a pool, which, through an inflow of water, every now and then possesses special powers of healing. Yet he has been so weak that he could not take the small step that might have saved him.

Jesus has singled out the crippled man, tried to rouse some hope, and made him acknowledge his impotence. Now he heals him: 'Rise, take up your stretcher, and walk.' At that command, the man who could hardly move himself gets up and carries off his bed. He is healed, and after so many years can resume a normal life.

But the story does not end there. The man is not yet fully healed. As the Gospel subtly puts it, he does not 'know' Jesus (5:13). Unless he really knows Jesus, he will not be truly saved. Jesus seeks him out, in order to heal him interiorly: 'See, you are well! Sin no more, so that nothing worse happens to you.' Does the man recognise his own sinfulness, come to know Jesus in faith, and spread that faith? Rather, he becomes the first betrayer, a kind of anticipation of Judas in the Fourth Gospel. He goes to the authorities who are outraged that this healing has occurred on the Sabbath. He informs them that it was Jesus of Nazareth who was responsible for his cure. This strengthens their desire to kill Jesus (5:18).

Here is the first time that John's Gospel clearly mentions any murderous plans to do away with Jesus. This chilling news comes in the aftermath of a loving initiative from Jesus, which has succeeded in touching a crippled man's body but not his heart. Meeting Jesus and even being physically healed by him do not infallibly and irresistibly transform a human life.

The woman caught in adultery

The next encounter with Jesus I want to discuss (7:53–8:11) has
no fixed and secure place in the text of John. Some ancient
authorities insert the story in the previous chapter or at the very
end of the Gospel. Others omit the passage altogether or give it a
home in Luke's Gospel. It is all rather like *the woman caught in
adultery* herself.[21]

Unlike the case of Nicodemus, the Samaritan woman, and
other individuals who encounter Jesus, we are told nothing
about her background. Has she been locked into a long-standing
affair? Was her act of adultery a sudden act of passion? Was her
husband out to catch her in the act? Has she ever heard of Jesus?
How will she relate to him later? About all that has gone on
before and what will follow afterwards, we are given no
information.

The woman meets Jesus because she is dragged or driven into
his presence. What does she expect? That he will lead the stoning
party? She says very little – just a brief 'No one, Lord,' when she
is left alone with Jesus and he asks: 'Woman, where are they?
Has no one condemned you?' Jesus himself refuses to condemn
or destroy her. He sends her away with one request, 'Do not sin
again.' From the threat of death, she has passed to the gift of new
life.

The passage has a precarious place in the New Testament. But
it records a very old story about an encounter with Jesus. That
lifts it from oblivion, just as the woman's meeting with Jesus
saves her too from oblivion. In Rome and its surroundings I
sometimes visited places that the Latin poet Horace wrote about,
and I recalled his confident hope, 'I shall not wholly die (*non
omnis moriar*)'. In a sense that Horace never entertained, the
thought can be applied to Jesus and ourselves. Like that woman
caught in adultery – provided we find ourselves in Jesus' presence, even if we have to be dragged or driven there – we can
hope that we will not wholly perish in oblivion but will be lifted
from destruction.

The man born blind

His disciples are with him when Jesus first meets *a man who has
been blind from birth* (9:1–41).[22] The disciples see the poor man
sitting there and begging, but show themselves quite blind to his

217

misery and also to the power of Jesus. They do not ask their Master to intervene. Instead, they treat the blind man as a good topic for a theological discussion: 'Rabbi, who sinned, this man or his parents, that he was born blind?' They do not show any feeling for the impoverished, apparently meaningless existence of the poor man. But by the end of the encounter with Jesus, the man born blind has not only received his physical sight but has also come to believe in Jesus and worship him as 'Lord'.

Chapter 9 of John's Gospel presents a scene of universal blindness. There is the man born blind himself. The disciples of Jesus do not see the truth (9:1–2). Some Pharisees are likewise spiritually blind (9:39–41). At the level of language, the chapter is dominated by words for blindness, eyes, and sight. Among all those terms one recurrent phrase, 'to open the eyes' (9:10, 14, 17, 21, 26, 30, 32), suggests a conclusion the evangelist wants his readers to grasp. They can believe themselves to see and presume themselves to have spiritual insight. But it is only when they acknowledge that they are spiritually blind and ask for help that their eyes will be opened by Jesus who is the Light of the world.

The raising of Lazarus

The raising of Lazarus depicts an encounter at the limit (11:1–44).[23] To be sure, Jesus also meets Martha and Mary. But the great encounter is with his friend Lazarus who is dead and decomposing in the grave.

Obviously Lazarus can have no expectations that Jesus will do something for him. Nor do his two sisters expect anything. Jesus has arrived too late. Martha goes straight to the point: 'Lord, if you had been here, my brother would not have died.' She then takes back somewhat the sting of that reproach by adding: 'Even now I know that whatever you ask from God, God will give you.' Nevertheless, when Jesus visits the tomb of Lazarus and asks for the stone to be taken away from the entrance, Martha protests: 'Lord, by this time there will be a stench, for he has been dead four days.' Humanly speaking, the situation is ultimately and absolutely helpless.

But with his loud cry, 'Lazarus, come forth,' Jesus intervenes to transform a family tragedy. We have seen him heal situations of *slavery* (the invalid in chapter 5) and of *darkness* (the blind man in chapter 9). Now he heals a situation of *death*. He reveals himself as 'the resurrection and the life'. Lazarus has 'fallen asleep' (11:11), and there is no way he will wake up unless Jesus steps in to bring him back from the sleep of death.

Various emotions colour the whole episode. The disciples of Jesus express their fear over the dangers involved in going to Bethany (11:8, 16). Mary weeps at the feet of Jesus. When he sees that, he also breaks down and cries. But the dominant feeling and force is neither fear nor grief, but love and the disclosure of love in action.

The chapter begins by remarking on the 'horizontal' love which binds Jesus to Martha, Mary, and their brother Lazarus (11:3, 5, 11), and goes on to suggest also Jesus' bond of 'vertical' love with the Father (11:41–42). That powerful love now sets Lazarus free from death and gives him new life. When he emerges from the tomb, he is still tied in the grave wrappings, and others have to 'unbind him and let him go'. But Jesus' love has already unbound Lazarus and loved him into life. Besides setting free and giving life, love also brings together what is separated. Sickness and death have broken up the family at Bethany. Jesus' love now reunites Lazarus with his sisters.

Such love is a high risk. Here its results provoke Caiaphas and other Jerusalem authorities into taking their decision of 'expediency' – Jesus must die (11:50). His love costs him his life. At the end of the Gospel, Peter protests his love ('Lord, you know everything; you know that I love you'), only to be warned at once that the price of such generous love is death (21:17–18).

After his return to life, Lazarus joins his sisters in hosting Jesus at a special, pre-Passover dinner (12:1–8). He too shares in the threat looming over Jesus' head: 'The chief priests planned to put Lazarus also to death, because on account of him many of the Jews were going away and believing in Jesus' (12:10–11). Lazarus has been raised from the dead, only to stand beside his friend Jesus as the passion bears down on them. It can be dangerous to be the object of Jesus' special love.

This distinguishes the story of Lazarus from the earlier encounters. The meetings with Andrew, the Samaritan woman, and the royal official highlight the path to *faith*. In chapter 9, a blind man comes to the *light*. In chapter 11, Jesus' *love* proves more powerful than the death which has overcome his friend Lazarus. One should not miss a further feature that also sets Lazarus apart: his silence. In the whole encounter with Jesus, Lazarus falls sick, dies, is buried, is raised, hosts a meal with his sisters, and is threatened, but never speaks. This silent interaction that marks his encounter with Jesus offers the readers of John another 'model' for being drawn to the side of Jesus and personally sharing in his story. This can happen in and through their silence.

In John's Gospel the pattern of meetings with individuals continues after the crucifixion and resurrection, and love characterises these encounters. Let me take two examples: *the disciple whom Jesus loves* and *Mary Magdalene*, who both meet and know Jesus through love.[24]

The beloved disciple

In two episodes (20:2–10; 21:1–14), the beloved disciple is mysteriously led by love to encounter Jesus risen from the dead. In the first episode, he enters the empty tomb, sees the grave cloths, *and believes*. Love makes the beloved disciple jump at once to the true conclusion: Jesus has risen and is alive. In the second scene the beloved disciple is one of seven disciples who have spent a night out fishing on Lake Tiberias. At dawn they look across the waters towards a stranger who calls to them from the beach. Love allows the beloved disciple to identify who it is that has come to meet them at daybreak: 'It is the Lord' (21:7). Once again love brings him to know the truth and recognise the living presence of Jesus.

The beloved disciple *sees* an empty tomb and reaches out in faith to the risen Lord. He *hears* a voice at dawn across the waters of a lake, and knows himself to be in the presence of Jesus. Love has turned some sights and sounds into moments when he cries out: 'It is the Lord.'

Mary Magdalene

Mary Magdalene meets the living Jesus because she has returned to the tomb and is looking for his dead body. The tears flood down her face (20:11, 13, 15). She now finds two angels sitting in the tomb like a guard of honour. She does not ask them for any help or information, but simply explains why she is weeping and turns her back on them. In her grief and love she is anxious only to locate the corpse of Jesus which 'they' have taken away and laid somewhere.

Then Mary sees the 'gardener' standing outside the new tomb where he had been buried (19:41). It is the risen Jesus, the new

Adam who is inaugurating his new creation. Artists like Beato Angelico and Rembrandt have sensed something about that encounter which theologians and biblical scholars have often missed: its joyful playfulness. They depict Jesus as wearing a gardener's hat or with a tool slung over his shoulder. His 'disguise' delays briefly the moment of recognition.

Mary imagines that the 'gardener' might for some unspecified reason have carried off the body, but expects that all the same he would be ready to help her: 'Sir, if you have carried him away, tell me where you have laid him, and I will take him away.' Then, with one word, Jesus changes her life for ever: 'Mary.'

In the Fourth Gospel no other encounter with Jesus matches the contrast between Mary Magdalene's expectations and their outcome. She expects at most to locate a missing corpse. Instead she finds that death has no final power over Jesus, and that she is to bring to the other disciples the ultimate good news: 'I have seen the Lord.' Through Jesus' words to her ('I am ascending to my Father and your Father, to my God and your God'), the evangelist speaks not only of the risen Lord's solidarity with all his brothers and sisters in the new family he has founded but also of a desire to draw them and the readers of the Gospel into a new, intimate relationship with Jesus – a relationship that Mary is pictured as learning and accepting.

The second section of this chapter has pulled in examples of encounters between Jesus and representative figures. Some meet him because they have gone looking for him (Nicodemus and the royal official). One person seemingly by chance blunders into the presence of Jesus (the Samaritan woman). Another is dragged or driven into his presence (the woman caught in adultery). Others again encounter him because he himself comes to them (the man crippled for thirty-eight years, the man blind from birth, and Lazarus). Andrew and his companion are directed towards Jesus by John the Baptist.

All in all, it does not seem to matter much to the evangelist *how* these and others in the Gospel happen to meet Jesus. The only important thing is that first they do find themselves in his presence, and that then they respond to his initiatives. Except for the invalid in 5:1–18, all the individuals whom we have looked at allow Jesus to take over. Andrew and his companion allow Jesus to lead them away for a quiet afternoon together. Nicodemus lets Jesus introduce some surprisingly new themes. The Samaritan woman lets Jesus not only raise the touchy topic of her irregular life but also gradually reveal himself to her. Lastly, Mary Magdalene lets Jesus interrupt her ecstatic union with him, so that she can bring to the other disciples the glorious news of the resurrection.

In every case what Jesus does goes far beyond the expectations of those who encounter him. Some, like the Samaritan woman, the man born blind, or, for that matter, the dead Lazarus, have no hopes or expectations whatsoever when they meet Jesus. Nicodemus wants only a little theological assurance. The royal official is looking only for a specific miracle of healing. Mary Magdalene merely expects a little help in locating a stolen corpse. Whatever the given expectations, Jesus always does something more, calls for something different, and dramatically changes the lives of those who meet him. The evangelist shows repeatedly how the presence of Jesus is transforming. If those who meet him let him take over, extraordinary things will follow.

THE DYNAMISM OF FAITH

In John's Gospel simple verbs like 'know', 'have', and 'see' dot the pages. Very often we can grasp a deeper meaning by substituting our contemporary verb 'experience'. Thus two individuals are invited: 'Come and *experience me* for yourselves' (1:39). Many people of Sychar tell the Samaritan woman who has brought them news about Jesus that she is now redundant: 'It is no longer because of your words that we believe, for we have heard for ourselves and *experienced* that this is indeed the Saviour of the world' (4:42). The whole Gospel is written that 'you may believe that Jesus is the Christ, the Son of God, and that believing *you may experience life* in his name' (20:31). One can readily think of further examples where 'experience' catches for us now something of the sense of the evangelist's 'know', 'have', and 'see'. This is part of the deeply experiential flavour of the Fourth Gospel.

One can add a further point: the use of such *verbs* is part of the dynamic quality of this Gospel, and belongs to the evangelist's portrayal of a personal relationship with Jesus. Of course, all interpersonal relationships can only be dynamic and changing. We live them, and can never store them up and possess them once and for ever. Even more so, the evangelist suggests to his readers, a relationship with Jesus is something that happens over and over again. They will spend a lifetime coming to him, seeing him, and experiencing him.

The evangelist brings this point out very nicely by the fact that his Gospel never uses the *noun* 'faith (*pistis*)', but always the verb 'to believe (*pisteuein*)'. Almost one hundred times that verb occurs – right up to the climactic invitation to *'believe* that Jesus is the Christ, the Son of God', so that *'believing* you may have life in his name'. To believe is to maintain a living, changing, dynamic relationship through the Holy Spirit with Jesus Christ who reveals to the world his Father.

John's Gospel introduces other verbs to express the act which puts its readers into an immediate relationship with the person of Jesus. If not totally synonymous with 'to believe', these further verbs are certainly parallel. We saw above examples where 'coming' expresses the state of someone 'believing' in Jesus, and 'seeing' proves equivalent to personally knowing in faith. To such examples we can add other such verbs: 'accepting' or 'receiving' Jesus (5:43) and 'hearing' and 'following' him (10:27). The verbal language is unmistakable and suggests the evangelist's conviction: no one should or can ever say, 'now I know Jesus and *have* faith in him'. No one *is* ever a believer, but at best only *becoming* a believer in him.

CONCLUSION

In sharing with readers his memories and experiences of Jesus, the evangelist whom I take to be the beloved disciple uses *questions* that Jesus puts and *encounters* that he has (with a notable range of people challenged by representative problems) to respond to what was and what remains a central issue for the evangelist's public: What was and what is Jesus like? By way of answer, the Fourth Gospel shows the remarkable impact of Jesus on various men and women facing recurrent human difficulties and even crises. It seems much easier for the evangelist to explain what the impact of Jesus was and is like and how it entailed a dynamic fidelity on the part of those who accepted him.

Unquestionably, this Gospel wants to recall for its readers moments that illustrate the two 'sides' of Christ: on the one hand, his human side expressed, for example, when he met the Samaritan woman because he was tired after a long journey and when he wept over the death of his friend Lazarus. His divine identity, on the other hand, shone through many moments in the Gospel narrative, not least on the occasion when he was arrested (see Chapter Ten above). In that sense this Gospel responds to the question 'What was he like?' by saying: 'He was genuinely human and truly divine.' In these terms, we can say that the story told by the beloved disciple is the human life of God, the one and only human life of God.

Another way of summarising the answer given by the Fourth Gospel to the question 'What was/is Jesus like?' would be to say: it was and is the story of Someone totally oriented towards others. Far from being self-regarding, Jesus reaches out to others: to his Father and to all human beings. The Jesus known and experienced by the beloved disciple is utterly centred on others – on the Father who has sent him and to whom he returns, and on all the men and women who cross his path and whom he can graciously transform. The Fourth Gospel displays and divulges Someone who is simply bent on doing everything he can for others and who never negotiates beneficial terms for himself. The high point in the self-revelation of Jesus comes with his 'I am' sayings. Yet those sayings, far from being exercises in ostentatious self-glorification, disclose his loving mission for others: 'I am [for them] the bread of life'; 'I am [for them] the light of the world'; 'I am [for them] the way, the truth, and the life.'

We could properly sum up the Jesus whom the beloved disciple knew and experienced as Someone who was completely and lovingly centred on others – on the will and work of his Father and on the crying needs of human beings. What we see in the story of Jesus is unqualified Love, the divine Love in person.

♦

EPILOGUE

Various questions posed by Jesus run through the Fourth Gospel. Yet the most famous question he ever asks in the Gospels is found elsewhere: 'Who do you say that I am?' (Mark 8:29). Being a 'relational' question, it calls for a self-involving reply from all who are ready to become or remain his disciples. It opens up a way of life. Those who respond to this question must put themselves into any answer they make. Their response will help them know who they are, how they identify themselves, and how they want to live.

Thus the question asked by Jesus put a daunting challenge to his disciples: How could they claim to know Jesus truly? How could they claim to be living according to what they believed him to be?

Those who profess to know Jesus and aim at producing a reliable portrait of him should remember a cautionary observation that came from St Augustine of Hippo on the deep connection between knowledge and love. In *De diversis quaestionibus* he wrote: '*nemo nisi per amicitiam cognoscitur*' (83.71.5). We might paraphrase this remark as, 'you need to be a friend of someone before you truly know him or her'. But who dares make the claim, 'I am a true friend of Jesus'?

Yet some measure of friendship with Jesus or at least a desire for such friendship is needed if anyone is to attempt the daunting task of describing and interpreting Jesus. Only those who wish to follow him as disciples and have a living relationship with him in prayer will be able, however haltingly and partially, to understand and interpret him.

The question put to the disciples at Caesarea Philippi remains the task of a lifetime in which Jesus is constantly encountered, trusted, and loved. No one can ever respond to that question by declaring: 'Now I truly and fully know who you are.' Even the holiest and wisest persons must continue to confess right through their lifetime: 'I am just beginning to know who you are.' We can only join Augustine in praying: 'Lord, that I might know myself, that I might know you.'

♦

NOTES

PREFACE

1. See Richard Bauckham, *Jesus and the Eyewitnesses. The Gospels as Eyewitness Testimony* (Grand Rapids, Mich.: Eerdmans, 2006).
2. See Gerald O'Collins, *Salvation for All. God's Other Peoples* (Oxford: Oxford University Press, 2008), pp. 142–61.
3. I have mentioned the portraits of Jesus provided by the four evangelists. But, rather than expound these four portraits, I intend to concentrate on developing my own portrait of Jesus. Hence I will not take up, for instance, the way in which each evangelist treats and contextualizes the miracles and parables of Jesus.
4. As Albert Schweitzer wisely remarked, 'the better we get to know each other, the more mystery we see in each other' (*Memoirs of Childhood and Youth*, New York: Macmillan, 1931, p. 70).

1: THE BEAUTY OF JESUS

1. St Augustine, *Confessions*, 10.38.
2. St Augustine, *Enarrationes in Psalmos*, 44.3.
3. St Augustine, *Tractatus CXXIV in Joannis Evangelium*.
4. Quoted in *The Idiot*, trans. R. Pevear and L. Volokhonsky, Everyman's Library (New York: Knopf, 2002), pp. xii–xiii.
5. J. Maritain, *Art and Scholasticism*, trans. J. F. Scanlan (London: Sheed & Ward, 1930), pp. 24–38, 159; Thomas Aquinas, *Summa theologiae*, 1.39. 8. See also Umberto Eco, *Art and Beauty in the Middle Ages* (New Haven/London: Yale University Press, 1986); id., *The Aesthetics of Thomas Aquinas* (London: Radius, 1988); Patrick Sherry, *Spirit and Beauty. An Introduction to Theological Esthetics* (Oxford: Oxford University Press, 1992).
6. See A. Louth, 'Beauty Will Save the World. The Formation of Byzantine Spirituality', *Theology Today* 61 (2004), 67–77, at 70.

7. See R. E. Brown, *The Birth of the Messiah* (New York: Doubleday, new edn, 1993).

8. The passage echoes what Ben Sirach says of the serenity with which Lady Wisdom has blessed his life (Sirach 51:23–27). See J. Nolland, *The Gospel of Matthew* (Grand Rapids, Mich.: Eerdmans, 2005), pp. 473–78.

9. On the wisdom theme in the preaching of Jesus, see Aidan O'Boyle, *Toward a Contemporary Wisdom Christology* (Rome: Gregorian University Press, 2003), pp. 121–49.

10. See C. R. Koester, *Hebrews* (New York: Doubleday, 2001), pp. 179–80, 186–90.

11. In John's Gospel a boy does something for Jesus, by producing the five barley loaves and two fish (John 6:9), from which Jesus creates enough for five thousand hungry people.

12. One should add that Jesus also showed himself a realistic friend of children; he knew that they could be petulant and hard to satisfy (Luke 7:32).

13. See Dorothy Lee, 'Transfiguration and the Gospel of John', in D. Kendall and G. O'Collins, *In Many and Diverse Ways. In Honor of Jacques Dupuis* (Maryknoll, NY: Orbis Books, 2003), pp. 158–69.

14. T. Casey, *Life and Soul: New Light on a Sublime Mystery* (Springfield, Ill.: Templegate, 2005), p. 107.

15. See A. C. Thiselton, *The First Epistle to the Corinthians* (Grand Rapids, Mich.: Eerdmans, 2000), pp. 169–75.

16. *Pensée* 736 (sometimes numbered 552 or 919).

17. Christopher Devlin (ed.), *The Sermons and Devotional Writings of Gerard Manley Hopkins* (Oxford: Oxford University Press, 1959), pp. 34–38.

18. See Gabriele Finaldi *et al.*, *The Image of Christ. The Catalogue of the Exhibition 'Seeing Salvation'* (London: National Gallery, 2000).

2: GOD'S KINGDOM IN PERSON

1. Like others, I hold that 'mulberry tree' goes back to Jesus, and that 'mountain' (Mark 11:23; Matthew 17:20) is a secondary development.

2. For more on the faith of Jesus, see G. O'Collins, *Christology. A Biblical, Historical, and Systematic Study of Jesus* (Oxford: Oxford University Press, rev. edn, 2004), pp. 250–68.

3. See R. E. Brown, *The Birth of the Messiah. A Commentary on the Infancy Narratives in the Gospels of Matthew and Luke* (New York: Doubleday, new edn, 1993), pp. 471–95.

4. J. Jeremias, *The Parables of Jesus* (London: SCM Press, rev. edn, 1963), p. 11.

5. See R. Arbesmann, 'The Concept of "Christus Medicus" in St Augustine', *Traditio* 10 (1954), 1–28.

6. Alert readers may recall that John's prologue twice writes of John the Baptist as having 'come'. But it does so immediately after introducing him as being 'sent': 'There was a man sent from God whose name was John'. Furthermore, John 'comes' to 'testify to the Light' and not to pursue an autonomous mission (John 1:6–8).

7. N. T. Wright, *Christian Origins and the Question of God*, vol. 2, *Jesus and the Victory of God* (London: SPCK, 1996), pp. 489–519; G. O'Collins, *Salvation for All. God's Other Peoples* (Oxford: Oxford University Press, 2008), pp. 109–11.

8. See G. S. Shogren, 'Forgiveness: New Testament', in D. N. Freedman (ed.), *Anchor Bible Dictionary*, vol. 2 (New York: Doubleday, 1992), pp. 835–38; hereafter *ABD*.

9. On some aspects of Jesus' claims to authority, see B. Chilton, 'Amen', *ABD*, vol. 1, pp. 184–86; G. E. Hasel, 'Sabbath', *ABD*, vol. 5, pp. 850–56; H. Weder, 'Disciple, Discipleship', *ABD*, vol. 2, pp. 207–10.

10. On 'Son of Man', see O'Collins, *Christology*, pp. 61–68; J. Nolland, *Luke 9:21–18:34* (Dallas, TX: Word, 1993), pp. 468–74; id., *The Gospel of Matthew* (Grand Rapids, Mich.: Eerdmans, 2005), pp. 365–66.

11. On Jesus as Son of God, see O'Collins, *Christology*, pp. 113–35.

12. (Sheffield: JSOT Press, 1989), p. 160.

13. For details, see G. O'Collins, *The Tripersonal God. Understanding and Interpreting the Trinity* (Mahwah, NJ: Paulist Press, 1999), pp. 14–23.

14. On the baptism of Jesus, see J. P. Meier, *A Marginal Jew. Rethinking the Historical Jesus*, vol. 2 (New York: Doubleday, 1994), pp. 100–16, 182–91. On Mark's version of the baptism, see J. Marcus, *Mark 1–9* (New York: Doubleday, 1999), pp. 158–67; on Matthew's version, see D. A. Hagner, *Matthew 1–13* (Dallas: Word Books, 1989), pp. 53–60; Nolland, *The Gospel of Matthew*, pp. 150–58; on Luke's version, see J. A. Fitzmyer, *The Gospel According to Luke I-IX* (Garden City, NY: Doubleday, 1981), pp. 479–87; J. Nolland, *Luke 1–9:20* (Dallas: Word Books, 1989), pp. 157–65.

15. Matthew depicts Jesus' baptism as a public manifestation for others, even if it is only Jesus who sees or experiences the descent of the Spirit (Matthew 3:16).

16. On baptism with 'Spirit and fire', see Nolland, *Luke 1–9:20*, pp.152–53; id., *The Gospel of Matthew*, pp. 145–48.

17. Meier, *A Marginal Jew*, vol. 2, pp. 108–109.

18. Ibid., 407–23.

19. *Summa theologiae*, 3, 45, art. 4, ad 2.

20. On Luke's version of the transfiguration, see Fitzmyer, *The Gospel according to Luke I-IX*, pp. 791–804; J. B. Green, *The Gospel of Luke* (Grand Rapids, Mich.: Eerdmans, 1997), pp. 376–84; for Matthew's version, see D. A. Hagner, *Matthew 14–28* (Dallas: Word Books, 1995), pp. 488–95; Nolland, *The Gospel of Matthew*, pp. 696–706.

21. For a helpful discussion of Matthew 11:25–30, see Hagner, *Matthew 1–13*, pp. 315–21; Nolland, *The Gospel of Matthew*, pp. 468–78; on the parallel in Luke 10:21–22, see Fitzmyer, *The Gospel according to Luke X–XXIV* (New York: Doubleday, 1985), pp. 864–76; Green, *The Gospel of Luke*, pp. 420–23.

22. On this parable see O'Collins, *Salvation for All*, pp. 101–103.

23. For details see O'Collins, *The Tripersonal God*, pp. 12–23.

24. See G. D. Fee, *God's Empowering Presence: The Holy Spirit in the Letters of St Paul* (Peabody, MA: Hendrickson, 1994), pp. 410–12; Meier, *A Marginal Jew*, vol. 2, pp. 358–59.

25. When reporting Jesus' prayer in Gethsemane, Matthew and Luke do not reproduce the Markan 'Abba', just as they drop other Aramaic expressions that Mark records (Mark 3:17; 5:41; 7:11, 34; 11:34; 15:34). The only Markan Aramaisms that survive in either Matthew or Luke are 'Hosanna' (Mark 11:9–10; par. in Matthew 21:9) and 'Golgotha' (Mark 15:22; par. in Matthew 27:33).

26. J. D. G. Dunn, *Christology in the Making* (London: SCM Press, 2nd edn 1989), p. 27.

27. On the Lord's Prayer, see G. O'Collins, *The Lord's Prayer* (London: Darton, Longman & Todd, 2006) and the bibliography, p. 130.

28. Obviously innumerable Christians accept Jesus as the Son of God incarnate without consciously basing this faith on the fact that he made claims to personal divine status during his lifetime. There is more to the making (and maintaining) of such faith in Christ than conclusions about claims he made during his earthly ministry. Nevertheless, it would seem strange to believe in him as truly divine but argue that during his lifetime he was in no way aware of his own divine identity.

29. One should also observe here that ancient Judaism displays no uniform system of messianic expectations. Along with the dominant notion of a Davidic Messiah or king who would restore the kingdom of Israel, there existed minor messianic strands that included a priestly messiah, an anointed prophet, and a heavenly Son of Man. One should also observe that figures promised in ancient Judaism were not necessarily *anointed* and so 'messianic'; conversely, someone who was anointed and so 'messianic' was not necessarily an eschatological figure (e.g. Psalm 45:7). In particular, pre-Christian Judaism offers no evidence that a/the 'Son of God' or 'son of God' was ever regarded as 'messianic', in the sense of being expected as the future, anointed agent of YHWH. On the evidence of 'Son of God' emerging as a messianic title at the time of Jesus, see my *Christology*, pp. 115–18.

3: DIVINE AND HUMAN

1. See M. Bockmuehl, *Seeing the Word. Refocusing New Testament Study* (Grand Rapids, Mich.: Baker Academic, 2006), p. 118.
2. For full details, see L. W. Hurtado, *Lord Jesus Christ: Devotion to Jesus in Earliest Christianity* (Grand Rapids, Mich.; Eerdmans, 2003).
3. Thus Matthew, in his version of Peter's confession at Caesarea Philippi, seems to have been responsible for enlarging the simpler statement in Mark 8:29 ('You are the Messiah') and making it read: 'You are the Messiah, the Son of the living God' (Matthew 16:16).
4. See note 10, Chapter Two above.
5. On this see G. O'Collins, *Christology. A Biblical, Historical and Systematic Study of Jesus* (Oxford: Oxford University Press, rev. edn, 2004), pp. 154–58.

4: JESUS THE HEALER

1. In another context Matthew glosses 'sheep without a shepherd' by recalling crowds of people who moved Jesus to pity because they were 'troubled and dejected' or, as the Revised English Bible renders the phrase, 'harassed and helpless' (Matthew 9:36).
2. Years ago I developed a case for acknowledging that miraculous activity truly characterised the ministry of Jesus and should not be dismissed as a later, legendary accretion: *Interpreting Jesus* (London: Geoffrey Chapman, 1983), pp. 54–59. Re-reading those pages, I would not take anything away, but only insist more on the personal style of Jesus (in particular, his compassion) that distinguished stories of his miracles from those attributed to wonder-workers in Greek and Jewish traditions.
3. See H. E. Remus, 'Miracle, New Testament', in *ABD*, vol. 4, pp. 856–69; D. Senior, 'The Miracles of Jesus', in R. E. Brown, J. A. Fitzmyer and R. E. Murphy (eds), *The New Jerome Biblical Commentary* (Englewood Cliffs, NJ: Prentice Hall, 1990), pp. 1360–73.
4. See J. P. Meier, *A Marginal Jew. Rethinking the Historical Jesus*, vol. 2 (New York: Doubleday, 1994), pp. 679–84, 728–29.
5. Ibid., pp. 680–84, 729–30.
6. See Richard Bauckham, *Jesus and the Eyewitnesses. The Gospels as Eyewitness Testimony* (Grand Rapids, Mich.: Eerdmans, 2006). As Bauckham rightly points out, 'vivid detail has no probative force – for or against – in an argument about eyewitness testimony' (ibid., p. 55). The presence of such eyewitness testimony must be established on other grounds, which he proceeds to do.
7. See Meier, *A Marginal Jew*, vol. 2, pp. 681–85, 730–33; J. Nolland, *Luke 9:21–18:34* (Dallas, TX: Word, 1993), pp. 721–25. On the healing of the crippled woman, see J. A. Fitzmyer, *The Gospel According to Luke X-XXIV* (New York: Doubleday, 1985), pp. 1009–14; J. B. Green, *The Gospel of Luke* (Grand Rapids, Mich.: Eerdmans, 1997), pp. 518–26.

8. See Meier, *A Marginal Jew*, vol. 2, pp. 700–701, 747–49.

9. See ibid., pp. 701–706, 749–53; Fitzmyer, *The Gospel According to Luke X-XXIV*, pp. 1148–56; Green, *The Gospel of Luke*, pp. 618–27; J. Nolland, *Luke 9:21–18:34*, 843–48.

10. During his lifetime and after his resurrection from the dead, people, especially suffering people, prayed to Jesus for help (e.g. Mark 9:22, 24; Acts 7:50; 2 Corinthians 12:8). In the Book of Revelation prayers of praise and adoration are addressed to him (Revelation 5:9–10, 12–14).

11. J. A. Fitzmyer, *The Gospel According to Luke I-IX* (New York: Doubleday, 1981), pp. 655–61, 742–50; Green, *The Gospel of Luke*, pp. 289–93, 342–51; Meier, *A Marginal Jew*, vol. 2, pp. 777–98, 841–60; J. Nolland, *Luke 1–9:20* (Dallas, TX: Word, 1989), pp. 319–25.

12. Narrative references to the earthly Jesus as 'Lord' will continue in Luke's Gospel. We should also note that, immediately before the episode at Nain, Jesus has been called 'Lord' (Luke 7:6) by the centurion in a scene that displays faith.

13. After losing her husband, the woman is now bereft of her son, presumably her means of financial support and certainly of legal representation in the public forums of society. Like Jesus, Luke evidently was concerned with the widows and their social disadvantages (e.g. Luke 4:24–26; 18:1–8; 21:1–4).

14. Since Roman troops were not yet stationed in Galilee, the officer probably belonged to the forces of Herod Antipas, who seemed to have employed foreigners in his service. On the healing of the centurion's son, see U. Luz, *Matthew 8–20* (Minneapolis: Fortress Press, 2001), pp. 8–12; J. P. Meier, *A Marginal Jew*, vol. 2, pp. 718–27, 763–72.

15. On the Syro-Phoenician woman and her daughter, see Luz, *Matthew 8–20*, pp. 336–42; Meier, *A Marginal Jew*, vol. 2, pp. 659–61, 674–77; J. Nolland, *The Gospel of Matthew* (Grand Rapids, Mich.: Eerdmans, 2005), pp. 628–36.

16. Some commentators argue that the two feedings are alternative versions of one and the same feeding miracle that the evangelist incorporated in his text in two different places. But see Meier, *A Marginal Jew*, vol. 2, pp. 950–66, 1022–38, at 956–58.

17. 'Satan laughs at Yugoslavia', *The Times*, 19 September 1991.

18. See Meier, *A Marginal Jew*, vol. 2, pp. 650–53, 664–67.

19. M. A. Chancey, *The Myth of Gentile Galilee* (Cambridge: Cambridge University Press, 2002), p. 178.

5: THE MEANINGS OF THE MIRACLES

1. Richard Bauckham's comment is worth recalling: 'we encounter once again the phenomenon of a character named by Mark, presumably because he was well known in the early Christian

movement, but whose name was dropped by one or both of the later
Synoptic Evangelists ..., presumably because they were not well
known when or where the Evangelists wrote' (*Jesus and the Eyewitnesses. The Gospels as Eyewitness Testimony* (Grand Rapids, Mich.:
Eerdmans, 2006), p. 53.

2. The Greek term in Mark 10:32 and 10:52 is the same '*he hodos* (way/
road)'. The Revised English Bible (REB) translates the word as 'the
road' in both cases, whereas the New Revised Standard Version
(NRSV) renders it as 'the road' in the first case but as 'the way' in the
second. This masks the connection for the reader who is without
Greek.

3. When he comes to the resurrection narratives, Luke, without
abandoning the language of resurrection (Luke 24:7), will show a
liking for the language of 'life' (e.g. Luke 24:5, 23; Acts 1:3). Here, as
in the case of some other themes, Luke prepares the way for John,
who will make 'life' a key theme in his Gospel – right from the
prologue and its confession of Jesus as the Life who is 'the Light of
human beings' (John 1:4).

4. R. Bultmann, *Jesus and the Word* (London: Collins Fontana, 1958), p.
173.

5. 'New Testament and Mythology', in H. W. Bartsch (ed.), *Kerygma
and Myth. A Theological Debate* (London: SPCK, 1972), p. 5.

6. P. Gwynne, *Special Divine Action: Key Issues in the Contemporary
Debate (1965–1995)* (Rome: Gregorian University Press, 1996), p. 326.
On the possibility and knowability of miracles and other special acts
of God, see also C. S. Evans, *Historical Christ and the Jesus of Faith*
(Oxford: Oxford University Press, 1996), pp.137–69.

6: JESUS THE STORY-TELLER

1. See J. R. Donahue, 'The Parables of Jesus', in R. E. Brown, J. A.
Fitzmyer and R. E. Murphy (eds), *The New Jerome Biblical Commen-
tary* (Englewood Cliffs, NJ: Prentice Hall, 1990), pp. 1364–69; R.
Etchells, *A Reading of the Parables* (London: Darton, Longman &
Todd, 1998); G. O'Collins, *Following the Way* (London: HarperCol-
lins, 1999).

2. On the Parable of the Mustard Seed, see J. Nolland, *The Gospel of
Matthew* (Grand Rapids, Mich.: Eerdmans, 2005), pp. 549–52.

3. Possibly we should describe passages about the Good Shepherd
(John 10:1–18) and the Vine and the Branches (John 15:1–10) as
having the character of parables.

4. On this parable see Nolland, *The Gospel of Matthew*, pp. 552–54.

5. On this parable see ibid., pp. 802–13.

6. In a lovely touch, Jesus expresses the owner's concern for the dis-
heartened men who are still waiting to be hired at 5 p.m.: 'Why are
you standing here?' For them it is now or never; otherwise they will

not share in the harvest, which hints fairly clearly at the abundant harvest of God's coming kingdom.

7. On this parable, see Nolland, *The Gospel of Matthew*, pp. 562–65.

8. On this parable, see ibid., pp. 565–66.

9. On this parable, see J. Nolland, *Luke 9:21–18:34* (Dallas, TX: Word, 1993), pp. 792–803.

10. On this parable, see Nolland, *The Gospel of Matthew*, pp. 233–34.

11. On this parable, see ibid., pp. 751–62.

12. On this parable, see Nolland, *Luke 9:21–18:34*, pp. 586–98.

13. The Parable of the Vineyard (Mark 12:1–12) introduced Jesus in the person of the owner's son. This was the only parable in which Jesus clearly spoke about himself. But a number of other parables point, at least implicitly, to Jesus: e.g. the Parable of the Wise and Foolish Bridesmaids (Matthew 25:1–13).

14. On this parable, see Nolland, *Luke 9:21–18:34*, pp. 823–33.

15. On this parable, see ibid., pp. 682–88.

7: THE PARABLE OF THE FATHER'S LOVE

1. See J. A. Fitzmyer, *The Gospel According to Luke X–XXIV* (New York: Doubleday, 1985), pp. 1071–82; J. B. Green, *The Gospel of Luke* (Grand Rapids, Mich.: Eerdmans, 1997), pp. 572–76; J. Nolland, *Luke 9:21–18:34* (Dallas, TX: Word, 1993), pp. 767–76.

2. In this context both parables differ from that of the Lost Son. Although he is 'lost' morally and religiously (Luke 15: 24, 32), the runaway son is still able to make his way home to his father and family. This parable does not introduce, let alone highlight, the *seeking out* of the lost, as do the previous two parables. No one comes in search of the prodigal, even though some news of his dissolute behaviour has reached home. The father speaks of his son being 'lost' and 'dead' (Luke 15:23, 32). The elder son is more specific: his younger brother has 'devoured' his inheritance 'with prostitutes' (Luke 15:30).

3. The stories of the Lost Coin and the Lost Sheep differ markedly from that of the Father's Love, in which a farmer loses one of his two sons – a 50 per cent loss and, much worse, the loss of a human being.

4. On this parable see Fitzmyer, *The Gospel According to Luke X–XXIV*, pp. 1082–94; Green, *The Gospel of Luke*, pp. 577–86; Nolland, *Luke 9:21–18:34*, pp. 777–91.

5. At the start of the parable when the younger son asks, 'Give me my share of the property,' the father has nothing to say. He does not ask: 'Are you sure you want it all now?' Still less does he say: 'What is the problem? Why do you want to leave home?'

6. Christian theology will later speak of the two-sided gift of salvation and revelation (the two distinguishable but inseparable dimensions

of God's self-communication), but will not always recall that this gift is inspired by self-forgetful love.

7. B. Pascal, *Pensées*, trans. A. J. Krailsheimer (London: Penguin Books, 1966), no. 423.

8. See J. A. Baker, *The Foolishness of God* (London: Darton, Longman and Todd, 1970).

9. The story of Lazarus suggests how dangerous it is not only to love but also, at times, to be loved. He had gone into the 'far country' of death, but the powerful love of Jesus brought him back to life. Lovingly and joyfully reunited with his dear friend Jesus and with his two sisters, Lazarus now found himself faced with a new threat of death, this time the threat of a violent death. Many people came to Bethany 'not only because of Jesus but also to see Lazarus, whom he had raised from the dead. So the chief priests planned to put Lazarus to death as well, since it was on account of him that many of the Jews were deserting and believing in Jesus' (John 12:9–10).

8: JESUS THE TEACHER

1. On the beatitudes (with an extensive bibliography) see J. P. Meier, *A Marginal Jew. Rethinking the Historical Jesus*, vol. 2 (New York: Doubleday, 1994), pp. 317–36, 377–89.

2. Poor, hungry, and covered with sores, Lazarus (Luke 16:19–31) epitomised those to whom Jesus addressed these beatitudes. Significantly, he was the only person given a name in any of Jesus' parables. The parables introduced a number of rich people; some were pictured as generous (like the landowner in the Labourers in the Vineyard, Matthew 20:1–15), some 'neutral' (like the employer in the Talents, Matthew 25:14–30), and some less than virtuous (like the farmer in the Rich Fool, Luke 12:16–21). But none of them is given a name by Jesus. Unlike Lazarus, they were all left anonymous.

3. See Mary Bosanquet, *The Life and Death of Dietrich Bonhoeffer* (London: Hodder and Stoughton, 1968), pp. 109–11.

4. See D. Bonhoeffer, *Discipleship, Dietrich Bonhoeffer Works*, vol. 4 (Minneapolis: Fortress, 2001), pp. 100–82 (on the entire Sermon on the Mount).

5. Quoted by Bosanquet, *The Life and Death of Dietrich Bonhoeffer*, pp. 277–78.

6. Here 'righteousness/justice' does not denote the salvation that comes from God, but is used in the other sense that recurs in Matthew's Gospel: doing the will of God in accordance with the teaching of Jesus.

7. Paul is thinking of the mirrors of his time, which were polished metal surfaces that did not provide a clear image.

8. B. Pasternak, *Doctor Zhivago*, trans. M. Hayward and M. Harari (New York: Pantheon Books, 1961), pp. 44–45; translation corrected.

9. On the 'Our Father', see G. O'Collins, *The Lord's Prayer* (London; Darton, Longman & Todd, 2006) and the bibliography provided (p. 130); J. Nolland, *The Gospel of Matthew* (Grand Rapids, Mich.: Eerdmans, 2005), pp. 279–94.

10. J. P. Meier, 'Jesus', in R. E. Brown, J. A. Fitzmyer and R. E. Murphy (eds), *The New Jerome Biblical Commentary* (Englewood Cliffs, NJ: Prentice Hall, 1990), p. 1323.

11. See J. A. Fitzmyer, *The Gospel According to Luke X-XXIV* (New York: Doubleday, 1985), pp. 876–82; J. Nolland, *The Gospel of Matthew*, pp. 907–13.

12. J. A. Fitzmyer, *The Gospel According to Luke X-XXIV*, p. 884.

9: FACING DEATH

1. For a well-documented account of how Jesus appears to have understood his death, see S. McKnight, *Jesus and His Death* (Waco, TX: Baylor University Press, 2005).

2. See J. Marcus, *Mark 1–8* (New York: Doubleday, 1999), pp. 232–39.

3. On the historicity of Jesus' baptism by John, see J. P. Meier, *A Marginal Jew. Rethinking the Historical Jesus*, vol. 2 (New York: Doubleday, 1994), pp. 100–104.

4. See J. A. Fitzmyer, *The Gospel According to Luke X-XXIV* (New York: Doubleday, 1985), pp. 941–53; D. A. Hagner, *Matthew 14–28* (Dallas: Word Books, 1995), pp. 678–81; U. Luz, *Matthew 21–28* (Minneapolis: Fortress Press, 2005), pp. 150–57; J. Nolland, *Luke 9:21–18:34* (Dallas: Word Books, 1993), pp. 659–72, 737–44.

5. For details see Fitzmyer, *The Gospel According to Luke X-XXIV*, p. 1032.

6. For details see M. Bockmuehl, *Seeing the Word. Refocusing New Testament Study* (Grand Rapids, Mich.: Baker Academic, 2006), pp. 215–20; J. R. Donahue and D. J. Harrington, *The Gospel of Mark* (Collegeville, Minn.: Liturgical Press, 2002), pp. 337–43; Fitzmyer, *The Gospel According to Luke X-XXIV*, pp. 1276–88; Hagner, *Matthew 14–28*, pp. 615–24; Luz, *Matthew 21–28*, pp. 615–24; Nolland, *Luke 9:21–18:34*, pp. 945–55.

7. See J. A. Fitzmyer, *The Gospel According to Luke I-IX* (New York: Doubleday, 1981), pp. 777–82; Nolland, *Luke 9:21–18:34*, pp. 557–68.

8. On further reasons for holding that this is an authentic saying of Jesus, see G. O'Collins, *Salvation for All. God's Other Peoples* (Oxford: Oxford University Press, 2008), pp. 106–107.

9. On 'after three days', see Nolland, *Luke 9:21–18:34*, pp. 466–67.

10. Donahue and Harrington, *The Gospel of Mark*, p. 331. On the 'royal' entry of Jesus into Jerusalem and his cleansing of the Temple see ibid., pp. 320–26 (entry) and pp. 326–33 (cleansing); Fitzmyer, *The*

Gospel According to Luke X-XXIV, pp. 1241–53 (entry) and pp. 1261–68 (cleansing); Hagner, *Matthew 14–28*, pp. 589–97 (entry) and pp. 597–603 (cleansing); Luz, *Matthew 21–28*, pp. 3–19 (entry and cleansing); J. Nolland, *Luke 18:35–24:53* (Dallas: Word Books, 1993), pp. 919–20 (entry) and pp. 933–38 (cleansing).

11. On this issue of dating, see Fitzmyer, *The Gospel According to Luke X-XXIV*, pp. 1264–65.

12. In John's Gospel, where the cleansing is located early in the story, it was the raising of Lazarus that finally motivated the authorities into having Jesus put to death (John 11:45–53). The raising of Lazarus could well have played its part in prompting the authorities to move. On Lazarus in the context of the passion, see Richard Bauckham, *Jesus and the Eyewitnesses. The Gospels as Eyewitness Testimony* (Grand Rapids, Mich.: Eerdmans, 2006), pp. 195–96.

13. Donahue and Harrington, *The Gospel of Mark*, p. 328. See O'Collins, *Salvation for All*, pp. 103–105.

14. Fitzmyer, *The Gospel According to Luke X-XXIV*, pp. 1254–55.

15. Hagner, *Matthew 14–28*, p. 798.

16. Even if Mark wrote his Gospel earlier, Matthew wrote after AD 70, and knew that it was the Romans, not Jesus, who had visibly destroyed the Temple.

17. For a discussion and extensive bibliography on Jesus and the kingdom of God, see Meier, *A Marginal Jew*, vol. 2, pp. 289–506.

18. See ibid., pp. 302–309, 366–71.

19. See O'Collins, *Salvation for All*, pp. 108–109.

20. R. Bauckham, *Jesus and the Eyewitnesses. The Gospels as Eyewitness Testimony* (Grand Rapids, Mich.: Eerdmans, 2006), pp. 183–201.

21. Ibid., p. 190.

22. Ibid., p. 193.

23. Ibid., pp. 187–89.

24. On the Last Supper, see Fitzmyer, *The Gospel According to Luke X-XXIV*, pp. 1385–1406; Luz, *Matthew 21–28*, pp. 364–85; Nolland, *Luke 18:35–24:53*, pp. 1035–57; A. C. Thiselton, *The First Epistle to the Corinthians* (Grand Rapids, Mich.: Eerdmans, 2000), pp. 848–91.

25. See Meier, *A Marginal Jew*, vol. 2, pp. 1035–37.

26. Marcus, *Mark 1–8*, pp. 446–47, 452–61.

27. See M. Hengel, *The Cross and the Son of God* (London: SCM Press, 1986), pp. 189–284; N. T. Wright, *The Climax of the Covenant* (Edinburgh: T. & T. Clark, 1991), pp. 60–61.

28. See K. Baltzer, *Deutero-Isaiah* (Minneapolis: Fortress Press, 2001), pp. 392–429; W. H. Bellinger and W. R. Farmer (eds), *Jesus and the Suffering Servant: Isaiah 53 and Christian Origins* (Harrisburg, Pa.: Trinity Press International, 1998).

10: JESUS THE SUFFERING SERVANT

1. On this verse, see G. O'Collins, *Jesus Our Redeemer. A Christian Approach to Salvation* (Oxford: Oxford University Press, 2007), p. 153.
2. See R. E. Brown, *The Death of the Messiah*, 2 vols. (New York: Doubleday, 1994).
3. See R. Bauckham, *Jesus and the Eyewitnesses. The Gospels as Eyewitness Testimony* (Grand Rapids, Mich.: Eerdmans, 2006), pp. 124–27.
4. See B. Chilton, 'Caiaphas', *ABD*, vol. 1, pp. 803–806.
5. See D. R. Schwartz, 'Pontius Pilate', *ABD*, vol. 5, pp. 395–401.
6. See W. Klassen, 'Judas Iscariot', *ABD*, vol. 3, pp. 1091–906. To sample the publications, popular and otherwise, that have appeared after the *ABD* (1992), see J. Archer and F. J. Moloney, *The Gospel According to Jesus* (London: Macmillan, 2007); W. Klassen, *Judas: Betrayer or Friend of Jesus?* (London: SCM Press, 1996); P. Perkins, 'Good News from Judas?', *America* magazine, 29 May 2006, 8–11.
7. On the young man who fled into the night, see Bauckham, *Jesus and the Eyewitnesses*, pp. 185–86, 197–201.
8. For a defence (against Dominic Crossan) of the historicity of Joseph of Arimathea and his action, see G. O'Collins and D. Kendall, 'Did Joseph of Arimathea Exist?', *Biblica* 75 (1994), 95–101. In his *Resurrecting Jesus. The Earliest Christian Tradition and Its Interpretation* (New York: Continuum, 2005), Dale Allison also musters sound arguments against Crossan and others and in favour of the historicity of Joseph's deed, but proposes the odd thesis of Joseph giving Jesus *dishonourable* burial in a tomb set aside for criminals (pp. 352–63).
9. On protective anonymity exercised by the Synoptic Gospels, see Bauckham, *Jesus and the Eyewitnesses*, pp. 183–201.
10. See F. Bigaouette, *Le cri de déréliction de Jésus en croix: Densité existentielle et salvifique* (Paris: Cerf, 2004); R. E. Brown, *The Death of the Messiah*, vol. 2 (New York: Doubleday, 1994), pp. 1085–88, 1455–67; O'Collins, *Jesus Our Redeemer*, pp. 140–48.
11. J. Limburg, *Psalms* (Louisville, Ky.: Westminster John Knox Press, 2000), p. 69.
12. Psalm 22 is the *only* psalm of lamentation that introduces the image of a mother who gives birth to and nourishes a child. In all the other psalms the closest parallel to this comes in a psalm for deliverance: 'Upon you [O Lord] I have leaned from my birth; it was you who took me from my mother's womb' (Psalm 71:6). In the setting of the crucifixion the image of a mother had its historical counterpart, and may have led Jesus to take this psalm for his final prayer. All Gospels testify that women were present at the death of Jesus, including married women who had children. John testifies that Jesus' own mother was present (19:25–27).
13. See A. Lacoque, 'My God, My God, Why Have You Forsaken Me?', in A. Lacoque and P. Ricoeur, *Thinking Biblically: Exegetical and*

Hermeneutical Studies (Chicago: University of Chicago Press, 1998), pp. 187–209, at 201.

14. On Simon of Cyrene as providing eyewitness testimony to the death of Jesus, see Bauckham, *Jesus and the Eyewitnesses*, pp. 51–52.

15. For further details see O'Collins, *Jesus Our Redeemer*, pp. 145–47.

16. Brown, *The Death of the Messiah*, vol. 2, p. 1051, n. 54; see p. 1045, n. 38.

17. See Bauckham, *Jesus and Eyewitnesses*, pp. 194–95.

18. Many have seen here a symbolic reference to the water of baptism (John 3:5) and the blood of the new covenant announced at the institution of the Eucharist (1 Corinthians 10:16; Mark 14:24). As is repeatedly the case, real events and symbolic meanings do *not* exclude each other: the water and blood that really came from the side of Christ can obviously also express a sacramental symbolism.

19. *God as the Mystery of the World* (Edinburgh: T. & T. Clark, 1983), p. 220.

20. *The First Epistle to the Corinthians* (Grand Rapids, Mich.: Eerdmans, 2000), p. 172.

21. *Pensée* no. 552 in the standard editions, but no. 919 in the order of *Pensées* in which Pascal left them at his death.

22. See David Brown, 'The Incarnation in Twentieth-Century Art', in S. T. Davis, D. Kendall and G. O'Collins (eds.), *The Incarnation* (Oxford: Oxford University Press, 2002), pp. 332–72; id., 'Images of Redemption in Art and Music', in S. T. Davis, D. Kendall and G. O'Collins (eds), *The Redemption* (Oxford: Oxford University Press, 2004), pp. 295–320.

11: JESUS THE LORD OF GLORY

1. See e.g. G. O'Collins, *Jesus Risen* (Mahwah, NJ/London: Paulist Press/Darton, Longman & Todd, 1987); id., *Easter Faith* (London/Mahwah, NJ: Darton, Longman & Todd/Paulist Press, 2003); S. T. Davis, D. Kendall, and G. O'Collins (eds), *The Resurrection* (Oxford: Oxford University Press, 1997).

2. C. F. Evans, *Resurrection and the New Testament* (London: SCM Press, 1970), p. 84. The verses contain several characteristic Matthean motifs: 'making disciples', 'the teaching aspect' of the Church's mission, Jesus' instructions which communicate the new law, the mission to 'all nations' prefigured by the names of Gentile women in Jesus' genealogy (Matthew 1:1–17) and by the visit of the Magi, and the enduring presence of Jesus which the Angel of the Lord had anticipated in the birth narrative (Matthew 1:23).

3. D. A. Hagner comments on Matthew 28:18–20: 'It is very clear that the words [of Jesus] are recast in Matthew's style and vocabulary ... This fact, however, does not amount to a demonstration that Matthew composed the passage *ex nihilo* ... He may simply have worked

over and re-presented a tradition available to him' (*Matthew 14–28*, Dallas: Word Books, 1995, p. 883).

4. On the psalms being interpreted as 'the voice of Christ to the Father (*vox Christi ad Patrem*)', see B. Fischer, 'Le Christ dans les Psaumes', *Le Maison Dieu* 77 (1951), 86–113.

5. Evans, *Resurrection and the New Testament*, p. 105.

6. See O'Collins, *Jesus Risen*, pp. 210–16; id., *Interpreting the Resurrection* (Mahwah, NJ: Paulist Press, 1988), pp. 5–21.

7. See The Constitution on Divine Revelation (*Dei Verbum*) of November 1965, nos. 2, 4, 14, 17; see also G. O'Collins, *Retrieving Fundamental Theology* (Mahwah, NJ: Paulist Press, 1993), p. 54.

8. For further details see O'Collins, *Interpreting the Resurrection*, pp. 61–67; id., *Easter Faith*, p. 114.

9. T. Dwyer, *The Motif of Wonder in the Gospel of Mark*, JSNT Supplement (Sheffield: Sheffield Academic Press, 1996.

10. Ibid., p. 188; see p. 192.

11. Ibid., p. 189.

12. Ibid., p. 192.

13. Ibid.

14. V. Bruemmer, *The Model of Love. A Study in Philosophical Theology* (Cambridge: Cambridge University Press, 1993), p.171.

15. In the next chapter we will spell this out in detail.

16. There may be a hint here of Jesus' words about 'working while it is day' (John 9:4).

17. Greek zoologists, it seems, reckoned that there were 153 kinds of fish; thus the catch of John 21 symbolises that with the help of Jesus the disciples have caught or will catch 'all kinds' of human beings; for details see R. Schnackenburg, *The Gospel According to John*, vol. 3 (London and Tunbridge Wells: Burns and Oates, 1982), p. 157.

18. R. Bauckham, *Jesus and the Eyewitnesses. The Gospels as Eyewitness Testimony* (Grand Rapids, Mich.: Eerdmans, 2006), pp. 391–93.

19. There is also an echo here of what Jesus has said to Peter at the Last Supper: 'Where I am going, you cannot follow' (John 13:36). Peter is now invited to do what was previously impossible – follow Jesus in accepting a violent death that would come in fact by crucifixion (see next chapter, note 15).

20. See Bauckham, *Jesus and the Eyewitnesses*, pp. 364–69, where he persuasively argues for chapter 21 being written by the author of the Fourth Gospel and not being a epilogue added by a later hand.

21. J. Rist, *Real Ethics* (Cambridge: Cambridge University Press, 2002), p. 108.

12: JESUS THE ABIDING PRESENCE

1. J. D. G. Dunn, *Jesus Remembered* (Grand Rapids, Mich.: Eerdmans, 2003). The other two major books on Jesus published that year were:

L. W. Hurtado, *Lord Jesus Christ: Devotion to Jesus in Early Christianity* (Grand Rapids, Mich.: Eerdmans, 2003); and N. T. Wright, *The Resurrection of the Son of God* (London: SPCK, 2003).

2. On John 1:35–39, see A. T. Lincoln, *The Gospel According to St John*, Black's New Testament Commentaries (London: Continuum, 2006), pp. 116–17.

3. Lincoln, *The Gospel According to St John*, p. 117.

4. C. K. Barrett, *The Gospel According to St John* (London: SPCK, 2nd edn, 1978), p. 181.

5. On John 6:67–71, see Lincoln, *The Gospel According to St John*, pp. 238–41.

6. On John 11:20–27, see ibid., pp. 323–35.

7. Ibid., p. 397.

8. Ibid., p. 372.

9. On John 20:13–17, see ibid., pp. 492–94.

10. Ibid., p. 493.

11. The evangelist exercises a similar discretion in the case of the raising of Lazarus (11:1–44). He has noted the tears and grief of Martha, Mary, and Jesus himself over the death of Lazarus, but discreetly declines to portray their happiness at his return to life.

12. On John 21:15–19, see Lincoln, *The Gospel According to St John*, pp. 316–20.

13. Ibid., p. 517.

14. Ibid., p. 518.

15. Barrett finds a clear reference to Peter's own crucifixion in Jesus' words about 'stretching out your hands' and being 'bound' or 'fastened' – i.e. to a cross (21:18–19); see Barrett, *The Gospel According to John*, p. 585.

16. Lincoln, *The Gospel According to St John*, p. 117.

17. On 3:1–21, see ibid., pp 145–57.

18. On 4:1–42, see ibid., pp. 167–82.

19. On 4:43–54, see ibid., pp. 183–90.

20. On 5:1–18, see ibid., pp. 190–200.

21. On the whole passage see ibid., pp. 524–36.

22. For a fuller treatment of this encounter with Jesus, see Chapter Five above.

23. On 11:1–53, see Lincoln, *The Gospel According to St John*, pp. 313–35.

24. On 20:1–18, see ibid., pp. 487–96.

◆

SELECT BIBLIOGRAPHY

Bauckham, R. *Jesus and the Eyewitnesses. The Gospels as Eyewitness Testimony* (Grand Rapids, Mich.: Eerdmans, 2006).

Benedict XVI, Pope, *Jesus of Nazareth* (London/New York: Bloomsbury/Doubleday, 2007).

Bockmuehl, M., *Seeing the Word. Refocusing New Testament Study* (Grand Rapids, Mich.: Baker Academic, 2006).

Brown, R. E., *The Birth of the Messiah* (New York: Doubleday, new edn, 1993).

Brown, R. E., *The Death of the Messiah*, 2 vols. (New York: Doubleday, 1994).

Cavadini, J. C. and Holt, L. (eds), *Who Do You Say That I Am?* (Notre Dame, Ind.: University of Notre Dame Press, 2004).

Donahue, J. R. and Harrington, D. J., *The Gospel of Mark* (Collegeville, Minn.: Liturgical Press, 2002).

Dunn, J. D. G., *Jesus Remembered* (Grand Rapids, Mich.: Eerdmans, 2003).

Davis, S. T., Kendall, D. and O'Collins, G. (eds), *The Incarnation* (Oxford: Oxford University Press, 2002).

Davis, S. T., Kendall, D. and O'Collins, G. (eds), *The Redemption* (Oxford: Oxford University Press, 2004).

Finaldi, G. *et al.*, *The Image of Christ* (London: National Gallery, 2000).

Fitzmyer, J. A., *The Gospel According to Luke*, 2 vols (New York: Doubleday, 1981–85).

Green, J. B., *The Gospel of Luke* (Grand Rapids, Mich.: Eerdmans, 1997).

Hagner, D. A., *Matthew*, 2 vols (Dallas: Word Books, 1993–95)

Hengel, M., *The Cross of the Son of God* (London: SCM Press, 1986).

Hurtado, L., *Lord Jesus Christ: Devotion to Jesus in Earliest Christianity* (Grand Rapids, Mich.: Eerdmans, 2003).

Keener, C. S., *A Commentary on the Gospel of Matthew* (Grand Rapids, Mich.: Eerdmans, 1999).

Lee, D., *Flesh and Glory. Symbolism, Gender and Theology in the Gospel of John* (New York: Herder & Herder, 2002).

Lincoln, A. T., *The Gospel According to St John* (London: Continuum, 2005).

Luz, U., *Matthew*, 3 vols (Minneapolis: Augsburg/Fortress Press, 1989–2005).

Marcus, J., *Mark 1-9* (New York: Doubleday, 1999).

McKnight, S., *Jesus and His Death* (Waco, TX: Baylor University Press, 2005).

Meier, J. P., *A Marginal Jew. Rethinking the Historical Jesus*, 3 vols (New York: Doubleday, 1991–2001).

Moltmann, J., *The Way of Jesus Christ* (London: SCM Press, 1990).

Nolland, J., *The Gospel of Matthew* (Grand Rapids, Mich.: Eerdmans, 2005).

Nolland, J., *Luke*, 3 vols (Dallas: Word Books, 1989–93).

O'Collins, G., *Christology: A Biblical, Historical and Systematic Study of Jesus* (Oxford: Oxford University Press, rev. edn 2004).

O'Collins, G., *The Lord's Prayer* (London: Darton, Longman & Todd, 2006).

O'Collins, G., *Salvation for All. God's Other Peoples* (Oxford: Oxford University Press, 2008).

Sanders, E. P., *The Historical Figure of Jesus* (London: Allen Lane [Penguin], 1993).

Sobrino, J., *Christ the Liberator: A View from the Victims* (Maryknoll, NY: Orbis Books, 2001).

Theissen, G. and Merz, A., *The Historical Jesus: A Comprehensive Guide* (London: SCM Press, 1998).

Thompson-Uberuaga, W., *Jesus and the Gospel Movement. Not Afraid to be Partners* (Columbia, Missouri: University of Missouri Press, 2006).

Wright, N. T., *Jesus and the Victory of God* (London: SPCK, 1996).

Wright, N. T., *The Resurrection of the Son of God* (London: SPCK, 2003).

INDEX OF NAMES

244